RAF Bomber Airfields
OF WORLD WAR 2

RAF Bomber Airfields
OF WORLD WAR 2

JONATHAN FALCONER

IAN ALLAN Publishing

Dedication

To my wife Annie.

First published 1992
Reprinted 1993

ISBN 0 7110 2080 9

© Jonathan Falconer 1992

Published by Ian Allan Ltd, Shepperton,
Surrey; and printed in Great Britain by
Ian Allan Printing Ltd, Coombelands
House, Addlestone, Surrey KT15 1HY

A catalogue record for this book is
available from the British Library.

Contents

Front cover:
**Lancasters of No 100 Squadron at Waltham
are prepared for a raid in 1943.** *From an
original painting by Michael Stride*

Left:
**Armourers at Woodhall Spa feed belted
.303in machine gun ammunition into the
nose turret of No 617 Squadron's Lancaster
III ED763 during 1944.** *IWM18175*

Introduction

They sprang up, as if overnight, like burgeoning clumps of field mushrooms dotted across the flat expanses of East Anglia, where the vast, unrelieved canvas of the lowering sky towers above all that lies beneath. High on the misty Lincolnshire Wolds and beyond to the flatlands surrounding the Humber Estuary they appeared, too, a creeping and uncontrollable rash across the face of mother nature. They thrust up and across the Vale of York, tearing down woodland and hedgerows, demolishing farms and diverting watercourses. And away to the south and west it was happening: they carved deep and indelible marks into the rolling countryside of Oxfordshire and Worcestershire. But without their intrusion the face of England would soon have borne a grave and implacable expression: that of the death mask of democracy.

'They' were the hundreds of airfields constructed for Bomber Command's front-line and training units before and during World War 2 to enable its bombers to take the fight back to Nazi Germany and, in the words of its Commander-in-Chief Sir Arthur Harris, 'to light a fire in the belly of the enemy and burn his black heart out'. And burn it out they did. In a hard fought conflict spanning six years, aircraft and crews of Bomber Command flew more than 374,500 sorties against enemy targets from airfields in Britain. But the cost in lives of bomber crews was high: some 47,000 aircrew perished.

In the pages that follow are quoted many facts and figures pertaining to the airfields, squadrons and aircraft of RAF Bomber Command during World War 2. When you read them, pause for a while and remember that behind every entry is a face and a name, some still living, many long dead — someone's father or son, husband or brother.

Author's Note

This book deals specifically with airfields, squadrons and units under the operational control of RAF Bomber Command between 1939 and 1945. On some airfields, squadrons and units took up residence before the outbreak of war; on others they remained after the war's end. With instances such as these, the dates pre-3 September 1939 and post-8 May 1945 have been included for the sake of clarity and accuracy, even though they fall outside the book's timeframe.

A number of different documentary sources have been consulted in the preparation of this book. Details, particularly dates, often vary from source to source when referring to individual squadrons and units, or when an airfield opened 'officially'. For this reason, some dates may be open to dispute. All airfields appear within the county boundaries as they were at the outbreak of war in 1939.

Some airfields hosted lodger squadrons and units from other Commands, eg Leeming, 6-10:40, No 219 Sqn Fighter Command. These are not included in this book. Neither are the numerous Beam Approach Training Flights which operated mainly Airspeed Oxfords and Avro Ansons from most airfields in the Command during the war years. From time to time, some Bomber Command squadrons were detached to operate from an airfield belonging to another Command, such as Coastal. These movements are not recorded. Pilots' and Observers' Advanced Flying Units — (P) and (O) AFUs — are not included because they came under the control of Flying Training Command.

Airfields operated a station flight for communications purposes, often using an Avro Anson for the task. These flights are not included. Most Operational Training Units (OTU) operated Vickers Wellingtons of a variety of marks, eg Mk I, Ia, Ic, Id. For the sake of space and clarity, these are all listed as Mk I. OTUs also operated a number of Ansons, Defiants, Lysanders and Hurricanes for navigational and gunnery training. Once more, for the sake of space and clarity, these secondary types are not listed.

Aircraft operated by a squadron or unit are listed in the order in which they served: Wellington I,III; Lancaster I,III. It does not necessarily mean that the squadron in question operated all of these types at the same time. Where a squadron or a unit's aircraft types are listed in the Orders of Battle thus: Wellington I/III, or Blenheim IV/Boston III, this denotes that the squadron or unit was in the process of converting from one mark or type of aircraft to another at that particular time.

Any work of this nature makes it an 'open season' on the author. As already stated, some dates, unit allocations and their equipment are open to varying interpretations, and errors can creep in, but all information contained in this book is, to the best of the author's knowledge, correct and true. Constructive comments will be welcomed.

Jonathan Falconer
Bath, February 1992

Acknowledgements

The following individuals and organisations have been a great help to me in the writing of this book: John Allison; Dick Armstrong for drawing many of the airfield maps; Owen Baum; Chaz Bowyer, for his kind help in supplying some of the photographs; Ron Clark, pilot, No 100 Squadron; Mrs Frances M. Davies, for her permission to reproduce letters written by her late fiancé, Sgt Jim Bowler; John Foreman; Steve Grant; my friend Andy Gray for his chauffeuring duties in Norfolk during September 1991; Colin Hawkesworth of the Construction Industry Training Board, Bircham Newton, Norfolk; Peter Holway; Bill Johnson, groundcrew, No 1666 HCU; Len Manning, air gunner, No 57 Squadron; Ken Merrick in Highbury, Australia, for his customary help and kindness in tracking down photographs; Simon Parry; Bruce Robertson for so kindly providing photographic and documentary material; Alan Thorpe, Company Archivist and Historian, John Laing Plc, for his kind assistance in providing photographs and documentary material relating to the airfield construction programme; Andrew Wadsted, Public Relations Manager, Costain Group Plc; Mrs Jean Yeomans, for her permission to reproduce letters from Flg Off Shaw; the staffs of the Commonwealth War Graves Commission, Imperial War Museum, Public Record Office and RAF Museum.

These newspapers kindly published my requests for help: *Cambridge Evening News, Derby Evening Telegraph, Eastern Evening News, East Anglian Daily Times, Grimsby Evening Telegraph, Hartlepool Mail, Leicester Mercury, Lincolnshire Echo, Liverpool Echo, Sunderland Echo, Yorkshire Evening Post.*

The Background

The cult of the bomber was very much a phenomenon of the interwar period. Its new role of mass destruction witnessed during the closing stages of World War 1, strongly affected military thinking in the years that immediately followed. Three men in particular can be credited with the original theories of air warfare: General Giulio Douhet of Italy, Air Marshal Sir Hugh Trenchard of Great Britain, and Brigadier-General William 'Billy' Mitchell of the USA. The early air theorists argued that the object of war was to destroy the will of the enemy as well as his ability to resist, and then to impose one's own will upon him. In the conflict of the future these three men believed naval and ground forces would no longer have the decisive role. With the advent of the aeroplane, the obstacle of the enemy's surface forces could be jumped and attacks could be staged by air to hit at the enemy's population, or at the industry and economy that supported it. Gone were the days of air forces being merely auxiliary to the army or navy.

In Douhet's view, the best way to attain victory was to destroy air bases, supply points and centres of production on which the enemy depended. His strategic bomber force would have two separable functions: it must be able to win command of the skies, and be able to exploit that command. The immediate aim of air warfare, as Douhet clearly saw, was the need to defeat totally the opposing air force.

Trenchard's theory was that the heart of air power lay in strategic bombing of an independent character. He argued that operations in direct support of the army and navy were subsidiary and diversionary.

'Billy' Mitchell too argued for an independent force, but his advocacy of autonomy for the air arm aroused American democracy's strong distaste for the military establishment and its theories of total war. This effectively put paid to any ideas of an independent air force in America for a long time to come.

Throughout the interwar period various international conventions were held with the intention of banning the bomber. In 1922 the Washington Conference on the

Right:
Zeppelin attack — the bomber's new role of mass destruction witnessed in the closing stages of World War 1 strongly affected military thinking in the years that followed.
via Jonathan Falconer

Ungainly in its appearance, the twin-engined Handley Page Heyford was the RAF's last biplane heavy bomber, entering service in November 1933. Illustrated here is Mk Ia K4024 of No 10 Squadron, Boscombe Down, in July 1935. *via Jonathan Falconer*

Limitation of Armaments strongly condemned aerial bombardment. The Hague Rules of Aerial Warfare of 1923, although never ratified, attempted to provide a definition of what constituted a military target, what could be suitably subjected to air bombardment, and what could not. Military targets included: '. . . military forces, works, establishments or depots, factories constituting important and well-known centres engaged in the manufacture of guns, munitions or distinctively military supplies; lines of communication or transportation for military purposes.'

One of the important reasons for the failure to reach an agreement can be attributed to the fact that the Hague Rules saw aerial bombardment as legitimate, but only when directed against military objectives. The difficulty lay in defining and reaching agreement on what constituted a military objective. The rules therefore left it to the discretion of the attacker as to whether a military target was important enough to warrant a bombardment. In 1928 Trenchard produced a paper in which he acknowledged that although bombing of civilians could be contrary to the rules of warfare, 'it is an entirely different matter to terrorise munitions workers (men and women) into absenting themselves from work or stevedores into abandoning the loading of a ship with munitions through fear of air attack upon the factory or dock concerned.'

From the early 1930s much of Britain lived in fear of a catastrophic blow from the air by bombers. The politician Harold Macmillan wrote in his memoirs: 'We thought of air warfare in 1938 rather as people think of nuclear warfare today.' Further attempts to restrict air warfare failed in 1932 when a disarmament conference organised by the League of Nations assembled in Geneva. By the time Germany withdrew from the conference in 1933 there had been no significant progress. Despite their decision to increase defence expenditure, it only gradually became obvious to the Prime Minister, Stanley Baldwin, and his Cabinet

that Germany, under Hitler, was re-arming at a rapid rate and preparing for war.

In 1934 the British Army's allocation of money was halved in the new re-armament programme since it was decided to rely primarily on the deterrent effect of a larger air force. The UK-based air force was to be increased to 84 squadrons by March 1939, as detailed in Expansion Scheme 'A' for the RAF which was approved by the Cabinet in July 1934. To concur with the policy of the Air Staff, 41 bomber squadrons — but only 28 fighter squadrons — were to be included. In July 1936 Bomber Command came into existence when the Air Defence of Great Britain was replaced by four Commands: Fighter, Bomber, Coastal and Flying Training.

Thus the bomber was cast to play the leading role in the Air Staff's plans for any future war. Such a large increase in the RAF's bomber force would inevitably cause problems with airfield accommodation. At the end of World War 1 there had been some 300 military aerodromes in the UK, yet by 1924 this number had diminished to 27. The need clearly existed for a rapid programme of airfield construction to accommodate the growing air force.

Even before the lengthening shadows of a bitter conflict yet to come had cast their blight on the Geneva Armament Conference, plans were afoot at home to construct new airfields for the RAF. In the early 1930s the Air Ministry Works Directorate (AMWD) was formed as the body responsible for the planning and organisation of these new airfields. A subsidiary of the AMWD, known as the Air Ministry Aerodromes Board (AMAB), was created in 1934. Its task was to work in close liaison with the Air Ministry Lands Branch (AMLB) in the selection of suitable sites for new airfields. An important part of the

AMAB's brief was to create a standard architectural style for both airfield and domestic facilities, and to prepare plans for the modification of existing airfields.

The environmental impact of all this new land development, much of it in the heart of the English countryside, attracted the attentions of a number of monitoring groups. All plans for permanent buildings on new airfields had to be approved by the Royal Fine Art Commission while the siting of airfields in the countryside involved consultations with the Society for the Preservation of Rural England.

In 1935 the RAF's prewar Expansion Scheme in terms of aircraft and airfields really took off. With a carefully planned airfield expansion programme totalling some 100 new military airfields, it continued unabated up to the outbreak of war four years later in 1939.

Work on the first of the Expansion Scheme bomber stations — Cranfield, Feltwell, Harwell, Marham, Stradishall and Waddington — was begun in 1935. At the same time a number of existing bomber stations, such as Upper Heyford, underwent a modernisation programme. More new permanent stations were started in 1936: Dishforth, Driffield, Finningley, Hemswell, Leconfield, Scampton, Upwood and Wyton — names that would soon assume well-earned chapters in the RAF's history book. The last permanent bomber stations to be built before the outbreak of war included Binbrook, Bramcote, Coningsby, Leeming, Middleton St George, Newton, North Luffenham, Oakington, Oulton, Swanton Morley, Swinderby, Syerston, Topcliffe and Waterbeach.

Of the 13 or so Expansion Schemes proposed before the war, Scheme 'C' approved in March 1935, emphasised the need for the bomber force to be able to reach Berlin in a latitudinally straight line. The eastern counties of England, in particular Lincolnshire and Yorkshire, were therefore the obvious choice for the construction of these new airfields, sowing the seeds for the rapid growth of what finally became known as the 'Bomber Counties' of World War 2.

Bomber Airfield Construction

As was also the case with airfields for other RAF Commands, the AMAB selected and inspected sites which were reasonably flat and free from obstructions, and between 50 and 600ft above mean sea level. Reconnaissance engineers were given a few days in which to examine the site in detail with particular attention being given to soil type, drainage and obstructions to flying. If the site was deemed suitable for development, the land was requisitioned under the Emergency Powers (Defence) Act of 1939 and civilian building contractors were invited to tender for the contract.

A number of companies were involved in the airfield construction programme, including John Laing & Son Ltd, Taylor-Woodrow Ltd, Richard Costain Ltd and George Wimpey & Co Ltd — household names in the construction industry today. A greater number of small contractors nationwide were also involved in the programme and in cases where such small firms had insufficient plant of their own, machinery was loaned to them by the AMWD so that all firms could play their fullest part in the huge programme of airfield construction. Once tenders had been accepted and issued, work commenced on clearing and levelling the site. Armies of workmen and heavy plant machinery moved in to transform one of many small corners of the English rural landscape into a home for hundreds of RAF servicemen and women, and a launch pad from which scores of Allied bomber aircraft could strike at the very heartland of Nazi Germany.

At the outbreak of war, Bomber Command was operating from some 33 permanent airfields in England and Scotland. A significant number of large, permanent airfields were nearing completion and formed part of the RAF's prewar Expansion Scheme. As a result of changing requirements, major extensions were undertaken at these semi-completed airfields to provide additional barrack blocks, bomb stores and sundry ancillary buildings.

The Expansion Scheme stations were characterised by their distinctive and comfortable neo-Georgian headquarters buildings, messes and married quarters. Elevational treatments could vary even around individual airfields, and also from airfield to airfield, offering a discreet mixture of neo-Georgian, Art Deco and Utilitarian styling. Accommodation was centralised and laid out to a roughly circular arrangement; it was not dispersed over a larger area like the hostilities-only temporary stations built during World War 2. Technical buildings were generally located alongside and to the rear of the hangars; bomber airfields, because of the large aircraft they operated, needed larger hangars and more technical accommodation than, say, a fighter airfield.

Airmen's quarters were located close to the hangars and technical buildings; the officers' and sergeants' messes generally occupied sites of a more secluded nature. All technical and domestic accommodation was built to a high standard of finish using brick, stone and roofing materials chosen to blend as harmoniously as possible with the hues of the surrounding countryside. With the outbreak of war, comprehensive airfield camouflage schemes were put into operation using paint, netting and other materials to make runways, hangars and other buildings as inconspicuous as possible from the air.

Airfields built before World War 2 had no paved runways: grass landing strips were the norm, as, for example, at Bircham Newton in Norfolk. With the introduction to service of heavier bomber aircraft, the need for paved runways to allow an unhindered all-weather operational capability became very clear. The grass airfields were generally quite adequate

Below:
Construction workers and plant are seen here at work on runway construction at an airfield 'somewhere in England' during World War 2. *John Laing Plc*

Above:
After the reconnaissance engineers had finished their job and the site had been requisitioned, the first task was to clear and level the ground. Here a 12cu yd Scraper drawn by a 90hp tractor works on runway excavation. *John Laing Plc*

Left:
Koehring Scrapers and their tractors often worked in teams of four on airfield regrading work, where areas of up to 600 acres required regrading to suitable levels. *John Laing Plc*

Below left:
Once regrading was completed, Sheepsfoot rollers were used to compact the soil before laying foundations for the runways. *John Laing Plc*

Bottom left:
Mechanical spreading and compacting machines like this one were used on runway construction. The compacting machine has a front screeding beam with a span of 20ft, a compacting beam capable of working at up to 3,000 impulses/min, and also a back finishing beam. *John Laing Plc*

during the summer months, but with the onset of winter with its attendant increase in rainfall, poor drainage of surface water led to water-logging and serious problems for an airfield's operational status. The necessity for concrete and tarmac runways became apparent, and work commenced in 1939 gradually to re-equip the majority of the Command's airfields with a new three-runway layout, perimeter tracks and concrete dispersal pans. From December 1940, all new bomber airfields in the UK were to be constructed with one paved main runway of 1,400yd and two subsidiaries of 1,100yd in length. By 1942 the requirements had changed still further, setting the standard for runway dimensions until the end of the war: a main runway length of 2,000yd with subsidiaries of 1,400yd (this also applied to any extensions to existing runways). However, towards the end of World War 2, doubts were expressed about the need for a three-runway layout on heavy bomber

Bomber Command and many of its squadrons. Such was the rapid rate of construction that in the peak year of 1942 an average of one new airfield was coming into use with the RAF every three days. In this year, some 127,000 men were employed on Air Ministry Works out of a total building and civil engineering workforce of 393,400 nationwide.

The following figures are typical of the quantity of work involved in the building of one RAF bomber airfield in 1942: 603,000sq yd total area of surfacing; 242,000cu yd of concrete; 1,030,000cu yd of excavation; 34 miles of drainage work; 10 miles of cable ducts; and 7 miles of water main.

During 1943, the RAF identified a number of its airfields as suitable for improvement to Very Heavy Bomber (VHB) standard in order to take the Boeing B-29 Superfortress (named 'Washington' in RAF service) and the projected Vickers Windsor (never to enter service). Lakenheath, Marham and Sculthorpe were earmarked to become the first VHB airfields and were closed during 1944-45 for major reconstruction work.

John Laing & Son Ltd began construction work at Sculthorpe in May 1944 on what was to become one of the most extensive RAF airfields in the country. The rebuilt Sculthorpe covered an area of some 750 acres, with a new main runway of 3,000yd in length and all three runways 100yd wide — twice the normal width. In order for the runways to bear the greater weight of the envisaged very heavy bombers, a sub-base of 4in of mass concrete was laid on a specially prepared sub-grade, and finished with 8-12in of high-grade quality concrete paving.

If the figures above are compared with those for the reconstruction at Sculthorpe in 1944, the enormity of the task can be appreciated: 1,100,000sq yd total area of surfacing; 566,300cu yd of concrete; 1,530,000cu yd of excavation; 34 miles of drainage work; and 32 miles of cable ducts. The work required the following materials: 120,764 tons of cement, 159 miles of heavy duty steel road forms; and 200 miles of sealing compound.

By the end of World War 2 over 170 airfields in England and Scotland had seen use by Bomber Command in its hard-fought battle against the Nazi war machine. Yet, within months of peace being declared, the RAF had begun to wind down. Its huge arsenal of aircraft and weapons, men and airfields became surplus to requirements almost overnight. Squadrons were disbanded and hundreds of perfectly serviceable aircraft scrapped; air and groundcrews were demobbed,

Top:
RAF station buildings of the prewar Expansion Scheme featured a high standard of design, construction and comfort. The elegant neo-Georgian façade of the Officers' Mess at Bircham Newton, Norfolk, is typical of the period. *Jonathan Falconer*

Above:
Just how fine the elevational treatment is can be seen from this view of the main entrance to the Officers' Mess at Bircham Newton, now in use as a conference centre by the Construction Industry Training Board. *Jonathan Falconer*

stations since, in practice, the subsidiary runways were very rarely used.

The new dispersal pan system allowed squadron aircraft to be scattered around an airfield perimeter to save them from damage or destruction in the event of enemy air attack. Aircraft were only returned to the central maintenance area or hangars for major engineering and repair work. Several contracts for permanent airfields were begun late in 1939 and included a number of modifications and economies which resulted in a considerable speeding up in construction. These were among the last of the so-called permanent airfields to be completed during the opening years of the war and some of the first to include a concrete perimeter track.

As the war progressed and Bomber Command's size and strength expanded, so too did the pace of the airfield construction programme. The need for rapid construction of airfields led to the development of many prefabricated building designs such as the Nissen and Romney hut, and the 'T' Type hangar, all of which combined ease and speed of erection with cost-effectiveness and durability.

Runway construction was speeded up with an average completion time, from foundations down to receiving the first bomber, of five to seven months. It would take a total of some 18 months for a labour force of 1,000 men to complete an entire 'A' class (Heavy Bomber) airfield with all facilities. Gone were the days of comfortable neo-Georgian elegance and centralisation of facilities; here, for the duration of hostilities, were the dispersed utilitarian quagmires that would serve

Left:
In contrast to the carefully planned peacetime accommodation, the dispersed sites of the utilitarian 'hostilities only' airfields like Ludford Magna in Lincolnshire offered little in the way of elegance or creature comforts. The nickname of 'Mudford Magna' will need little explanation. *P. Holway*

11

Left:
Concrete dispersal pans were an innovation in World War 2 airfield design which allowed squadron aircraft to be scattered around an airfield's perimeter, minimising their vulnerability to damage in the event of enemy air attack.

This Halifax VI of No 426 (RCAF) Squadron is pictured on its dispersal at Linton-on-Ouse during the spring of 1945. In the right foreground can be seen a hut typical of many used by a squadron's groundcrews who carried out all the maintenance on their charges except for major overhauls.
K. Merrick

Right:
As dusk falls and the shadows lengthen, the bomber airfield assumes its true identity and comes to life. In this atmospheric photograph taken at Scampton, Lincolnshire, in February 1943, No 57 Squadron's Lancasters wait for their crews to board them during the Battle of the Ruhr. And the target for tonight? Essen, Dusseldorf, maybe, or perhaps the Barmen-Elberfeld conurbation?
Imperial War Museum (IWM) CH8785

Left:
Today, in September 1991, the Nissen huts on the former technical site at North Creake, Norfolk, are still standing and in use for storage. *Jonathan Falconer*

returning to the comparatively humdrum life of civvy street. Dozens of airfields were downgraded to Care & Maintenance status before their eventual closure and return to the more peaceable ways of agriculture.

A number of permanent airfields such as Coningsby, Lossiemouth and Marham, which had played key roles in the bomber offensive, have survived into the 1990s to see use by the RAF's force of Tornados, Jaguars, Buccaneers and Hawks — jet-age successors to the legendary Lancaster, Mosquito and their other contemporaries. An even greater number of these airfields have succumbed to the ravages of time and nature.

North Creake was once a thriving home to several squadrons of men and aircraft in No 100 Group. Once its runways and dispersals echoed to the throaty sound of its resident Stirlings running up their engines before finally getting airborne. Today it is a forlorn shadow of its former self, bordered by thick swathes of scented pines on high, gently rolling ground in the north Norfolk countryside. Noisy lorries carrying animal feed from a factory on the airfield's former technical site, grate and grumble their ponderous ways along what remains of the perimeter track, the runways having fallen to the ploughshare years ago. Once the nerve centre of wartime operations, the control tower seems ill at ease with its conscience in its peacetime guise as a private dwelling, complete with clothes line in place of the wind sock.

Such a picture can be seen repeated across the countryside as Britain's wartime airfields crumble and decay, mute testimonies to an age when they were homes to the most powerful conventional bomber force the world had ever seen.

Above right:
Close to the watchtower at North Creake, this old Maycrete hut was formerly used as an MT shed but is now derelict. *Jonathan Falconer*

Right:
The watchtower at Little Snoring, Norfolk, is now a derelict shell and the airfield has long since been returned to agriculture. However, the lonely watchtower and the ploughed earth on which it stands must still hold memories of the momentous events which its squadrons of Lancasters and Mosquitoes helped carve all those years ago. *Jonathan Falconer*

Hangar Designs Commonly Seen at RAF Bomber Command Airfields 1939-45

'A' Type (1924)
Open span: 120ft; length: 250ft; max door height clearance: 25ft.
With the expansion of the RAF during the 1930s, and the anticipation of larger aircraft entering service, the 'A' Type proved ultimately to be unsuitable and thus a larger hangar was required.

'C' Type (1934)
'C' Type Gabled (1934) — Max door height: 35ft.
'C' Type Hipped (1938) — Max door height: 30ft.
Open span: 152ft; length: 300ft; max door height clearance: 35ft.
The width of the 'C' Type was standard although the length could vary according to local requirements. It was of brick and steel construction with steel plate doors at each end and came with either a gabled or hipped roof design. Single or two-storey offices and workshops were built externally along the length of the hangar on either side.

'C1' Type (1939)
The same as the 'C', but making extensive use of asbestos sheeting instead of brickwork to save time and construction costs.

'D' Type (1936)
Open span: 150ft; length: 300ft; max door height: 30ft.
Constructed predominantly from reinforced concrete topped by a curved roof.

Bellman (8349/37) (1937)
Open span: 87ft 9in; length: 175ft; max door height: 26ft.
Of steel construction with steel doors at each end, the Bellman was the most common steel hangar on RAF airfields up until 1940 when it was superseded by the 'T' Types.

'J' and 'K' Types (1939)
Open span: 150ft; length: 300ft; max door height: 30ft.
Predominantly of metal and brick construction with a curved roof of 0.25in steel plate. Offices and workshops were built externally along the length of the hangar on either side.

'T' Types (1940/41/42)
The main types were the 'T2' and 'T2' (Home).
Open spans of 90ft or 97ft 2in; length: 239ft 7in; max door height: 25ft. Lengths could vary according to local requirements.
'T' stood for Transportable. The type was a transportable metal hangar which was quick to erect. 'T2s' were by far the most ubiquitous type of hangar to be seen on wartime bomber airfields, superseding the prewar Bellman design.

'B1' and 'B2' Types (1942)
Open span: 120ft; length: 227ft 6in; max door height: 27ft (B1), 20ft 6in (B2).
A MAP design used at many of Bomber Command's frontline stations and OTUs for the major servicing of aircraft. Steel construction with doors at each end.

The Airfields:
An A to Z

Opened: The date on which the airfield opened officially for flying operations during World War 2 (eg: Downham Market, 07/42) or, in the case of an old-established airfield or one which had seen almost continuous use up until then, the date on which it first saw use for flying (eg: Waddington, 11/16).

Closed: The date on which operational flying from the airfield by the RAF ceased (eg: Barford St John, 03/46); or, in the case where military flying has continued since the war's end on a regular or semi-regular basis, or activities directly or closely related to flying are still undertaken, the current use of the airfield in 1992 (eg: currently in use by RAF, USAF, Army, British Aerospace Plc, as civil airport, etc).

Elevation: The airfield's height in feet above mean sea level.

Pundit code: In order to identify airfields from the air a system of two-letter codes was adopted, usually taken from letters making up the airfield's name (eg: 'AY' for Alconbury). However, with the proliferation of airfields during the war

years the number of code permutations became exhausted and so new codes with apparently little or no connection to the airfields they represented were introduced (eg: 'AL' for Blyton or 'AC' for Breighton). These were displayed on the ground in 10ft-high white capital letters adjacent to the signals area or in the signals square near to the control tower. At night this method of airfield identification was obviously unworkable so a mobile beacon situated several miles away from the airfield, known as a Pundit, was used to flash in red light the identity letters in Morse code.

Main contractor: The civil engineers and building contractors who undertook the majority of the construction work at the airfield. In some cases this was undertaken by a consortium of smaller contractors instead of one of the bigger firms like Laing or Costain.

Below:
In common with the other Battle squadrons of No 1 Group, No 226 Squadron moved to France from its base at Harwell on the outbreak of war. Squadron Battles are seen here at Reims in early 1940.
via Jonathan Falconer

Runways: The flying surfaces at the airfield, generally made of concrete or tarmac, or a combination of the former with a tarmac surfacing, on a compacted hardcore base. Some runways were also surfaced with wood or rubber chippings or pine needles. They were usually laid to a triangular pattern with the main runway orientated roughly SW/NE to suit the prevailing wind.

Hangars: Large purpose-built weatherproof structures for aircraft storage and overhaul (see the earlier section on 'Hangar Designs Commonly Seen at RAF Bomber Command Airfields').

User sqns/units: The RAF frontline squadrons (sqn) and secondline training units, ie: Operational Training Units (OTU), Heavy Conversion Units (HCU), and their parent groups (Gp), permanently based at the airfield (not including squadrons and units on temporary detachment) and their dates of occupancy.

The notes following this entry refer to significant changes in the airfield's status during the war years (eg: Alconbury, became satellite to Wyton 09/39), and to any awards of the Victoria Cross to aircrew of based squadrons (eg: Bardney, Flt Sgt G. Thompson, 9 Sqn, 01/01/45).

ABINGDON, Berks

Opened: 01/09/32
Closed: Currently in use by RAF
Elevation: 245ft
Pundit code: AB
Main contractor: Various
Runways: 2 concrete
Hangars: C Type (1), A Type (4)
User sqns/units:

97 Sqn (6 Gp)
16/09/39-02/04/40
Whitley II

166 Sqn (6 Gp)
16/09/39-02/04/40
Whitley I, III

10 OTU (6/91 Gp)
02/04/40-10/09/46
Whitley I-III, V, VII; Wellington III, X

Opened with full station status 01/09/32

ALCONBURY, Cambs

Opened: 17/05/38
Closed: Currently in use by USAF
Elevation: 165ft
Pundit code: AY
Main contractor: Various
Runways: 3 concrete
Hangars: T2 (2)
User sqns/units:

15 Sqn (2 Gp)
14/04-15/05/40
Blenheim IV; Wellington I

40 Sqn (3 Gp)
02/02/41-14/02/42
Wellington I

156 Sqn (3 Gp)
14/02/42-07/08/42
Wellington I, III

Opened as satellite to Upwood 17/05/38
Became satellite to Wyton 09/39
Transferred to USAAF control 08/42

ATTLEBRIDGE, Norfolk

Opened: 06/41
Closed: 15/03/59
Elevation: 165ft
Pundit code: AT
Main contractor: Richard Costain Ltd
Runways: 3 concrete
Hangars: T2 (2)
User sqns/units:

88 Sqn (2 Gp)
01/08/41-30/09/42
Blenheim IV; Boston III

320 Sqn (2 Gp)
30/03/43-30/08/43
Hudson VI; Mitchell II

ATTLEBRIDGE continued

Opened as satellite to Swanton Morley 06/41
Closed for rebuilding 09/43
Transferred to USAAF control 03/44

BALDERTON, Notts

Opened: 06/41
Closed: 1954
Elevation: 67ft
Pundit code: BL
Main contractor: Various
Runways: 3 tarmac
Hangars: T2 (2), B1 (1)
User sqns/units:

25 OTU (7 Gp)
06/41-11/41
Hampden

408 Sqn (5 Gp)
09/12/41-14/09/42
Hampden

1668 HCU (5 Gp)
15/08/43-17/11/43
Lancaster I; Halifax II, V

227 Sqn (5 Gp)
21/10/44-05/04/45
Lancaster I, III

Opened as satellite to Finningley 06/41
Became satellite to Syerston 12/41
Transferred to USAAF control 02/01/44
Returned to RAF control as No 56 Base substation 10/44

BARDNEY, Lincs

Opened: 04/43
Closed: 1963
Elevation: 40ft
Pundit code: BA
Main contractor: Various
Runways: 3 concrete
Hangars: T2 (2), B1 (1)
User sqns/units:

9 Sqn (5 Gp)
14/04/43-06/07/45
Lancaster I, III

227 Sqn (5 Gp)
07/10/44-12/10/44
Lancaster I, III

189 Sqn (5 Gp)
15/10/44-02/11/44
08/04/45-15/10/45
Lancaster I, III

Opened as No 53 Base substation 04/43
*Flt Sgt G. Thompson, 9 Sqn, awarded posthumous VC, Dortmund-Ems Canal, 01/01/45

BARFORD St JOHN, Oxon

Opened: 06/41
Closed: 03/46
Elevation: 380ft
Pundit code: BJ
Main contractor: Various
Runways: 3
Hangars: T2 (1), B1 (1)
User sqns/units:

16 OTU (92 Gp)
15/12/42-03/46
Wellington III, X; Mosquito III, X, XVI, XX, XXV, TIII

Opened under Flying Training Command control 06/41
Transferred to Bomber Command control as satellite to Upper Heyford 15/12/42

BASSINGBOURN, Cambs

Opened: 03/38
Closed: Currently in use by the Army
Elevation: 78ft
Pundit code: BS
Main contractor: John Laing & Son Ltd
Runways: 3
Hangars: C Type (4)
User sqns/units:

104 Sqn (6 Gp)
02/05/38-17/09/39
Blenheim I; Anson I

108 Sqn (6 Gp)
02/05/38-17/09/39
Blenheim I; Anson I

215 Sqn (6/3 Gp)
24/09/39-08/04/40
Harrow II; Wellington I

35 Sqn (6 Gp)
07/12/39-01/02/40
Battle; Blenheim IV; Anson I

11 OTU (6/7/92 Gp)
08/04/40-02/10/42
Wellington I; Anson I

Opened with full station status 03/38
Transferred to USAAF control 10/42

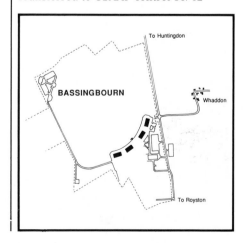

1 ABINGDON
The twin-engined Wellington X equipped the majority of Bomber Command's Operational Training Units (OTUs) by the latter stages of the war. An external distinguishing feature of many was the faired-over nose turret, as seen in this picture of a No 10 OTU machine. *via Chaz Bowyer*

2 ALCONBURY
The view from the cockpit as a Wellington makes its final approach to Alconbury in 1941. *J. O. Lancaster via Chaz Bowyer*

3 ATTLEBRIDGE
A No 88 Squadron Blenheim IV receives the attention of its groundcrew at Attlebridge in the autumn of 1941. The squadron operated Blenheim IVs and Boston IIIs alongside each other from Swanton Morley and Attlebridge until the Blenheims were finally retired in February 1942. *via Chaz Bowyer*

4 ATTLEBRIDGE
On 8 March 1942, 12 Boston III light bombers of No 88 Squadron (Attlebridge) and No 226 Squadron (Swanton Morley) were detailed to make a low-level daylight attack on the Matford factory at Poissy, 10 miles northwest of Paris. Eight Bostons actually bombed the target which was beyond Allied fighter cover, although one crashed soon afterwards — the first operational loss of a Boston. *via Jonathan Falconer*

5 BALDERTON
In the bleak midwinter: a No 408 (Goose) Squadron Hampden is run up at its dispersal in the thick snow of early 1942. *IWM CH4738*

6 BARDNEY
In the early evening of 20 June 1943, the crew of No 9 Squadron's Lancaster III ED831 prepare to board their aircraft at its dispersal before taking off for the night's target, Friedrichshafen in southern Germany. ED831 went missing six nights later on a trip to the Ruhr target of Gelsenkirchen. *B. Robertson*

9 BENSON
Fairey Battle light bombers of Nos 52 and 63 Squadron (illustrated) moved to Benson during September 1939 and became part of No 1 Group Pool before both squadrons merged to form No 12 OTU in April 1940. *via Jonathan Falconer*

7 BARDNEY
A scene in the leafy bomb dump at Bardney on 9 September 1944 where armourers show off a 12,000lb 'Tallboy' earthquake bomb to the photographer, with a 40lb GP bomb beside it for comparison. Flying from a forward airfield at Yagodnik in northern Russia, 18 Lancasters from No 9 Squadron, together with 20 from No 617 Squadron carried 'Tallboys' and 'Johnny Walker' 500lb air-dropped oscillating mines to bomb the German battleship *Tirpitz* in Tromso Fjord, Norway, in Operation 'Paravane' on 15 September. *via Chaz Bowyer*

8 BASSINGBOURN
No 21 Squadron flew a detachment of Blenheim IVs from here between the outbreak of war and June 1940. Flying from another airfield, V6240:B was shot down by flak on 16 July 1941 and crashed at Waalhaven, Rotterdam, during an attack on the docks by 36 No 2 Group Blenheims from Nos 18, 21, 105, 139 and 226 Squadrons. No 21 Squadron was detached three times to Coastal Command between the outbreak of war and December 1941. *via Chaz Bowyer*

BENSON, Oxon

Opened: 04/39
Closed: Currently in use by RAF
Elevation: 215ft
Pundit code: EB
Main contractor: John Laing & Son Ltd
Runways: 2
Hangars: C Type (4)
User sqns/units:

103 Sqn (1 Gp)
01/04-02/09/39
Battle

150 Sqn (1 Gp)
03/04-02/09/39
Battle

52 Sqn (6 Gp)
18/09/39-06/04/40
Battle

63 Sqn (6 Gp)
09/09/39-06/04/40
Battle

207 Sqn (6 Gp)
04/40
Battle

12 OTU (6 Gp)
06/04/40-09/41
Battle; Wellington

1 PRU
11/40-18/10/42
Spitfire; Blenheim; Mosquito

Opened with full station status 04/39
Transferred to Coastal Command control 09/41

BICESTER, Oxon

Opened: 1917
Closed: Currently in use by RAF
Elevation: 270ft
Pundit code: BC
Main contractor: Various
Runways: 3 grass
Hangars: A Type (2), C Type (2)
User sqns/units:

104 Sqn (6 Gp)
12/09/39-08/04/40
Blenheim I, IV; Anson I

108 Sqn (6 Gp)
12/09/39-08/04/40
Blenheim I, IV; Anson I

13 OTU (6/7/92 Gp)
08/04/40-01/06/43
Blenheim IV, V

1551 Flt (92 Gp)
20/11/42-15/04/43
Anson; Oxford; Master

307 FTU (92 Gp)
24/12/42-18/03/43
Blenheim V

BICESTER continued

Re-opened with full station status
17/08/36
Transferred to Fighter Command control
06/43

BINBROOK, Lincs

Opened: 06/40
Closed: 06/88
Elevation: 373ft
Pundit code: BK
Main contractor: Various
Runways: 3
Hangars: C Type (5)
User sqns/units:

12 Sqn (1 Gp)
03/07/40-08/40
09/40-24/09/42
Battle; Wellington II

142 Sqn (1 Gp)
03/07/40-12/08/40
06/09/40-26/11/41
Battle; Wellington II, IV

460 Sqn (1 Gp)
14/05/43-28/07/45
Lancaster I, III

Opened with full station status 06/40
Became No 12 Base HQ 01/43

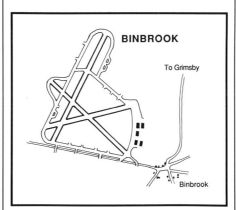

BIRCOTES, Notts

Opened: 11/41
Closed: 08/44
Elevation: 110ft
Pundit code: BR
Main contractor: Various
Runways: 3 grass
Hangars: T2 (1), B1 (1), Bessoneau (1)
User sqns/units:

25 OTU (7/93 Gp)
06/41-07/01/43
Wellington III, X

18 OTU (93 Gp)
10/43-08/44
Wellington III, X

Opened as satellite to Finningley 11/41
Closed 1944

BITTESWELL, Leics

Opened: 02/42
Closed: Currently in use by British Aerospace
Elevation: 420ft
Pundit code: BT
Main contractor: Various
Runways: 3
Hangars: T2 (1), B1 (1)
User sqns/units:

18 OTU (7/93 Gp)
02/42-06/43
Wellington III, X

29 OTU (92 Gp)
06/43-11/44
Wellington III, X

Opened as satellite to Bramcote 02/42
Became satellite to Bruntingthorpe 06/43
Transferred to Transport Command control 11/44

BLYTON, Lincs

Opened: 11/42
Closed: 1954
Elevation: 70ft
Pundit code: AL
Main contractor: Various
Runways: 3
Hangars: T2 (2), B1 (1)
User sqns/units:

199 Sqn (1 Gp)
07/11/42-03/02/43
Wellington III

1662 HCU (1/7 Gp)
02/43-04/45
Halifax, I, II, V; Manchester; Lancaster I, III

Opened as satellite to Lindholme 11/42
Became No 11 Base substation 01/43
Became No 71 Base substation 11/44

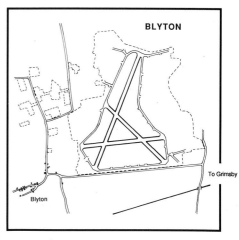

BODNEY, Norfolk

Opened: 03/40
Closed: 11/45
Elevation: 149ft

BODNEY continued

Pundit code: BO
Main contractor: Various
Runways: 3 grass
Hangars: T2 (2)
User sqns/units:

82 Sqn (2 Gp)
03/40-04/41
Blenheim IV

105 Sqn (2 Gp)
21/05/41-07/41
Blenheim IV

21 Sqn (2 Gp)
14/03-31/10/42
Blenheim IV; Ventura I, II

Opened as satellite to Watton 03/40
Transferred to USAAF control 05/43

BOTTESFORD, Lincs

Opened: 10/09/41
Closed: 1945
Elevation: 110ft
Pundit code: AQ
Main contractor: Various
Runways: 3 concrete
Hangars: T2 (9), B1 (1)
User sqns/units:

207 Sqn (5 Gp)
17/11/41-20/09/42
Manchester; Lancaster I

90 Sqn (3 Gp)
07/11-29/12/42
Stirling I

467 Sqn (5 Gp)
22/11/42-13/11/43
Lancaster I, III

1668 HCU (5/7 Gp)
07/44-03/46
Lancaster I, II, III

Opened with full station status 10/09/41
Transferred to USAAF control 11/43
Returned to RAF control 07/44
Became No 72 Base HQ 11/44

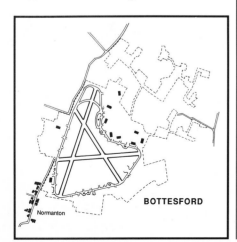

BOURN, Cambs

Opened: 04/41
Closed: 1948
Elevation: 235ft
Pundit code: AU
Main contractor: Various
Runways: 3 concrete
Hangars: T2 (2), B1 (1)
User sqns/units:

101 Sqn (1 Gp)
11/02-11/08/42
Wellington I, III

15 Sqn (3 Gp)
13/08/42-14/04/43
Stirling I, III

97 Sqn (5 Gp)
18/04/43-18/04/44
Lancaster I, III

105 Sqn (2 Gp)
23/03/44-29/06/45
Mosquito IV

162 Sqn (8 Gp)
16/12/44-10/07/45
Mosquito XX, XXV

Opened as satellite to Oakington 04/41
Upgraded to full station status 08/42

BRAMCOTE, Warks

Opened: 04/06/40
Closed: Currently in use by the Army
Elevation: 378ft
Pundit code: RT
Main contractor: John Laing & Son Ltd
Runways: 3 steel matting
Hangars: C Type (5)
User sqns/units:

18 OTU (6/91 Gp)
15/06/40-07/03/43
Wellington I, III

300 Sqn (1 Gp)
01/07-22/08/40
Battle

301 Sqn (1 Gp)
22/07-29/08/40
Battle

304 Sqn (1 Gp)
22/08-02/12/40
Battle; Wellington I

305 Sqn (1 Gp)
29/08-02/12/40
Battle; Wellington I

Opened with full station status 06/40
Transferred to Transport Command
control 04/43

BREIGHTON, Yorks

Opened: 01/42
Closed: 1946
Elevation: 24ft

BREIGHTON continued

Pundit code: AC
Main contractor: Various
Runways: 3 tarmac
Hangars: T2 (2), B1 (1)
Runways: 3 tarmac
User sqns/units:

460 Sqn (1 Gp)
04/01/42-14/05/43
Wellington IV; Halifax II; Lancaster I, III

1656 HCU (5 Gp)
07-26/10/42
Manchester; Lancaster I

78 Sqn (4 Gp)
16/06/43-20/09/45
Halifax II, III, VI

Opened as satellite to Holme-on-Spalding
Moor 01/42
Became No 44 Base substation 11/44

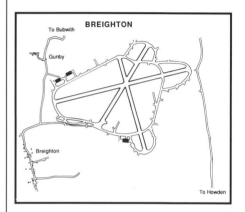

BRUNTINGTHORPE, Leics

Opened: 11/42
Closed: 1962
Elevation: 450ft
Pundit code: BP
Main contractor: Various
Runways: 3 concrete
Hangars: T2 (4), B1 (1)
User sqns/units:

29 OTU (92 Gp)
06/43-19/06/45
Wellington III, X

Opened as satellite to North Luffenham
11/42
Upgraded to full station status 06/43

BURN, Yorks

Opened: 11/42
Closed: 1946
Elevation: 20ft
Pundit code: AZ
Main contractor: Various
Runways: 3 concrete/tarmac
Hangars: T2 (2), B1 (1)
User sqns/units:

10 BICESTER
Blenheim Is equipped No 90 Squadron which was stationed at Bicester from March 1937 until it moved to West Raynham shortly before the outbreak of war. On 16 September the squadron moved to Upwood as a part of No 2 Group Pool before it disbanded in April 1940 and merged into No 17 OTU.
via Jonathan Falconer

11 BINBROOK
The winter of 1940-41 was a harsh one, particularly so at exposed airfields like Binbrook up on the Lincolnshire Wolds where No 142 Squadron's Wellington II W5359:B is pictured in the snow.
R. Bonser via Chaz Bowyer

12 BOTTESFORD
No 207 Squadron became the first squadron to operate the ill-fated twin-engined Avro Manchester, initially from Waddington then Bottesford. L7515:S is pictured here early in 1942 before its transferral to No 106 Squadron at Coningsby. No 207 Squadron remained under No 5 Group control, from its re-formation in November 1940 until the end of the war.
Hawker Siddeley Aviation Ltd, Neg No A9/50, via Chaz Bowyer

13 BURN
No 578 Squadron was formed at Snaith in January 1944 from 'C' Flight of No 51 Squadron. The following month it moved to Burn, near Selby, which became its home until the squadron's disbandment in April 1945. In this picture, Halifax III LL558:R can be seen taking off from Burn. Skippered by 21 year-old Flt Lt Gordon Powell, she failed to return from Hemmingstadt on 7-8 March 1945. *K. Kemp via Jonathan Falconer*

14 BURN
An unidentified crew, most probably that of Flg Off I. Denley RAAF, pose for the camera next to No 578 Squadron's Halifax III NA618:N at Burn late in 1944. This aircraft, with Denley's crew, failed to return from Reisholz on 21 February 1945.
K. Kemp via Jonathan Falconer

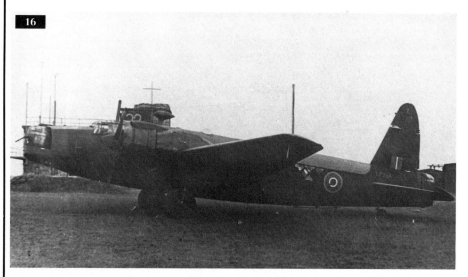

15   CHEDBURGH
The wheelbrakes have been nipped and the undercarriage begins to retract as No 218 Squadron's Lancaster I, LM257:P, piloted by Flg Off R. G. Walker, climbs away from the runway on the last op of Walker's tour, destination Oberhausen, 4 December 1944. The two horizontal yellow colour bars on the tail fin reveal the aircraft to be a G-H leader. *via Chaz Bowyer*

16   CHURCH BROUGHTON
Wellington X LP264, pictured in October 1942, served at Church Broughton with No 1429 Operational Training Flight (OTF) which trained Czech aircrews in conjunction with No 27 OTU. *Z. Hurt via Chaz Bowyer*

17   CONINGSBY
Skippered by Sgt A. J. Moore, No 106 Squadron's Hampden P1228:L was one of 13 aircraft that failed to return from a raid on Hamburg on 30 November/1 December 1941. It is believed to have ditched in the North Sea. No 106 Squadron suffered the highest percentage of losses of all the Hampden squadrons. *via Chaz Bowyer*

BURN continued

1653 HCU (4 Gp)
06-10/42
Halifax I

431 Sqn (4/6 Gp)
13/11/42-15/07/43
Wellington X

578 Sqn (4 Gp)
06/02/44-15/04/45
Halifax III

Opened as satellite to Pocklington 11/42
Became No 42 Base substation 11/44
*Plt Off C.J. Barton, 578 Sqn, awarded posthumous VC, Nuremberg 30-31/03/44

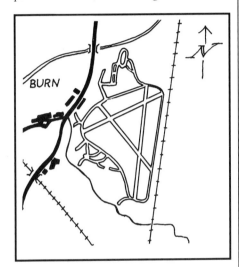

CARNABY, Yorks
Opened: 26/03/44
Closed: 1963
Elevation: 35ft
Pundit code: KQ
Main contractor: John Laing & Son Ltd
Hangars: None
Runways: 1 bitumen, 3,000yd x 250yd with undershoots and overshoots of 500 yd each
User sqns/units:

None: FIDO-equipped Emergency Diversion Runway under control of 4 Gp

CASTLE DONINGTON, Leics
Opened: 01/43
Closed: Currently in use as East Midlands Airport
Elevation: 290ft
Pundit code: CD
Main contractor: Various
Runways: 3 concrete
Hangars: T2 (1), B1 (1)
User sqns/units:

28 OTU (92 Gp)
01/01/43-15/10/44
Wellington I, III, X

CASTLE DONINGTON continued

Opened as satellite to Wymeswold 01/43
Transferred to Transport Command control 10/44

CHEDBURGH, Suffolk
Opened: 07/09/42
Closed: 10/52
Elevation: 410ft
Pundit code: CU
Main contractor: John Laing & Son Ltd
Runways: 3 concrete
Hangars: T2 (2), B1 (1)
User sqns/units:

214 Sqn (3 Gp)
01/10/42-10/12/43
Stirling I, III

620 Sqn (3 Gp)
17/06-23/11/43
Stirling I, III

1653 HCU (3/7 Gp)
21/11/43-12/44
Stirling I, III

218 Sqn (3 Gp)
05/12/44-10/08/45
Lancaster I, III

Opened as satellite to Stradishall 09/42
Became No 31 Base substation 06/43

CHEDDINGTON, Bucks
Opened: 03/42
Closed: Currently in use by MOD
Elevation: 304ft
Pundit code: CZ
Main contractor: George Wimpey & Co Ltd
Runways: 3 concrete
Hangars: T2 (4)
User sqns/units:

26 OTU (7/92 Gp)
15/03-03/09/42
Wellington I

Opened as temporary satellite to Wing 03-09/42
Transferred to USAAF control 10/42

CHIPPING WARDEN, Oxon
Opened: 08/41
Closed: 12/46
Elevation: 457ft
Pundit code: CW
Main contractor: Various
Runways: 3 concrete
Hangars: T2 (4), J Type (1)

CHIPPING WARDEN continued

User sqns/units:

12 OTU (6/92 Gp)
07/41-14/06/45
Wellington III, X

Opened with full station status 08/41

CHURCH BROUGHTON, Derby
Opened: 08/42
Closed: 06/45
Elevation: 225ft
Pundit code: CB
Main contractor: Various
Runways: 3 concrete/tarmac
Hangars: T2 (1), B1 (1)
User sqns/units:

27 OTU (93 Gp)
08/42-22/06/45
Wellington III, X

1429 OTF (93 Gp)
31/08/42-06/45
Wellington III, X

93 Gp Instructors' Pool
04/43-06/45
Wellington III, X

Opened as satellite to Lichfield 08/42

CONINGSBY, Lincs
Opened: 04/11/40
Closed: Currently in use by RAF
Elevation: 25ft
Pundit code: CY
Main contractor: Various
Runways: 3 concrete/asphalt
Hangars: T2 (3), B1 (1), J Type (2)
User sqns/units:

106 Sqn (5 Gp)
23/02/41-01/10/42
Hampden; Manchester; Lancaster I

97 Sqn (5 Gp)
10/03/41-02/03/42
18/04/44-12/11/46
Hampden; Manchester; Lancaster I, III

617 Sqn (5 Gp)
30/08/43-10/01/44
Lancaster I, III

619 Sqn (5 Gp)
09/01/44-17/04/44
Lancaster I, III

61 Sqn (5 Gp)
12/01/44-15/04/44
Lancaster I, III

83 Sqn (8/5 Gp)
18/04/44-05/11/46
Lancaster I, III; Lincoln 2

Opened with full station status 04/11/40
Became No 54 Base HQ 08/43

COTTESMORE, Rutland

Opened: 03/38
Closed: Currently in use by RAF
Elevation: 460ft
Pundit code: CT
Main contractor: George Wimpey & Co
Ltd
Runways: 3 tarmac
Hangars: C Type (4), T2 (1)
User sqns/units:

185 Sqn (5/6 Gp)
24/08/39-08/04/40
08/04-17/05/40
Hampden

106 Sqn (5 Gp)
01/09-06/10/39
Hampden

14 OTU (6/92 Gp)
08/04/40-01/08/43
Hampden; Hereford; Wellington I; Anson I

Opened with full station status 03/38
Transferred to USAAF control 09/43

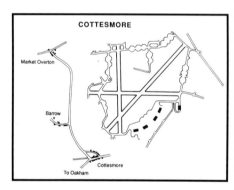

CRANFIELD, Beds

Opened: 07/37
Closed: Currently in use as Institute of
Technology
Elevation: 336ft
Pundit code: CX
Main contractor: John Laing & Son Ltd
Runways: 3 concrete
Hangars: C Type (4), T3 (1)
User sqns/units:

35 Sqn (6 Gp)
25/08-07/12/39
Battle

207 Sqn (6 Gp)
24/08-09/12/39

05/04/40-19/04/40
Battle

Opened with full station status 07/37
Transferred to Fighter Command control
05/41

CROFT, Yorks

Opened: 10/41
Closed: 1946
Elevation: 182ft
Pundit code: CR
Main contractor: Various
Runways: 3 tarmac
Hangars: T2 (2), B1 (1)
User sqns/units:

419 Sqn (4 Gp)
01/10-10/11/42
Wellington II

427 Sqn (4/6 Gp)
07/11/42-05/05/43
Wellington III, X

1664 HCU (6 Gp)
10/05-07/12/43
Halifax V; Lancaster I

431 Sqn (6 Gp)
10/12/43-07/06/45
Halifax V, III; Lancaster X

434 Sqn (6 Gp)
11/12/43-10/06/45
Halifax V, III; Lancaster I, III, X

Opened as satellite to Middleton St George
10/41
Became No 64 (RCAF) Base substation
03/43

CROUGHTON, Northants

Opened: 06/41
Closed: 05/46
Elevation: 450ft
Pundit code: AW
Main contractor: Various
Runways: 3 grass
Hangars: T2 (4)
User sqns/units:

16 OTU (7/92 Gp)
06/41-07/42
Hampden

Opened as satellite for Upper Heyford
06/41
Transferred to Flying Training Command
control 07/42

DALTON, Yorks

Opened: 11/41
Closed: 12/45
Elevation: 79ft

Pundit code: DA
Main contractor: Various
Runways: 3 tarmac
Hangars: T2 (2), B1 (1)
User sqns/units:

102 Sqn (4 Gp)
15/11/41-07/06/42
Halifax II

1652 HCU (4 Gp)
13/07-31/08/42
Halifax I, II

428 Sqn (4/6 Gp)
07/11/42-04/06/43
Wellington III, X

424 Sqn (6 Gp)
3-16/05/43
Wellington III, X

1666 HCU (6 Gp)
15/05-21/10/43
Halifax II

420 Sqn (6 Gp)
06/11-12/12/43
Halifax III

Opened as satellite to Topcliffe 11/41
Became No 61 (RCAF) Base substation
03/43
Became No 76 Base substation 11/44

DESBOROUGH, Northants

Opened: 01/09/43
Closed: 1946
Elevation: 460ft
Pundit code: DS
Main contractor: Various
Runways: 3 tarmac
Hangars: T2 (4), B1 (1)
User sqns/units:

84 OTU (92 Gp)
15/09/43-14/06/45
Wellington III, X

Opened with full station status 09/43

DISHFORTH, Yorks

Opened: 09/36
Closed: Currently in use by RAF
Elevation: 106ft
Pundit code: DH
Main contractor: Various
Runways: 3 concrete/tarmac
Hangars: C Type (5)
User sqns/units:

10 Sqn (4 Gp)
25/01/37-08/07/40
Heyford; Whitley I

18 COTTESMORE
Handley Page Herefords (illustrated) equipped No 14 OTU between April 1940 and May 1941, jointly with their stablemate the Hampden. The Hereford was identical in construction to the Hampden, except for the engines which were the in-line Napier Dagger VIII in place of the Bristol Pegasus XVIII. *via Jonathan Falconer*

19 CROFT
No 431 (Iroquois) Squadron operated the Halifax III with No 6 (RCAF) Group from Croft between March and October 1944, when it converted to the Lancaster X. Three of the squadron's Halifax IIIs are pictured on dispersal during mid-1944; SE-N is probably MZ600.
Public Archives of Canada PL40972 via K. Merrick

20 DALTON
In this specially posed photograph taken in 1942, a No 102 Squadron crew pore over a map, discussing route details with their skipper in the shadow of a Halifax II.
via Jonathan Falconer

21 DISHFORTH
No 425 (Alouette) Squadron's Wellington X HZ303:H soars away from Dishforth during September 1942. From its formation in No 4 Group on 22 June 1942, the squadron operated Wellingtons from Dishforth until its transferral to the new No 6 (RCAF) Group in January 1943. It was then detached to the Middle East from May to November as a part of No 331 Wing and on its return converted to Halifaxes. The squadron operated from Tholthorpe until the end of the war.
via Jonathan Falconer

22 DOWNHAM MARKET
An engine failure on take-off for its 14th op on 17 May 1943, caused No 218 Squadron's Stirling I EF353 to swing and then plough into the station Ops block, overturning the station commander's car. *J. McIlhinney*

23 DRIFFIELD
On the night of 20-21 May 1940 five crews from No 102 Squadron, Driffield, were sent to attack bridges over the River Oise in one of many last-ditch attempts to halt the German Blitzkrieg. Whitley V N1380:R, skippered by Flt Lt D. H. W. Owen, was the only one that failed to return that night. *via Chaz Bowyer*

24 DRIFFIELD
In this photograph, which was probably taken at Driffield in the closing months of the war, most of No 467 (RAAF) Squadron's Halifax IIIs can be seen lined up.
RAAF Official via K. Merrick

DISHFORTH continued

78 Sqn (4 Gp)
01/02/37-13/12/39
16/07/40-07/04/41
Heyford III; Whitley I, IVa

51 Sqn (4 Gp)
09/12/39-06/05/42
Whitley II, III, IV

425 Sqn (4/6 Gp)
25/06/42-16/05/43
06/11-09/12/43
Wellington III, X; Halifax III

426 Sqn (4/6 Gp)
15/10/42-17/06/43
Wellington III, X

Opened with full station status 09/36
Became No 61 Base substation 01/43
Became No 76 Base substation 11/44

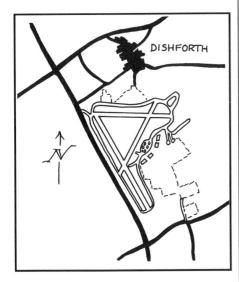

DONCASTER, Yorks

Opened: 01/16
Closed: 05/54
Elevation: 25ft
Pundit code: None
Main contractor: Various
Runways: 2 grass, 1 metal sheeting
Hangars: Bellman (3)
User sqns/units:

18 OTU (93 Gp)
06/43-01/45
Wellington III,X

Used as satellite to Finningley 06/43

DOWNHAM MARKET, Norfolk

Opened: 07/42
Closed: 24/10/46
Elevation: 117ft
Pundit code: DO
Main contractor: Various

DOWNHAM MARKET continued

Runways: 3 concrete
Hangars: T2 (2), B1 (1)
User sqns/units:

218 Sqn (3 Gp)
10/07/42-07/03/44
Stirling I, III

623 Sqn (3 Gp)
10/08-06/12/43
Stirling III

214 Sqn (3 Gp)
01/12/43-17/01/44
Stirling III

635 Sqn (8 Gp)
20/03/44-01/09/45
Lancaster III, VI

571 Sqn (LNSF) (8 Gp)
07-24/04/44
Mosquito XVI

608 Sqn (8 Gp)
01/08/44-24/08/45
Mosquito XVI, XX, XXV

Opened as satellite to Marham 07/42
Raised to full station status 03/44
*Flt Sgt A. A. Aaron DFM, 218 Sqn, awarded posthumous VC, Turin 12-13/08/43
*Sqn Ldr I. W. Bazalgette DFC, 635 Sqn, awarded posthumous VC, Troissy St Maxim 04/08/44

DRIFFIELD, Yorks

Opened: 30/07/36
Closed: Currently in use by Army
Elevation: 63ft
Pundit code: DR
Main contractor: Various
Runways: 3 concrete
Hangars: C Type (5)
User sqns/units:

102 Sqn (4 Gp)
11/07/38-25/08/40
Heyford II, III; Whitley III, V

77 Sqn (4 Gp)
25/07/38-28/08/40
Wellesley; Whitley III, V

97 Sqn (6 Gp)
30/04-20/05/40
Whitley

88 Sqn (2 Gp)
14-23/06/40
Battle

104 Sqn (4 Gp)
07/04/41-14/02/42
Blenheim IV; Wellington II

405 Sqn (4 Gp)
23/04-20/06/41
Wellington II

DRIFFIELD continued

158 Sqn (4 Gp)
14/02-06/06/42
Wellington II

466 Sqn (4 Gp)
15/10-22/12/42
03/06/44-06/09/45
Wellington II, X; Halifax II, III, VI

196 Sqn (4 Gp)
07/11-22/12/42
Wellington III

462 Sqn (4 Gp)
12/08-22/12/44
Halifax III

Opened with full station status 30/07/36
Became No 43 Base HQ 06/06/43

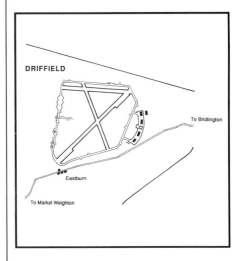

DUNHOLME LODGE, Lincs

Opened: 05/43
Closed: 11/44
Elevation: 100ft
Pundit code: DL
Main contractor: Various
Runways: 3 concrete/tarmac
Hangars: T2 (2), B1 (1)
User sqns/units:

44 Sqn (5 Gp)
31/05/43-30/09/44
Lancaster I, III

619 Sqn (5 Gp)
17/04-28/09/44
Lancaster I, III

170 Sqn (1 Gp)
22/10-29/11/44
Lancaster I, III

Opened with full station status 05/43
Closed 11/44

EAST KIRKBY, Lincs

Opened: 20/08/43
Closed: 04/70
Elevation: 40ft

EAST KIRKBY continued

Pundit code: EK
Main contractor: John Laing & Son Ltd
Runways: 3 concrete
Hangars: T2 (6), B1 (1)
User sqns/units:

57 Sqn (5 Gp)
27/08/43-27/11/45
Lancaster I, III

630 Sqn (5 Gp)
15/11/43-18/07/45
Lancaster I, III

Opened with full station status 20/08/43
Became No 55 Base HQ 15/04/44

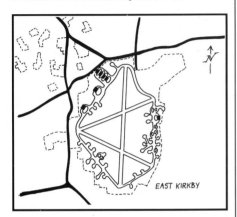

EAST MOOR, Yorks

Opened: 06/42
Closed: 06/46
Elevation: 91ft
Pundit code: EM
Main contractor: Various
Runways: 3 concrete
Hangars: T2 (2), B1 (1)
User sqns/units:

158 Sqn (4 Gp)
06/06-06/11/42
Halifax II

429 Sqn (4/6 Gp)
07/11/42-13/08/43
Wellington III, X

432 Sqn (6 Gp)
19/09/43-15/05/45
Wellington X; Lancaster II; Halifax III, VII

1679 HCU (6 Gp)
20/05-13/12/43
Lancaster II

415 Sqn (6 Gp)
26/07/44-15/05/45
Halifax III, VII

Opened as satellite to Linton-on-Ouse
06/42
Became No 62 Base substation 04/43

28

EAST WRETHAM, Norfolk

Opened: 03/40
Closed: 07/46
Elevation: 135ft
Pundit code: UT
Main contractor: Various
Runways: 3 grass
Hangars: Bellman (2)
User sqns/units:

311 Sqn (3 Gp)
16/09/40-28/04/42
Wellington I

1429 Flt (3 Gp)
01-07/42
Wellington, Oxford

115 Sqn (3 Gp)
08/11/42-06/08/43
Wellington III; Lancaster II

1678 HCU (3 Gp)
03-08/43
Lancaster II

Opened as satellite to Honington 03/40
Closed to C&M 08/42
Reopened as satellite to Mildenhall 11/42
Transferred to USAAF control 10/43

EDGEHILL, Warks

Opened: 10/41
Closed: 06/45
Elevation: 628ft
Pundit code: EH
Main contractor: Various
Runways: 3 concrete/tarmac
Hangars: T2 (2), B1 (1)
User sqns/units:

21 OTU (6/91 Gp)
21/10/41-12/04/43
Wellington I

12 OTU (6/92 Gp)
12/04/43-06/45
Wellington I, III, X

Opened as satellite to Moreton-in-Marsh
10/41
Became satellite to Chipping Warden
04/43

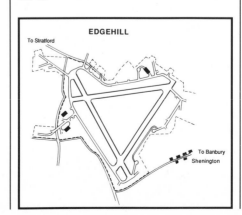

ELGIN, Moray

Opened: 06/40
Closed: 1947
Elevation: 100ft
Pundit code: Not known
Main contractor: Various
Runways: 3 grass
Hangars: T2 (1), B1 (1)
User sqns/units:

21 Sqn (2 Gp)
24/06-30/10/40
Blenheim IV

57 Sqn (2 Gp)
23/06-14/08/40
Blenheim IV

20 OTU (6/91 Gp)
06/40-06/45
Wellington III, X

Opened as satellite to Lossiemouth 06:40

ELSHAM WOLDS, Lincs

Opened: 07/41
Closed: 1947
Elevation: 241ft
Pundit code: ES
Main contractor: Various
Runways: 3 concrete
Hangars: J1 (1), T2 (5)
User sqns/units:

103 Sqn (1 Gp)
11/07/42-26/11/45
Wellington I; Halifax II; Lancaster I, III

576 Sqn (1 Gp)
25/11/43-31/10/44
Lancaster I, III

100 Sqn (1 Gp)
01/04-03/12/45
Lancaster I, III

Opened with full station status 07/41
Became No 13 Base 1943

ELVINGTON, Yorks

Opened: 10/42
Closed: Currently in use by RAF
Elevation: 44ft
Pundit code: EV
Main contractor: Various
Runways: 3 asphalt
Hangars: T2 (2), B1 (1)
User sqns/units:

77 Sqn (4 Gp)
05/10/42-15/05/44
Whitley; Halifax II, V

346 Sqn (4 Gp)
16/05/44-20/10/45
Halifax V, III, VI

25 EAST KIRKBY
Lancaster I W4232:B joined No 57 Squadron
at East Kirkby early in 1943, serving later
with No 1660 Heavy Conversion Unit (HCU),
Swinderby, and No 50 Squadron,
Skellingthorpe. It finished its life with No 5
Lancaster Finishing School (LFS) at Syerston,
where it suffered structural failure and
broke up in mid-air on 17 April 1944.
via Jonathan Falconer

26 EAST MOOR
Sqn Ldr A. Ennis DSO, DFC, poses with his
crew and groundcrew in front of No 158
Squadron's Halifax II W1108:E 'The Menace',
during July 1942, a few weeks after the
squadron had moved to the base. Ennis was
killed in action on 17 June 1944 whilst
serving with No 99 Squadron in India.
via Chaz Bowyer

27 EAST WRETHAM
The only Czech squadron in Bomber
Command, No 311 (Czechoslovak) Squadron
spent 18 months at East Wretham with No 3
Group before moving to Aldergrove in April
1942 to join Coastal Command. Here
Wellington Ic R1598:C receives the attention
of its groundcrew at its dispersal. 'C-Charlie'
crashed at East Wretham on 23 October
1941. *B. M. Rynhout via Chaz Bowyer*

28 EAST WRETHAM
This Lancaster II of No 115 Squadron
skippered by Sgt Jolly was attacked
returning from Cologne on the night of
28 June 1943 by two Focke-Wulf Fw190
nightfighters. The rear turret and its gunner
were completely shot away in the ensuing
combat, but the Lanc's other gunners
claimed one Fw190 as a probable. *IWM CE79*

No 77 Squadron moved to Elvington on
5 October 1942 and remained there until
15 May 1944, operating Halifax IIs and Vs.
Here the squadron's MkII Srs I (Special)
JB911:X beats up the airfield to the delight of
the watching groundcrews during July 1943.
IWM CH10594

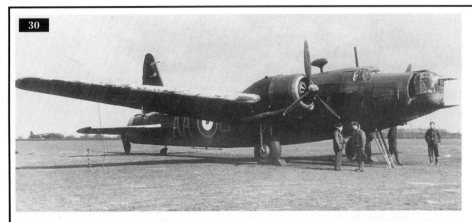

30   FELTWELL
Pictured here ready for the off, this
somewhat battered Wellington Ic, T2835:C,
belongs to No 75 (New Zealand) Squadron.
The starboard wing leading edge bears
evidence of liberal applications of Kilfrost
de-icing paste. Later, T2835 went on to serve
with No 12 OTU at Chipping Warden.
via Chaz Bowyer

31   FISKERTON
Flying Control at Fiskerton on the night of
2-3 January 1944, awaiting the return of the
base's resident squadron, No 49, and its
Lancasters, from Berlin. From left to right:
Flt Lt L. Bone; ?;?; Cpl Brown, WAAF; and
AC1 K. G. Clarke.   *IWM CH12207*

32   FISKERTON
Fiskerton as it was in 1978, with its derelict
control tower seen against the backdrop of
the airfield's sole B1 hangar. *via Chaz Bowyer*

33   FISKERTON
Skippered by Flt Sgt J.Paddison, No 1668
HCU's Lancaster III JB228 suffered an engine
fire on a cross-country training flight and
force-landed at Fiskerton on 10 March 1945,
where it burned. *via B. Robertson*

ELVINGTON continued

347 Sqn (4 Gp)
20/06/44-20/10/45
Halifax V, III, VI

Opened as satellite to Pocklington 10/42
Became No 42 Base substation 1943

ENSTONE, Oxon
Opened: 09/42
Closed: 1947
Elevation: 550ft
Pundit code: EN
Main contractor: Various
Runways: 3 concrete
Hangars: T2 (1), B1 (1)
User sqns/units:

21 OTU (6/91 Gp)
12/04/43-08/45
Wellington I, III, X

Became satellite to Moreton-in-Marsh
04/43

FALDINGWORTH, Lincs
Opened: 10/43
Closed: 11/72
Elevation: 48ft
Pundit code: FH
Main contractor: John Laing & Son Ltd
Runways: 3 concrete
Hangars: T2 (2), B1 (1)
User sqns/units:

300 Sqn (1 Gp)
01/03/44-11/10/46
Lancaster I, III

1667 HCU (1 Gp)
10:43-02:44
Lancaster I, III; Halifax

Became No 14 Base substation 12/43

FELTWELL, Norfolk
Opened: 04/37
Closed: 05/58
Elevation: 25ft
Pundit code: FL
Main contractor: Various
Runways: 3 grass
Hangars: C Type (5)
User sqns/units:

37 Sqn (3 Gp)
26/04/37-13/11/40
Wellington I

75 Sqn (3 Gp)
08/04/40-15/08/42
Wellington I, III

57 Sqn (3 Gp)
18/11/40-04/09/42
Wellington I, II, III

FELTWELL continued

464 Sqn (2 Gp)
15/08/42-03/04/43
Ventura I, II

487 Sqn (2 Gp)
15/08/42-03/04/43
Ventura II

192 Sqn (3 Gp)
05/04-25/11/43
Mosquito IV, Wellington X

Bombing Development Unit (BDU)
04-11/43;
01-06/45
Halifax III, VI; Lancaster I,III; Mosquito
IX, XVI, XX

320 Sqn (2 Gp)
04-05/43
Mitchell II

1473 RCM Flt (3 Gp)
14/09-11/43
Leopard Moth; Wellington; Anson;
Whitley

3 LFS (3 Gp)
11/43-01/45
Lancaster I, III

Opened with full station status 04/37
*Sgt J. A. Ward, 75 Sqn, awarded VC,
Munster 07-08/07/41

FINMERE, Bucks
Opened: 1941
Closed: 07/45
Elevation: 405ft
Pundit code: FI
Main contractor: Various
Runways: 3 concrete
Hangars: T2 (1), B1 (1)
User sqns/units:

13 OTU (92 Gp)
08/42-11/43
Blenheim I, IV; Mitchell II; Boston IIIa;
Mosquito

307 FTU (92 Gp)
18/03-05/43
Havoc; Boston

Satellite for Bicester 08/42
Transferred to Flying Training Command
control 11/43

FINNINGLEY, Yorks
Opened: 09/36
Closed: Currently in use by RAF
Elevation: 28ft
Pundit code: FV
Main contractor: Various
Runways: 3 concrete/tarmac
Hangars: C Type (5)

FINNINGLEY continued

User sqns/units:

76 Sqn (5 Gp)
12/04/37-23/09/39
Hampden; Anson

106 Sqn (5 Gp)
06/10/39-22/02/41
Hampden

98 Sqn (2 Gp)
19/03-16/04/40
Battle

7 Sqn (6 Gp)
30/04-20/05/40
15-23/09/40
Hampden

12 Sqn (2 Gp)
16/06-03/07/40
Battle

25 OTU (7/93 Gp)
01/03/41-07/01/43
Hampden; Manchester; Wellington

18 OTU (7/93 Gp)
07/03/43-01/45
Wellington III, X

*Bomber Command Instructors' School
(BCIS) (7 Gp)*
05/12/44-22/01/47
Wellington X; Lancaster I, III; Halifax III;
Spitfire; Master; Oxford

Opened with full station status 09/36

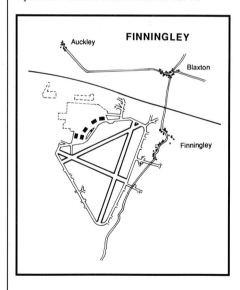

FISKERTON, Lincs
Opened: 01/43
Closed: 12/45
Elevation: 50ft
Pundit code: FN
Main contractor: Various
Runways: 3 concrete/tarmac
Hangars: T2 (2), B1 (1)

FISKERTON continued

User sqns/units:

49 Sqn (5 Gp)
31/10/44-13/09/45
Lancaster I, III

576 Sqn (1 Gp)
31/10/44-13/09/45
Lancaster I, III

150 Sqn (1 Gp)
01-23/11/44
Lancaster I, III

Opened as No 52 Base substation 01/43

FORRES, Moray
Opened: 04/40
Closed: 10/44
Elevation: 50ft
Pundit code: Not known
Main contractor: Various
Runways: 2 grass
Hangars: T2 (1)
User sqns/units:

19 OTU (6/91 Gp)
27/04/40-22/10/44
Whitley

Opened as satellite for Lossiemouth 04/40

FOULSHAM, Norfolk
Opened: 05/42
Closed: 1945
Elevation: 173ft
Pundit code: FU
Main contractor: Various
Runways: 3 tarmac
Hangars: T2 (9), B1 (1)
User sqns/units:

98 Sqn (2 Gp)
15/10/42-18/08/43
Mitchell II

180 Sqn (2 Gp)
19/10/42-18/08/43
Mitchell II

514 Sqn (3 Gp)
01/09-23/11/43
Lancaster II

1678 HCU (3 Gp)
16/09-23/11/43
Lancaster II

192 Sqn (100 Gp)
25/11/43-22/08/45
Halifax III, V; Mosquito XVI; Wellington X

462 Sqn (100 Gp)
22/12/44-24/09/45
Halifax III

Opened with full station status 05/42

34

FULBECK, Lincs
Opened: 1940
Closed: 1970
Elevation: 50ft
Pundit code: FK
Main contractor: Various
Runways: 3 concrete/tarmac
Hangars: T2 (5)
User sqns/units:

49 Sqn (5 GP)
16/10/44-22/04/45
Lancaster I, III

189 Sqn (5 Gp)
02/11/44-08/04/45
Lancaster I, III

Opened as satellite for Syerston 1940
Transferred to USAAF control 01/10/43
Returned to RAF control 17/10/44 as No
56 Base substation

FULL SUTTON, Yorks
Opened: 05/44
Closed: 04/63
Elevation: 49ft
Pundit code: FS
Main contractor: Various
Runways: 3 concrete/tarmac
Hangars: T2 (2), B1 (1)
User sqns/units:

77 Sqn (4 Gp)
15/05/44-31/08/45
Halifax II, III, V, VI

Opened as No 42 Base substation 05/44

GAMSTON, Notts
Opened: 12/42
Closed: 1957
Elevation: 90ft
Pundit code: GB
Main contractor: Various
Runways: 3 concrete/tarmac
Hangars: T2 (4), B1 (1)
User sqns/units:

82 OTU (93 Gp)
01/06/43-01/06/44
Wellington III, X

86 OTU (93 Gp)
01/06-10/44
Wellington III, X

30 OTU (93/91 Gp)
02-06/45
Wellington III, X

Opened as satellite to Ossington in Flying
Training Command 12/42
Transferred to Bomber Command control
as satellite to Ossington in 93 Gp 05/43
Transferred to 7 Gp control 11/44
Transferred to 91 Gp control 02/45

GAYDON, Warks
Opened: 13/06/42
Closed: 31/10/74
Elevation: 41ft
Pundit code: GP
Main contractor: John Laing & Son Ltd
Runways: 3 concrete/tar
Hangars: T2 (1), B1 (1)
User sqns/units:

12 OTU (91 Gp)
13/06-01/09/42
Wellington I, III, X

22 OTU (91 Gp)
01/09/42-01/07/45
Wellington I, III, X

Opened as satellite to Chipping Warden
13/06/42
Became satellite to Wellesbourne
Mountford 01/09/42

GRANSDEN LODGE, Beds
Opened: 04/42
Closed: 1955
Elevation: 248ft
Pundit code: GL
Main contractor: John Laing & Son Ltd
Runways: 3 concrete
Hangars: T2 (2), B1 (1)
User sqns/units:

1418 Flt (3 Gp)
08/04-20/07/42
Wellington

1474 Flt (3 Gp)
04/07/42-04/01/43
Wellington

*No 1 Bombing Development Unit (BDU)
(3 Gp)*
20/07/42-04/43
Stirling; Lancaster; Halifax; Wellington III;
Proctor

192 Sqn (3 Gp)
04/01-05/04/43
Wellington I, III, X; Mosquito IV

*PFF Navigation Training Unit (NTU)
(8 Gp)*
04-06/43
Halifax II

405 Sqn (8 Gp)
19/04/43-26/05/45
Halifax II; Lancaster I, III

97 Sqn (5 Gp)
08-09/43
Lancaster I, III

142 Sqn (LNSF) (8 Gp)
25/10/44-28/09/45
Mosquito XVI, XXV, B5

Opened as satellite to Tempsford 04/42
Became satellite to Oakington 04/43
Achieved full station status 06/43

GRAVELEY, Hunts

Opened: 03/42
Closed: 12/68
Elevation: 177ft
Pundit code: GR
Main contractor: Various
Runways: 3 concrete
Hangars: T2 (3), B1 (1)
User sqns/units:

161 Sqn (3 Gp)
01/03-08/04/42
Lysander IIIa; Hudson I; Whitley V

35 Sqn (8 Gp)
15/08/42-16/09/46
Halifax II, III; Lancaster I, III

692 Sqn (LNSF) (8 Gp)
01/01/44-04/06/45
Mosquito IV, XVI

571 Sqn (LNSF) (8 Gp)
05-24/04/44
Mosquito XVI

Opened as satellite to Tempsford 03/42
Became satellite to Wyton 08/42
Achieved full station status 05/43

GREAT MASSINGHAM, Norfolk

Opened: 09/40
Closed: 04/58
Elevation: 295ft
Pundit code: GM
Main contractor: Various
Runways: 3 concrete
Hangars: T2 (4), B1 (1)
User sqns/units:

18 Sqn (2 Gp)
09/09/40-03/04/41
Blenheim IV

107 Sqn (2 Gp)
11/05/41-20/08/43
Blenheim IV; Boston III, IIIa

90 Sqn (2 Gp)
15/05-30/08/41
Fortress I

98 Sqn (2 Gp)
12/09-19/10/42
Mitchell II, III

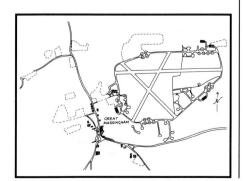

GREAT MASSINGHAM continued

342 Sqn (2 Gp)
19/07-06/09/43
Boston IIIa

1692 Bomber Support Training Unit (BSTU)
22/05/44-15/06/45
Beaufighter; Mosquito VI; Wellington XVIII; Anson; Oxford

169 Sqn (100 Gp)
04/06/44-10/08/45
Mosquito II, VI, XIX

Opened as satellite to West Raynham 09/40
Achieved full station status 03/06/44

GRIMSBY/WALTHAM, Lincs

Opened: 11/41
Closed: 1946
Elevation: 67ft
Pundit code: GY
Main contractor: John Laing & Son Ltd
Runways: 3 concrete/tarmac
Hangars: T2 (2), B1 (1)
User sqns/units:

142 Sqn (1 Gp)
26/11/41-19/12/42
Wellington II, III

100 Sqn (1 Gp)
15/12/42-01/04/45
Lancaster I, III

550 Sqn (1 Gp)
20/10/43-03/01/44
Lancaster I, III

Opened as satellite to Binbrook 11/41
Became No 12 Base substation 1943

HAMPSTEAD NORRIS, Berks

Opened: 09/40
Closed: 1945
Elevation: 376ft
Pundit code: HR
Main contractor: Various
Runways: 3 concrete/tarmac
Hangars: T2 (1), B1 (1), Bessoneau (1)
User sqns/units:

15 OTU (6/91 Gp)
09/40-03/44
Wellington I, III, X

Opened as satellite to Harwell 09/40
Transferred to No 38 Gp control 01/03/44

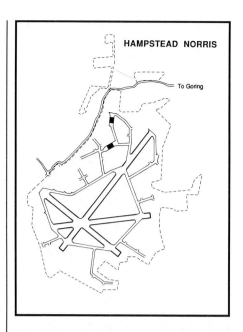

HARRINGTON, Northants

Opened: 09/11/43
Closed: 23/01/63
Elevation: 520ft
Pundit code: HR
Main contractor: Various
Runways: 3 concrete
Hangars: T2 (4)
User sqns/units: none

Opened as satellite to Desborough (92 Gp) 09/11/43
Declared surplus to RAF requirements and transferred to USAAF control 28/03/44

HARWELL, Oxon

Opened: 02/37
Closed: 1945
Elevation: 384ft
Pundit code: HW
Main contractor: John Laing & Son Ltd
Runways: 3 concrete
Hangars: C Type (4)

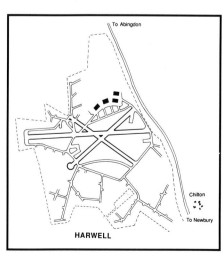

37   GREAT MASSINGHAM

On 25 July 1942, Plt Off Burghley and crew flew a No 107 Squadron Boston III from Great Massingham, unescorted and in daylight, to bomb the Dutch inland port of Sluiskil. This dramatic photograph taken at rooftop height shows a bomb from Burghley's aircraft exploding on a gantry on the wharf. *via Jonathan Falconer*

34   FOULSHAM

No 180 Squadron flew the North American Mitchell right through from September 1942 until September 1945. It was based at Foulsham from 19 October 1942 before moving to Dunsfold on 18 August 1943. Mitchell II FL218:W is pictured here during 1943. *RAF Museum 5972-5 via Chaz Bowyer*

35   GRAVELEY

With a two-man crew, a Mosquito armed with a 4,000lb HC 'Cookie' blast bomb could fly to Berlin in two hours at 27,000ft, compared with some four hours for a seven-crew Lancaster or Halifax at heights of around 20,000ft. The first 'Cookie' to be dropped by a Mosquito was from a No 692 Squadron Light Night Striking Force (LNSF) aircraft flying from Graveley, skippered by Sqn Ldr S.D.Watts on 23 February 1944, the target Dusseldorf.

In this April 1944 picture, armourers wheel a 'Cookie' up to No 692 Squadron's Mosquito BIV Srs II DZ637 at Graveley, ready for loading into the bomb bay. *via Chaz Bowyer*

36   GRAVELEY

A Pathfinder Force Lancaster of No 35 Squadron takes off between two bands of flame during a FIDO test early in 1945. FIDO burner installations equipped 15 of the RAF's wartime airfields in England, using a staggering total of 30 million gallons of petrol to heat and disperse fog from airfield runways to let aircraft take off and land in safety.

FIDO was installed at Carnaby, Fiskerton, Foulsham, Graveley, Ludford Magna, Melbourne, Metheringham, Sturgate, Tuddenham and Woodbridge. Non-Bomber Command airfields so equipped were Blackbushe, Bradwell Bay, Manston and St Eval. *IWM CH15271*

HARWELL continued

User sqns/units:

75 Sqn (6 Gp)
17/09/39-04/04/40
Wellington I

148 Sqn (6 Gp)
17/09/39-08/04/40
Wellington I

15 OTU (6/91 Gp)
08/04/40-03/03/44
Wellington I, X

Opened with full station status 02/37
Transferred to No 38 Gp control 01/04/44

HEMSWELL, Lincs
Opened: 01/37
Closed: 1967
Elevation: 180ft
Pundit code: HL
Main contractor: Various
Runways: 3 concrete/tarmac
Hangars: C Type (4), T2 (1)
User sqns/units:

61 Sqn (5 Gp)
08/03/37-17/07/41
Anson; Audax; Blenheim I; Hampden;
Manchester

144 Sqn (5 Gp)
09/03/37-17/07/41
Anson; Audax; Blenheim I; Hampden

300 Sqn (1 Gp)
18/07/41-18/05/42;
31/01-22/06/43
Wellington I, III, IV, X

301 Sqn (1 Gp)
18/07/41-07/04/43
Wellington I, IV

305 Sqn (1 Gp)
22/07/42-22/06/43
Wellington II, IV, X

83 Sqn (5 Gp)
18/04/44-01/01/56
Lancaster I, III; Lincoln

1 LFS (1 Gp)
01-11/44
Lancaster I, III

150 Sqn (1 Gp)
22/11/44-07/11/45
Lancaster I, III

170 Sqn (1 Gp)
29/11/44-14/11/45
Lancaster I, III

Opened with full station status 01/37
Became No 13 Base substation 10/44

HINTON-IN-THE-HEDGES, Northants
Opened: 11/40
Closed: 07/45
Elevation: 470ft
Pundit code: HI
Main contractor: Various
Runways: 3 concrete/tarmac
Hangars: B1 (1), T1 (1)
User sqns/units:

13 OTU (7/92 Gp)
11/40-07/42
Blenheim

16 OTU (92 Gp)
07/42-04/43
Wellington I

1478 Flt (26 Gp)
15/04/43-07/44
Whitley V

Signals Development Unit (SDU) (26 Gp)
06/43-07/44
Oxford; Anson; Master

Opened as satellite for Bicester 11/40
Satellite to Upper Heyford 07/42

HIXON, Staffs
Opened: 05/42
Closed: 11/57
Elevation: 267ft
Pundit code: HX
Main contractor: Various
Runways: 3 concrete/tarmac
Hangars: T2 (4), B1 (1)
User sqns/units:

30 OTU (93 Gp)
28/06/42-02/02/45
Wellington III, X

Opened as satellite to Lichfield 05/42
Achieved full station status 07/42

HOLME-ON-SPALDING-MOOR, Yorks
Opened: 08/41
Closed: 10/45
Elevation: 12ft
Pundit code: HM
Main contractor: Various
Runways: 3 tarmac
Hangars: J Type (1), T2 (5)
User sqns/units:

458 Sqn (4 Gp)
25/08/41-23/03/42
Wellington I, IV

101 Sqn (1 Gp)
29/09/42-15/06/43
Wellington III; Lancaster I, III

HOLME continued

76 Sqn (4 Gp)
16/06/43-08/08/45
Halifax III, V, VI

Opened with full station status 08/41
Became No 44 Base HQ 06/43
Transferred to Transport Command
control 07/05/45

HONEYBOURNE, Worcs
Opened: 10/41
Closed: 01/46
Elevation: 178ft
Pundit code: HQ
Main contractor: John Laing & Son Ltd
Runways: 3 concrete
Hangars: J Type (1), T2 (4)
User sqns/units:

24 OTU (6/91 Gp)
15/03/42-24/07/45
Whitley V, VII; Wellington III, X; Anson

Opened with full station status in Ferry
Command 10/41
Transferred to Bomber Command control
03/42

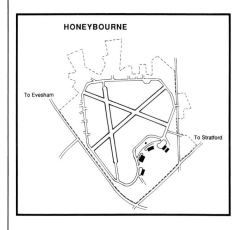

HONILEY, Warks
Opened: 05/41
Closed: 03/58
Elevation: 426ft
Pundit code: HY
Main contractor: John Laing & Son Ltd
Runways: 3 tarmac
Hangars: Bellman (3), Blister (12)
User sqns/units:

Signals Flying Unit (26 Gp)
07/44-06/46
Anson; Beaufighter; Wellington; Oxford

Opened under Fighter Command control
05/41
Transferred to Bomber Command control
07/44

38 GREAT MASSINGHAM

Flt Sgt 'Nick' Nicholls of No 107 Squadron was awarded the DFM for his skill in bringing a damaged Boston III home from the daylight raid on the Philips works at Eindhoven, Holland, on 6 December 1941. Nicholls brought AL754 D-Donald home to its Norfolk base from Operation 'Oyster' on one engine for a wheels-up landing in which the aircraft overshot the airfield and was written off. The crew managed to escape with minor bruising.
via Chaz Bowyer

HONILEY continued

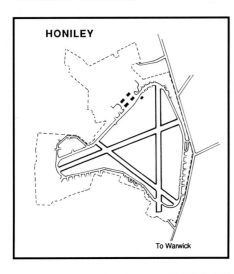

HONILEY

To Warwick

HONINGTON, Suffolk

Opened: 03/05/37
Closed: Currently in use by RAF
Elevation: 174ft
Pundit code: HT
Main contractor: John Laing & Son Ltd
Runways: 3 grass
Hangars: C Type (4)
User sqns/units:

9 Sqn (3 Gp)
15/07/39-08/08/42
Wellington I, II, III

103 Sqn (2 Gp)
18/06-03/07/40
Battle

105 Sqn (2 Gp)
14/06-10/07/40
Blenheim IV

311 Sqn (3 Gp)
29/07-16/09/40
Wellington I

214 Sqn (3 Gp)
05-12/01/42
Wellington I

Opened with full station status 05/37
Transferred to USAAF control 09/42

HORSHAM St FAITH, Norfolk

Opened: 05/40
Closed: Currently in use as Norwich
Airport
Elevation: 102ft
Pundit code: HF
Main contractor: Various
Runways: 3 concrete
Hangars: C Type (5)
User sqns/units:

139 Sqn (2 Gp)
10/06/40-13/07/41;
23/10-09/12/41
Blenheim IV

HORSHAM St FAITH continued

114 Sqn (2 Gp)
10/06-10/08/40
Blenheim IV

18 Sqn (2 Gp)
13/07-05/11/41;
05-09/12/41
Blenheim IV

105 Sqn (2 Gp)
09/12/41-22/09/42
Mosquito IV

Opened with full station status 05/40
Transferred to USAAF control 09/42

HUSBANDS BOSWORTH, Leics

Opened: 1943
Closed: 1956
Elevation: 510ft
Pundit code: HZ
Main contractor: Various
Runways: 3 concrete
Hangars: T2 (4)
User sqns/units:

14 OTU (92 Gp)
08/43-15/06/44
Wellington III, X

85 OTU (92 Gp)
06/44-??/45
Wellington III, X

Opened as satellite to Market Harborough
08/43

INGHAM, Lincs

Opened: 05/42
Closed: 01/45
Elevation: 200ft
Pundit code: Not known
Main contractor: Various
Runways: 3 grass
Hangars: T2 (2), B1 (1)
User sqns/units:

300 Sqn (1 Gp)
05/42-01/43;
22/06/43-01/03/44
Wellington III, X

199 Sqn (1 Gp)
03/02-21/06/43
Wellington III, X

305 Sqn (1 Gp)
22/06-05/09/43
Wellington III, X

Opened as satellite for Hemswell 05/42
Became No 13 Base substation 03/44

KELSTERN, Lincs

Opened: 09/43
Closed: 05/45
Elevation: 415ft
Pundit code: KS
Main contractor: Various
Runways: 3 concrete/tarmac
Hangars: T2 (2), B1 (1)
User sqns/units:

625 Sqn (1 Gp)
01/10/43-05/04/45
Lancaster I, III

170 Sqn (1 Gp)
15-22/10/44
Lancaster I, III

Opened as No 12 Base substation 09/43

KIMBOLTON, Cambs

Opened: 11/41
Closed: 1946
Elevation: 241ft
Pundit code: KI
Main contractor: Various
Runways: 3 concrete/asphalt
Hangars: T2 (2)
User sqns/units:

460 Sqn (1 Gp)
29/11/41-04/01/42
Wellington IV

Opened as satellite to Molesworth 11/41
Transferred to USAAF control 07/42

KINLOSS, Moray

Opened: 1939
Closed: Currently in use by RAF
Elevation: 19ft
Pundit code: KW
Main contractor: Various
Runways: 3 concrete/tarmac
Hangars: K Type (2), L Type (9), Bellman (2)
User sqns/units:

19 OTU (7/91 Gp)
17/05/40-26/06/45
Whitley III, V; Wellington III, X

Opened with full station status in Flying
Training Command 1939
Transferred to Bomber Command control
04/40

KIRMINGTON, Lincs

Opened: 10/42
Closed: Currently in use as Humberside
Airport
Elevation: 86ft
Pundit code: KG
Main contractor: Various
Runways: 3 concrete/tarmac
Hangars: T2 (2), B1 (1)

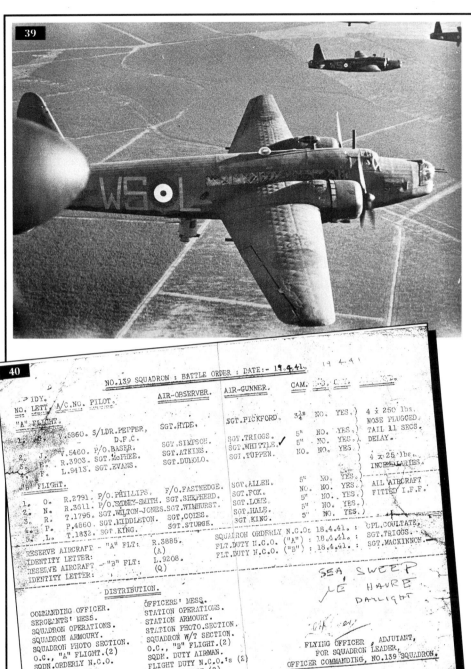

39 HONINGTON

No 9 Squadron moved to Honington from Stradishall with its Heyford IIIs and Wellington Is on 15 July 1939, remaining there until August 1942. The antiquated Heyford biplane bombers were all replaced by May 1939 with the new 'geodetic' Vickers Wellington I. Mk Ia N3000:L is pictured here near its base during early 1940; note the ventral 'dustbin' gun turret which was a feature on early Wellingtons, but one which was soon discontinued on subsequent marks. *via Chaz Bowyer*

40 HORSHAM St FAITH

The Battle Order for No 139 Squadron, Horsham, 19 April 1941, for a daylight anti-shipping sweep in the Le Havre area. No aircraft were lost from this daylight coastal operation by 34 Blenheim IVs of No 2 Group and two Hampdens, but two large enemy merchant ships were hit and believed sunk. *via Jonathan Falconer*

41 HORSHAM St FAITH

No 139 Squadron reformed at Horsham on 8 June 1942 with Blenheim Vs and Mosquito IVs, the second RAF squadron to operate the Mosquito. It was not until some four months later that the squadron received its own aircraft, until then flying the Blenheim V as a stop-gap and Mosquitoes borrowed from No 105 Squadron. *via Chaz Bowyer*

42 INGHAM

Flt Lt Marian Wlodarczyk of No 300 (Masovian) Squadron fell foul of the German defences over Bremen on 4-5 September 1942, but still made it home to Ingham. The stripped rear fuselage of his twin-Wasp Wellington IV, Z1407 'Z-Zoska', bears testimony to the ferocity of the German defences and the strength of the Wimpy's geodetic construction. No 300 Squadron was twice based at Ingham. *Sikorski Institute via Chaz Bowyer*

User sqns/units:

150 Sqn (1 Gp)
10-12/42
Wellington I, III

142 Sqn (1 Gp)
19/12/42-27/01/43
Wellington III

166 Sqn (1 Gp)
27/01/43-18/11/45
Lancaster I, III

153 Sqn (1 Gp)
07-15/10/44
Lancaster I, III

Opened as satellite to Elsham Wolds
10/42
Became No 13 Base substation 1943

LAKENHEATH, Suffolk
Opened: 06/41
Closed: Currently in use by USAF
Elevation: 50ft
Pundit code: LK
Main contractor: Various
Runways: 3 concrete
Hangars: T2 (2), B1 (1)
User sqns/units:

20 OTU (6/91 Gp)
24/11/41-12/01/42
Wellington I

149 Sqn (3 Gp)
06/04/42-15/05/44
Stirling I, III

199 Sqn (3 Gp)
21/06/43-01/05/44
Wellington III, X; Stirling III

Opened as satellite to Mildenhall 06/41
Became No 31 Base substation 12/42
Closed for rebuilding to Very Heavy
Bomber (VHB) station standard 05/44
*Flt Sgt R.H.Middleton, 149 Sqn, awarded
posthumous VC, Turin 28-29/11/42

LANGAR, Notts
Opened: 09/42
Closed: 09/68
Elevation: 118ft
Pundit code: LA
Main contractor: Various
Runways: 3 concrete/tarmac
Hangars: T2 (2)
User sqns/units:

207 Sqn (5 Gp)
20/09/42-12/10/43
Lancaster I, III

1669 HCU (7 Gp)
11/44-03/45
Lancaster I, III; Halifax

Opened as satellite to Bottesford 09/42
Transferred to USAAF control 18/10/43
Returned to RAF Bomber Command
control 10/44
Became No 72 Base substation 11/44

LECONFIELD, Yorks
Opened: 03/12/36
Closed: Currently in use by RAF
Elevation: 25ft
Pundit code: LC
Main contractor: Various
Runways: 3 concrete
Hangars: C Type (5)
User sqns/units:

97 Sqn (6 Gp)
07/01/37-17/09/39
Whitley II, III

196 Sqn (4 Gp)
22/12/42-19/07/43
Wellington X

466 Sqn (4 Gp)
22/12/42-03/06/44
Wellington X; Halifax II, III

640 Sqn (4 Gp)
07/01/44-07/05/45
Halifax III, VI

51 Sqn (4 Gp)
20/04-21/08/45
Halifax III; Stirling V

Opened as satellite to Driffield 03/12/36
Transferred to Fighter Command control
10/39
Closed for runway building 12/41
Reopened under Bomber Command
control 02/12/42
Became No 43 Base substation 06/06/43

LEEMING, Yorks
Opened: 06/40
Closed: Currently in use by RAF
Elevation: 109ft
Pundit code: LG
Main contractor: Various
Runways: 3 concrete/tarmac
Hangars: C Type (5)
User sqns/units:

7 Sqn (3 Gp)
01/08-29/10/40
Stirling I

10 Sqn (4 Gp)
08/07/40-19/08/42
Whitley V; Halifax

102 Sqn (4 Gp)
25/08-01/09/40
Whitley V

35 Sqn (4 Gp)
20/11-05/12/40
Halifax I

77 Sqn (4 Gp)
05/09/41-06/05/42
Whitley V

419 Sqn (4 Gp)
13-17/08/42
Wellington III

408 Sqn (4/6 Gp)
14/09/42-26/08/43
Halifax V, II

1659 HCU (6 Gp)
06/10/42-06/03/43
Halifax

405 Sqn (6 Gp)
06/03-18/04/43
Halifax II

424 Sqn (6 Gp)
07/04-02/05/43
Wellington III, X

427 Sqn (6 Gp)
05/05/43-31/05/46
Halifax V, III; Lancaster III, X

429 Sqn (6 Gp)
13/08/43-31/05/46
Halifax II, V, III; Lancaster III, X

Opened with full station status 06/40
Became No 63 (RCAF) Base HQ 01/01/43

LICHFIELD, Staffs
Opened: 01/08/40
Closed: 04/58
Elevation: 220ft
Pundit code: LF
Main contractor: Various
Runways: 3 tarmac
Hangars: J Type (3), K Type (4), L Type
(8), B1 (1), T2 (2)
User sqns/units:

27 OTU (6/93/91 Gp)
23/04/41-08/07/45
Wellington III, X

Opened in Maintenance Command
01/08/40
Achieved full station status 05/41

LINDHOLME, Yorks
Opened: 01/06/40
Closed: Currently in use as HM Prison
Elevation: 20ft
Pundit code: LB
Main contractor: Various
Runways: 3 concrete/tarmac
Hangars: C Type (5)
User sqns/units:

50 Sqn (5 Gp)
10/07/40-20/07/41
Hampden

43 LAKENHEATH
Stirling crews of No 149 Squadron, just back from an op, unwind with cigarettes and mugs of tea before their debriefing at Lakenheath in the early spring of 1944. *IWM CH12689*

44 LAKENHEATH
Lino polished to a glassy finish and spartan utility furniture grace the Sergeants' Mess at Lakenheath in April 1944. A homely touch has been added by the provision of a few pot plants down the middle of the room.
Stirling Aircraft Association (SAA)

45 LEEMING
The position preferred by a German nightfighter pilot for a successful attack — behind and below. If the rear gunner of the bomber was not vigilant, allowing the nightfighter to creep into position in the darkness, then the end came swiftly, violently and without warning when the hunter emptied rounds of machine gun and cannon fire into the bomb-bay and fuel tanks of his quarry.

No 10 Squadron's Whitley V Z9226:K demonstrates this position. Note the rear gunner traversing his turret from left to right, scanning the sky for enemy fighters.
IWM CH4446

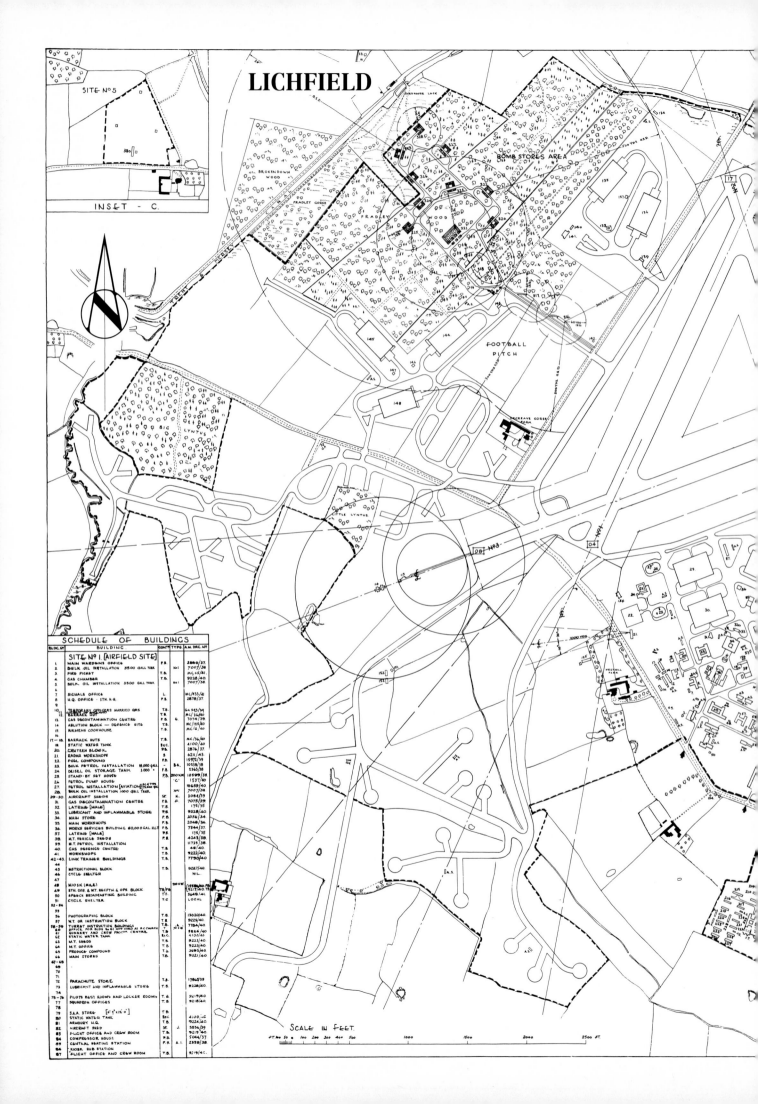

LICHFIELD

SITE Nº 5

INSET - C.

BOMB STORES AREA

BROKENDOWN WOOD

FRADLEY GORSE

FRADLEY WOOD

FOOTBALL PITCH

DECREAVE GORSE FARM

BIG LYNTUS

LITTLE LYNTUS

PESHILL FARM

SCHEDULE OF BUILDINGS

BLDG Nº	BUILDING	CONTR	TYPE	A.M. DRG Nº
	SITE Nº 1 [AIRFIELD SITE]			
1	MAIN WARDENS OFFICE		P.B.	2880/37
2	BULK OIL INSTALLATION 3500 GALL TANK		Nº1	7007/38
3	FIRE PICKET		T.B.	MC/65/41
4	GAS CHAMBER			9228/40
5	BULK OIL INSTALLATION 3500 GALL TANK		Nº1	7007/38
6				
7	SIGNALS OFFICE		L	MC/433/41
8	H.Q. OFFICE - STN. H.Q.		P.B.	2878/37
9				
10	TEMPORARY OFFICERS MARRIED QRS		T.B.	GA 543/34
11	BARRACK HUTS		T.B.	MC/36/40
12				
13	GAS DECONTAMINATION CENTRE		P.B.	7074/39
14	ABLUTION BLOCK — DEFENCE SITE			MC/125/40
15	AIRMENS COOKHOUSE		T.B.	MC/6/40
16				
17 - 18	BARRACK HUTS		T.B.	MC/36/40
19	STATIC WATER TANK		B.&C.	4100/40
20	CANTEEN BLOCK		T.B.	2876/37
21	RADAR WORKSHOPS		S	621/43
22	FUEL COMPOUND		B.4.	15972/39
23	BULK PETROL INSTALLATION 18,000 GALL		P.B.	10338/38
24	DEISEL OIL STORAGE TANK 3,000		P.B.	1363/38
25	STAND-BY SET HOUSE		200 KW	10599/38
26	PETROL PUMP HOUSE		'C'	1537/40
27	PETROL INSTALLATION [AVIATION]			10689/40
28	BULK OIL INSTALLATION 1000 GALL TANK		Nº1	7007/38
29 - 30	AIRCRAFT SHEDS		Sr.	3084/39
31	GAS DECONTAMINATION CENTRE		P.B.	7075/39
32	LATRINE [MALE]			175/35
33	LUBRICANT AND INFLAMMABLE STORE		P.B.	9228/40
34	MAIN STORE		P.B.	2056/34
35	MAIN WORKSHOPS		P.B.	2048/34
36	WORKS SERVICES BUILDING 60,000 GAL H.L.T		P.B.	7364/41
37	LATRINE [MALE]			175/35
38	M.T. VEHICLE SHEDS		P.B.	4243/38
39	M.T. PETROL INSTALLATION			11735/38
40	GAS DEFENCE CENTRE		T.B.	48/40
41	WORKSHOPS		T.B.	9222/40
42 - 43	LINK TRAINER BUILDINGS		T.B.	7730/40
44				
45	INSTRUCTIONAL BLOCK		T.B.	9227/40
46	CYCLE SHELTER			NIL.
47				
48	KIOSK [M.E.]			
49	STN. OFF. & M.T. RECPTN & OPS BLOCK		T.B./P.B	9217/40,15
50	SPEECH BROADCASTING BUILDING		T.C	5648/41
51	CYCLE SHELTER		T.C	LOCAL
52 - 54				
55				
56	PHOTOGRAPHIC BLOCK		T.B.	13020/40
57	W.T. OR INSTRUCTION BLOCK		T.B.	9225/40
58 - 59	TURRET INSTRUCTION BUILDINGS		T.B.	
60	OFFICE, FOR BLDG Nº 61 NOW USED AS R.C CHURCH			5856/40
61	GUNNERY AND CREW PROCER. CENTRE			4103/40
62	STATIC WATER TANK		B.&C.	
63	M.T. SHEDS		T.B.	9223/40
64	M.T. OFFICE		T.B.	9223/40
65	PRODUCE COMPOUND		T.B.	3693/40
66	MAIN STORES		T.B.	9221/40
67 - 68				
69				
70				
71	PARACHUTE STORE		T.B.	17865/39
73	LUBRICANT AND INFLAMMABLE STORE		T.B.	9228/40
74				
75 - 76	PILOTS REST ROOMS AND LOCKER ROOMS		T.B.	9219/40
77	SQUADRON OFFICES		T.B.	9218/40
78				
79	S.A.A STORE [6'7"x12'0"]		B.&C.	4100/-/
80	STATIC WATER TANK		T.B.	9224/40
81	ARMOURY H.Q.		St.	5836/39
82	AIRCRAFT SHED		St.	J.	5836/39
83	FLIGHT OFFICE AND CREW ROOM		T.B.	9219/40
84	COMPRESSOR HOUSE		P.B.	5044/39
85	CENTRAL HEATING STATION		A.1.	2358/38
86	KIOSK, SUB STATION			
87	FLIGHT OFFICE AND CREW ROOM		T.B.	9219/40

SCALE IN FEET.

FT. Ins 50 0   100   200   300   400   500   1000   1500   2000   2500 FT.

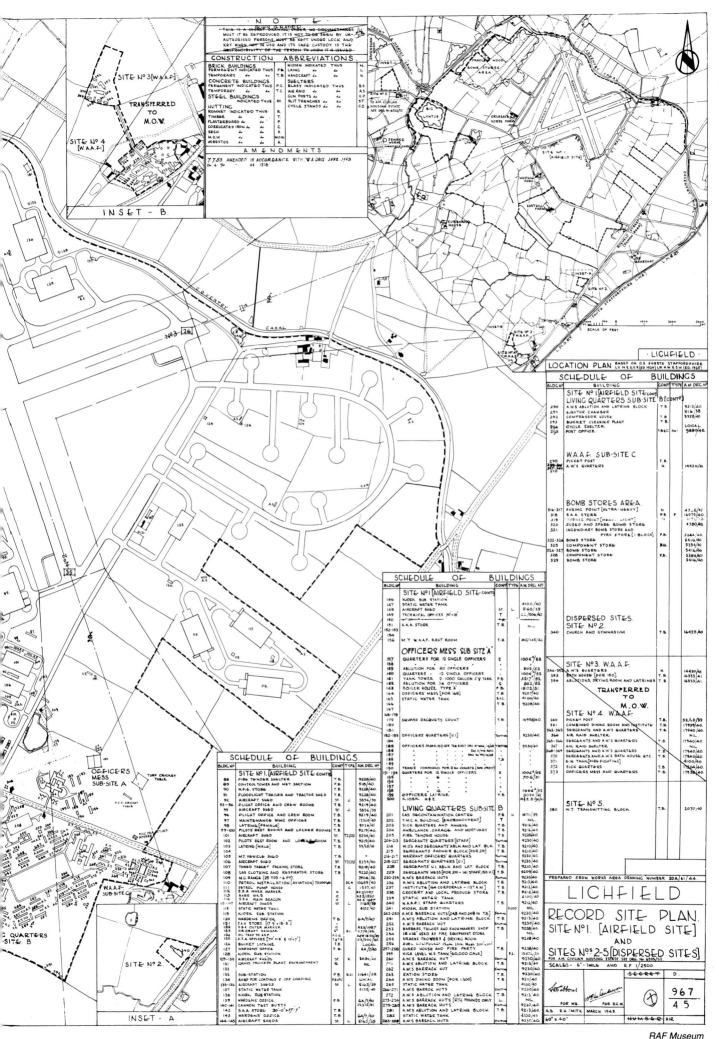

LINDHOLME continued

408 Sqn (5 Gp)
24/06-19/07/41
Hampden

304 Sqn (1 Gp)
19/07/41-10/05/42
Wellington I

305 Sqn (1 Gp)
20/07/41-22/07/42
Wellington I

1656 HCU (1/7 Gp)
10/42-11/45
Manchester; Halifax II, V; Lancaster I, III

1667 HCU (1 Gp)
06-10/43
Lancaster I, III; Halifax II, V

1 LFS (1 Gp)
11/43-01/44
Lancaster I, III

Opened with full station status as Hatfield
Woodhouse 01/06/40
Name changed to Lindholme 18/08/40
Became No 11 (Training) Base HQ 09/43
Became No 71 (Training) Base HQ
03/11/44

LINTON-ON-OUSE, Yorks

Opened: 13/05/37
Closed: Currently in use by RAF
Elevation: 43ft
Pundit code: LO
Main contractor: Various
Runways: 3 concrete
Hangars: C Type (5)
User sqns/units:

51 Sqn (4 Gp)
20/04/38-09/12/39
Whitley II, III, IV

58 Sqn (4 Gp)
20/04/38-30/09/39;
14/02/40-08/04/42
Heyford III; Whitley II, III, V

78 Sqn (4 Gp)
13/12/39-16/07/40;
16/09/42-16/06/43
Whitley V; Halifax II

77 Sqn (4 Gp)
28/08-05/10/40
Whitley V

102 Sqn (4 Gp)
10/10-15/11/40
Whitley V

35 Sqn (4 Gp)
05/12/40-15/08/42
Halifax I, II

LINTON-ON-OUSE continued

76 Sqn (4 Gp)
01/05-04/06/41;
16/09/42-16/06/43
Halifax I, II, V

426 Sqn (6 Gp)
18/06/43-25/05/45
Lancaster II; Halifax III, VII

408 Sqn (6 Gp)
27/08/43-14/06/45
Halifax II, III, VII; Lancaster II, X

405 Sqn (8/6 Gp)
26/05-16/06/45
Lancaster III, X

Opened with full station status 05/37
Became No 62 (RCAF) Base HQ 07/43

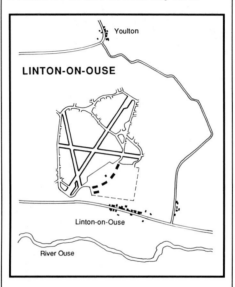

LISSETT, Yorks

Opened: 02/43
Closed: 08/45
Elevation: 23ft
Pundit code: LT
Main contractor: Various
Runways: 3 concrete
Hangars: T2 (2)
User sqns/units:

158 Sqn (4 Gp)
28/04/43-17/08/45
Halifax II, III, VI

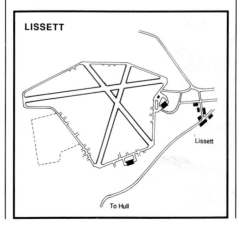

LISSET continued

640 Sqn (4 Gp)
07/01/44-07/05/45
Halifax III, VI

Opened as satellite to Driffield 02/43
Became No 43 Base substation 06/06/43

LITTLE HORWOOD, Bucks

Opened: 09/42
Closed: 01/46
Elevation: 385ft
Pundit code: LH
Main contractor: Various
Runways: 3 concrete
Hangars: T2 (1), B1 (1)
User sqns/units:

26 OTU (92 Gp)
09/42-26/08/44;
10/44-03/46
Wellington III, X

Opened as satellite to Wing 09/42

LITTLE SNORING, Norfolk

Opened: 07/43
Closed: 10/58
Elevation: 191ft
Pundit code: LS
Main contractor: Taylor Woodrow Ltd
Runways: 3 concrete
Hangars: T2 (2), B1 (1)
User sqns/units:

115 Sqn (3 Gp)
06/08/43-26/11/43
Lancaster II

1678 HCU (3 Gp)
08-09/43
Lancaster II

23 Sqn (100 Gp)
02/06/44-25/09/45
Mosquito VI, XXX

169 Sqn (100 Gp)
07/12/43-04/06/44
Beaufighter VI; Defiant II; Mosquito II

515 Sqn (100 Gp)
15/12/43-10/06/45
Beaufighter II; Blenheim V; Mosquito II

Opened as a satellite to Foulsham 07/43
Achieved full station status 08/43
Transferred to 100 Gp control 12/43

46 LINDHOLME
Wellington Ic aircraft of No 304 (Silesian) Squadron stand alongside one of Lindholme's C Type (hipped) hangars. The squadron operated Wellingtons with No 1 Group from Syerston and Lindholme until transferred to Coastal Command control in May 1942. In the foreground is Mk Ic DV441:Q.
J. B. Cynk Polish Aircraft Archives via Chaz Bowyer

47 LINDHOLME
No 1656 HCU's Lancaster I, L7532:C, saw almost continuous service from December 1941 until it was struck off charge (SOC) in October 1946. *via Chaz Bowyer*

48 LINTON-ON-OUSE
Whitleys of Nos 51 and 58 Squadrons were based at Linton between April 1938 and April 1942. Here a Mk V of No 58 Squadron is bombed up with 250lb GP bombs during the summer of 1940. *IWM CH227*

49 LISSETT
Flt Sgt 'Chuck' Freeman and his crew sit astride a bomb trolley in front of their No 158 Squadron Halifax B Mk II Srs I (Special) JD300:G during the summer of 1943.
During a raid on Nuremburg on 10-11 August 1943, 'Chuck' Freeman's gunners claimed a Dornier Do217 nightfighter as destroyed, 25 miles northwest of Ludwigshafen. *G. Smith via K. Merrick*

As a safeguard against a possible shortage of Rolls-Royce Merlin engines, development of a Bristol Hercules-engined Lancaster variant was put in hand during late 1941. Some 300 Mk IIs were built and equipped six squadrons in Bomber Command — Nos 61, 115, 408, 426, 432 and 514 Squadrons — between January 1943 and September 1944.

No 408 (Goose) Squadron at Linton-on-Ouse operated the Mk II from October 1943 until September 1944. Here, groundcrew refuel EQ-Z 'Zombie' in preparation for a raid on Cologne, 24 April 1944.
Public Archives of Canada PL29074 via B. Robertson

51 LITTLE SNORING
The gaping eye sockets of Little Snoring's derelict Type 12779/41 watchtower gaze out over a silent sea of sugar beet in September 1991. Taxi tracks remain, but only one of the three runways survives today for private flying. *Jonathan Falconer*

52 LITTLE SNORING
Where once Lancasters and Mosquitoes received their overhauls, this T2 hangar on the airfield perimeter at Little Snoring survives today as a grain store. *Jonathan Falconer*

54 LUDFORD MAGNA
Ron Holmes' No 101 Squadron crew pose beside their Lancaster III, ME837:L, at Ludford Magna in the summer of 1944. From left to right, top to bottom: Sid Davison, wireless op; Norman Smith, rear gunner; Peter Holway, special operator; Stan Waind, flight engineer; Tom Wade, bomb-aimer; Charlie, radio technician; Alex Kabbash, navigator; 'Titch', groundcrew; Ron Holmes, pilot; Bill, groundcrew. *P. Holway*

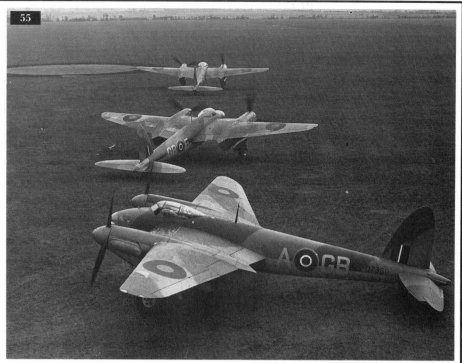

55 MARHAM
No 105 Squadron carried out more bombing operations than any other squadron in Bomber Command during World War 2. Initially under the control of No 2 Group, the squadron was retained in Bomber Command when the Group left in May 1943 to join the 2nd Tactical Air Force (2 TAF), and flew 'Oboe' Mosquito night bomber ops with the Pathfinders until the war's end. The squadron introduced the Mosquito to Bomber Command service in November 1941 and moved to Marham in September 1942. From Marham, three Mosquitoes carried out the first daylight raid on Berlin on 30 January 1943.

In this photograph, Mosquito IVs of No 105 Squadron taxi out at Marham in December 1942. DZ360:A in the foreground was shot down by flak at Dunkirk on 22 December 1942; while DZ353:E also served with Nos 139 and 627 Squadrons, failing to return from a raid on the marshalling yards at Rennes on 8 June 1944 when serving with the latter. *via Chaz Bowyer*

53 LUDFORD MAGNA
No 101 Squadron's 'C-Charlie' crash-landed at its base, Ludford Magna, on return from a RCM sortie on 22 February 1944, tearing up part of the airfield's FIDO pipeline system in the process.

From October 1943, the squadron operated specially equipped Lancasters in the 'Airborne Cigar' (ABC) radio countermeasures role with an extra, German-speaking crewmember (Special Operator) to jam communications between German nightfighters and their controllers. *via Chaz Bowyer*

LITTLE STAUGHTON, Hunts

Opened: 12/42
Closed: 12/45
Elevation: 225ft
Pundit code: LX
Main contractor: Various
Runways: 3 concrete/tarmac
Hangars: T2 (3), Robin (8)
User sqns/units:

582 Sqn (8 Gp)
01/04/44-10/09/45
Lancaster I, III

109 Sqn (8 Gp)
02/04/44-30/09/45
Mosquito XVI

Opened as USAAF bomber station 12/42
Transferred to RAF Bomber Command control 01/03/44
*Sqn Ldr R. A. M. Palmer DFC, 109 Sqn, posthumously awarded VC, Cologne 23/12/44
*Capt E. E. Swales, 582 Sqn, posthumously awarded VC, Pforzheim 23-24/02/45

LONG MARSTON, Gloucs

Opened: 11/41
Closed: 1954
Elevation: 145ft
Pundit code: JS
Main contractor: John Laing & Son Ltd
Runways: 3 tarmac
Hangars: T2 (2), B1 (1)
User sqns/units:

24 OTU (6/91 Gp)
03/42-07/45
Whitley; Wellington III, X

23 OTU (91 Gp)
1943
Wellington III, X

Became satellite to Honeybourne 03/42

LOSSIEMOUTH, Moray

Opened: 1939
Closed: Currently in use by RAF
Elevation: 19ft
Pundit code: OL
Main contractor: Various
Runways: 3 concrete/tarmac
Hangars: C Type (3), J Type (1), K Type (4), L Type (7)
User sqns/units:

20 OTU (6/91 Gp)
27/05/40-07/45
Wellington III, X

21 Sqn (2 Gp)
24/06-30/10/40;
Blenheim IV

LOSSIEMOUTH continued

57 Sqn (2 Gp)
23/06-14/08/40
Blenheim IV

Opened with full station status 1939

LUDFORD MAGNA, Lincs

Opened: 06/43
Closed: 05/63
Elevation: 428ft
Pundit code: LM
Main contractor: George Wimpey & Co Ltd
Runways: 3 concrete
Hangars: T2 (6), B1 (1)
User sqns/units:

101 Sqn (1 Gp)
15/06/43-01/10/45
Lancaster I, III

Opened with full station status 06/43
Became No 14 Base HQ 12/43

MARHAM, Norfolk

Opened: 01/04/37
Closed: Currently in use by RAF
Elevation: 70ft
Pundit code: MR
Main contractor: Various
Runways: 3 concrete
Hangars: C Type (5)
User sqns/units:

38 Sqn (3 Gp)
05/05/37-12/11/40
Hendon; Wellington I

115 Sqn (3 Gp)
15/06/37-24/09/42
Harrow; Wellington I, III

218 Sqn (3 Gp)
25/11/40-10/07/42
Wellington I; Stirling I

1418 Flt (3 Gp)
06/01-01/03/42
Wellington III

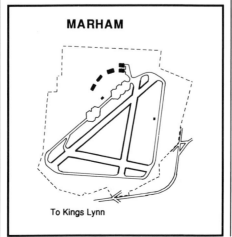

MARHAM

To Kings Lynn

MARHAM continued

105 Sqn (2/8 Gp)
29/09/42-23/03/44
Mosquito IV

139 Sqn (2/8 Gp)
29/09/42-04/07/43
Blenheim V; Mosquito IV

1655 Mosquito Training Unit (MTU) (2 Gp)
29/09/42-01/05/43
Blenheim; Mosquito

109 Sqn (8 Gp)
05/07/43-02/04/44
Mosquito IV, IX, XVI

Opened with full station status 01/04/37
Closed for redevelopment to VHB station standard 03/44

MARKET HARBOROUGH, Leics

Opened: 05/43
Closed: 05/47
Elevation: 360ft
Pundit code: MB
Main contractor: J. Mowlem & Co Ltd
Runways: 3 concrete/tarmac
Hangars: T2 (4), B1 (1)
User sqns/units:

14 OTU (92 Gp)
01/08/43-22/06/45
Wellington III, X

Opened with full station status 01/05/43

MARSTON MOOR, Yorks

Opened: 20/11/41
Closed: 11/45
Elevation: 68ft
Pundit code: MA
Main contractor: John Laing & Son Ltd
Runways: 3 concrete
Hangars: T2 (6), B1 (1)
User sqns/units:

1652 HCU (4/7 Gp)
03/01-07/42;
08/42-25/06/45
Halifax I, II, III, V

Opened with full station status 20/11/41
Became No 41 Base HQ 09/43
Became No 74 Base HQ 12/44

MELBOURNE, Yorks

Opened: 1940
Closed: 03/46
Elevation: 25ft
Pundit code: ME
Main contractor: Various
Runways: 3 concrete/tarmac
Hangars: T2 (2), B1 (1)

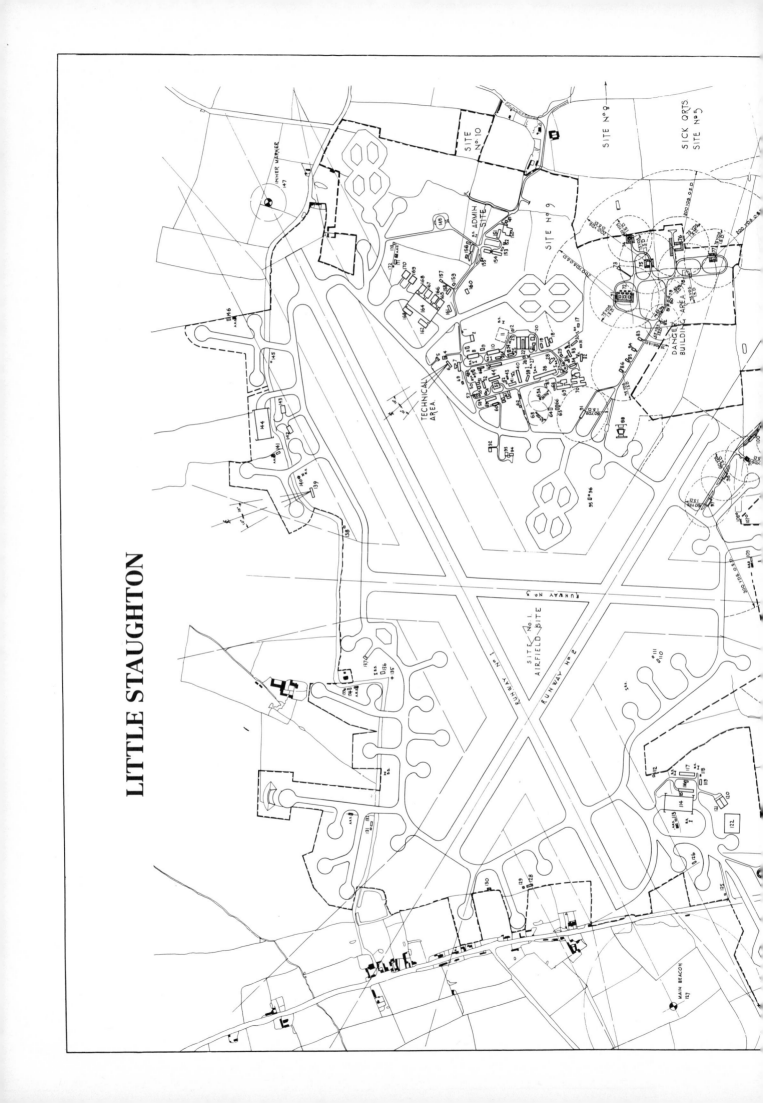

LITTLE STAUGHTON

MELBOURNE continued

User sqns/units:

10 Sqn (4 Gp)
19/08/42-06/08/45
Halifax II, III

Opened as satellite to Leeming 1940
Became No 44 Base substation 06/43

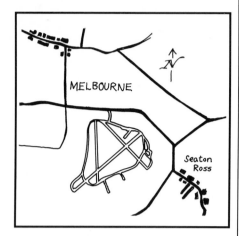

MEPAL, Cambs

Opened: 06/43
Closed: 1963
Elevation: 80ft
Pundit code: MP
Main contractor: Various
Runways: 3 concrete
Hangars: T2 (2), B1 (1)
User sqns/units:

75 Sqn (3 Gp)
28/06/43-21/07/45
Stirling III; Lancaster I, III

Opened as No 33 Base substation 06/43

METHERINGHAM, Lincs

Opened: 10/43
Closed: 02/46
Elevation: 63ft
Pundit code: MN
Main contractor: Various
Runways: 3 concrete
Hangars: T2 (2), B1 (1)

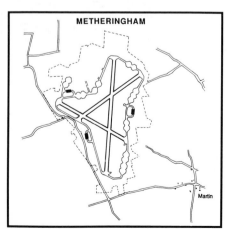

METHERINGHAM continued

User sqns/units:

106 Sqn (5 Gp)
11/11/43-18/02/46
Lancaster I, III

Opened as No 54 Base substation 10/43
*Sgt N. C. Jackson, 106 Sqn, awarded VC,
Schweinfurt 26-27/04/44

METHWOLD, Suffolk

Opened: 09/39
Closed: 06/58
Elevation: 50ft
Pundit code: ML
Main contractor: Various
Runways: 3 concrete
Hangars: T2 (4), B1 (1)
User sqns/units:

214 Sqn (3 Gp)
03/09/39-14/02/40
Wellington I

21 Sqn (2 Gp)
31/10/42-01/04/43
Ventura I, II

57 Sqn (3 Gp)
01-09/42
Wellington I, III

320 Sqn (2 Gp)
15-30/03/43
Hudson VI

464 Sqn (2 Gp)
03/04-20/07/43
Ventura I, II

487 Sqn (2 Gp)
03/04-20/07/43
Ventura II

149 Sqn (3 Gp)
15/05/44-04/46
Stirling III; Lancaster I, III

218 Sqn (3 Gp)
04/08-05/12/44
Stirling III; Lancaster I, III

Opened as satellite to Feltwell 09/39
Became No 31 Base substation 07/43
*Sqn Ldr L. H. Trent, 487 Sqn, awarded
VC, Amsterdam power station 03/05/43

MIDDLETON St GEORGE, Co Durham

Opened: 15/01/41
Closed: Currently in use as Teesside
Airport
Elevation: 115ft
Pundit code: MG
Main contractor: Various
Runways: 3 tarmac

MIDDLETON St GEORGE continued

Hangars: C Type (1), B1 (1), J Type (1), T2
(2)
User sqns/units:

78 Sqn (4 Gp)
07/04-20/10/41;
10/06-16/09/42
Whitley V; Halifax II

76 Sqn (4 Gp)
04/06/41-16/09/42
Halifax I, II

420 Sqn (4/6 Gp)
16/10/42-16/05/43
Wellington III

419 Sqn (4/6 Gp)
10/11/42-01/06/45
Halifax II; Lancaster X

428 Sqn (6 Gp)
04/06/43-31/05/45
Halifax V, II; Lancaster X

Opened with full station status 01/41
Became No 64 (RCAF) Base HQ 01/43
*Plt Off A.C.Mynarski, 419 Sqn, awarded
posthumous VC, Cambrai 12-13/06/44

MILDENHALL, Suffolk

Opened: 16/10/34
Closed: Currently in use by USAF
Elevation: 15ft
Pundit code: MI
Main contractor: Various
Runways: 3 concrete
Hangars: C Type (3), A Type (2), T2 (2)
User sqns/units:

149 Sqn (3 Gp)
12/04/37-06/04/42
Heyford; Wellington I, II; Stirling I

419 Sqn (3 Gp)
15/12/41-13/08/42
Wellington I, III

115 Sqn (3 Gp)
24/09/42-08/11/42
Wellington III

15 Sqn (3 Gp)
14/04/43-19/08/46
Stirling III; Lancaster I, III

622 Sqn (3 Gp)
10/08/43-15/08/45
Stirling III; Lancaster I, III

Opened with full station status 16/10/34
Became No 32 Base HQ 12/42
*Harry Watt's film *Target for Tonight*
made here during 1941 by Crown Film
Unit featuring Wellingtons and crews of
149 Sqn

56 MEPAL
Returning from Hanover on its 14th op, No 75 (New Zealand) Squadron's Stirling III, EH936 'W-Willy', crash-landed on Mepal's runway and was written off. *C. Dickenson*

57 METHERINGHAM
An unidentified Lancaster III of No 106 Squadron sits on its dispersal during the summer of 1944. Note the exhaust staining on the engine nacelles caused by leaded fuel and the American-built 500lb bombs in the left foreground. These were used by Bomber Command in the summer of 1944 to make up for the shortage in British-made 500lb and 1,000lb bombs. They differed only in that they were built with two suspension lugs instead of one. No 106 Squadron was based at Metheringham from November 1943 until it was disbanded in February 1946.
via Jonathan Falconer

58 METHWOLD
The Lockheed Vega Ventura was introduced into RAF service by No 21 Squadron in June 1942. Similar in appearance to the Lockheed Hudson, it equipped only three squadrons in No 2 Group as a Blenheim replacement but was not popular with its crews. Ventura I AE774:V, pictured here at Methwold, served with No 21 Squadron from 18 November 1942 until 21 February 1943, and took part in the famous Operation 'Oyster' on 6 December 1942. *via Chaz Bowyer*

59 MIDDLETON St GEORGE
The most northerly of Bomber Command's frontline airfields, Middleton St George hosted the Whitley Vs of No 78 Squadron between April and October 1941.
via Jonathan Falconer

Seasons Greetings FROM

106 Squadron, R.A.F. Metheringham.

60 MILDENHALL
The layout of a prewar Expansion Scheme airfield can be appreciated in this view of Mildenhall from the air taken in July 1945. *via Chaz Bowyer*

61 MILDENHALL
Aircrew of No 149 Squadron pose for the Press at Mildenhall after returning from the first raid by British bombers on Berlin, 25/26 August 1940. *IWM HU44271*

62 MILDENHALL
Stirlings of Nos 15, 149 and 622 Squadrons were resident at Mildenhall at various times between November 1941 and January 1944. Here, groundcrew Sgt Bobby Gault sits for the camera on the port inner engine cowling of No 15 Squadron's Stirling III BK611 'Te Kooti'. *D. Mepham via A. Edgley*

63 MORETON-IN-MARSH
Preparations are in hand to salvage No 21 OTU's Wellington Ic R1090:K after she bellied-in. She went on to serve with Nos 18, 15 and 105 OTUs before being SOC on 15 August 1944. *via Chaz Bowyer*

MOLESWORTH, Hunts

Opened: 05/41
Closed: Currently in use by USAF
Elevation: 240ft
Pundit code: MX
Main contractor: Various
Runways: 3
Hangars: T2 (2), J Type (1)
User sqns/units:

460 Sqn (1 Gp)
15/11/41-04/01/42
Wellington IV

Opened with full station status 05/41
Transferred to USAAF control 06/42

MORETON-IN-MARSH, Gloucs

Opened: 01/41
Closed: Currently in use as Fire Service College
Elevation: 420ft
Pundit code: MO
Main contractor: Various
Runways: 3 concrete/tarmac
Hangars: J Type (1), T2 (4)
User sqns/units:

21 OTU (6/91 Gp)
03/41-11/46
Wellington I, III, X

1446 Flt (91 Gp)
05/42-01/05/43
Wellington

Opened with full station status 01/41

MOUNT FARM, Oxon

Opened: 07/40
Closed: 07/46
Elevation: 180ft
Pundit code: MF
Main contractor: John Laing & Son Ltd
Runways: 3 concrete
Hangars: Blister (8)
User sqns/units:

12 OTU (6 Gp)
07/40-07/41
Battle; Wellington I

140 Sqn (106 Gp)
20/05/42-16/03/43
Spitfire Ia, Vg; Blenheim IV

Opened as satellite to Benson 07/40
Became satellite to Harwell 07/41
Became satellite to Benson 01/42 under
Coastal Command control
Transferred to USAAF control 02/43

NEWMARKET, Suffolk

Opened: 1939
Closed: 05/45
Elevation: 96ft
Pundit code: NM
Main contractor: Various
Runways: 3 grass
Hangars: B1 (3), T2 (3), Blister (3)
User sqns/units:

99 Sqn (3 Gp)
01/09/39-08/03/41
Wellington I

7 Sqn (3 Gp)
16/03-27/04/41
Stirling I

138 Sqn (3 Gp)
25/08-16/12/41
Lysander; Whitley V; Halifax II

215 Sqn (3 Gp)
09/12/41-05/01/42
Wellington I

161 Sqn (3 Gp)
14/02/42-01/03/42
Lysander IIIa; Hudson I; Whitley V

75 Sqn (3 Gp)
01/11/42-29/06/43
Wellington III; Stirling I, III

Bombing Development Unit
11/09/43-25/02/45
Lancaster; Halifax; Stirling; Wellington;
Spitfire; Mosquito; Beaufighter; Anson;
Proctor

Opened as satellite to Mildenhall 09/39
Became No 31 Base HQ 12/42

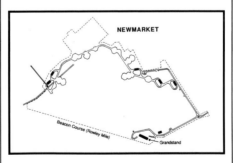

NEWTON, Notts

Opened: 1937
Closed: Currently in use by RAF
Elevation: 151ft
Pundit code: NA
Main contractor: Various
Runways: 3 grass
Hangars: C Type (5)
User sqns/units:

103 Sqn (1 Gp)
03/07/40-11/07/41
Battle; Wellington I

NEWTON continued

150 Sqn (1 Gp)
03/07/40-10/07/41
Battle; Wellington I

Operational with full station status 07/40
Transferred to Flying Training Command
07/41

NORTH CREAKE, Norfolk

Opened: 23/11/43
Closed: 09/47
Elevation: 240ft
Pundit code: NO
Main contractor: Taylor Woodrow Ltd
Runways: 3 concrete
Hangars: T2 (2), B1 (1)
User sqns/units:

199 Sqn (100 Gp)
01/05/44-29/07/45
Stirling III; Halifax III

171 Sqn (100 Gp)
08/09/44-27/07/45
Stirling III; Halifax III

Opened as satellite to Foulsham 11/43
Achieved full station status 04/44

NORTH KILLINGHOLME, Lincs

Opened: 11/43
Closed: 10/45
Elevation: 31ft
Pundit code: NK
Main contractor: John Laing & Son Ltd
Runways: 3 concrete
Hangars: T2 (2), B1 (1)
User sqns/units:

550 Sqn (1 Gp)
03/01/44-31/10/45
Lancaster I, III

Opened as No 13 Base substation 11/43

NORTH LUFFENHAM, Rutland

Opened: 12/40
Closed: Currently in use by RAF
Elevation: 350ft
Pundit code: NL
Main contractor: John Laing & Son Ltd
Runways: 3 concrete
Hangars: B1 (1), J Type (2), T2 (3)
User sqns/units:

61 Sqn (5 Gp)
07-09/41
Hampden; Manchester

57

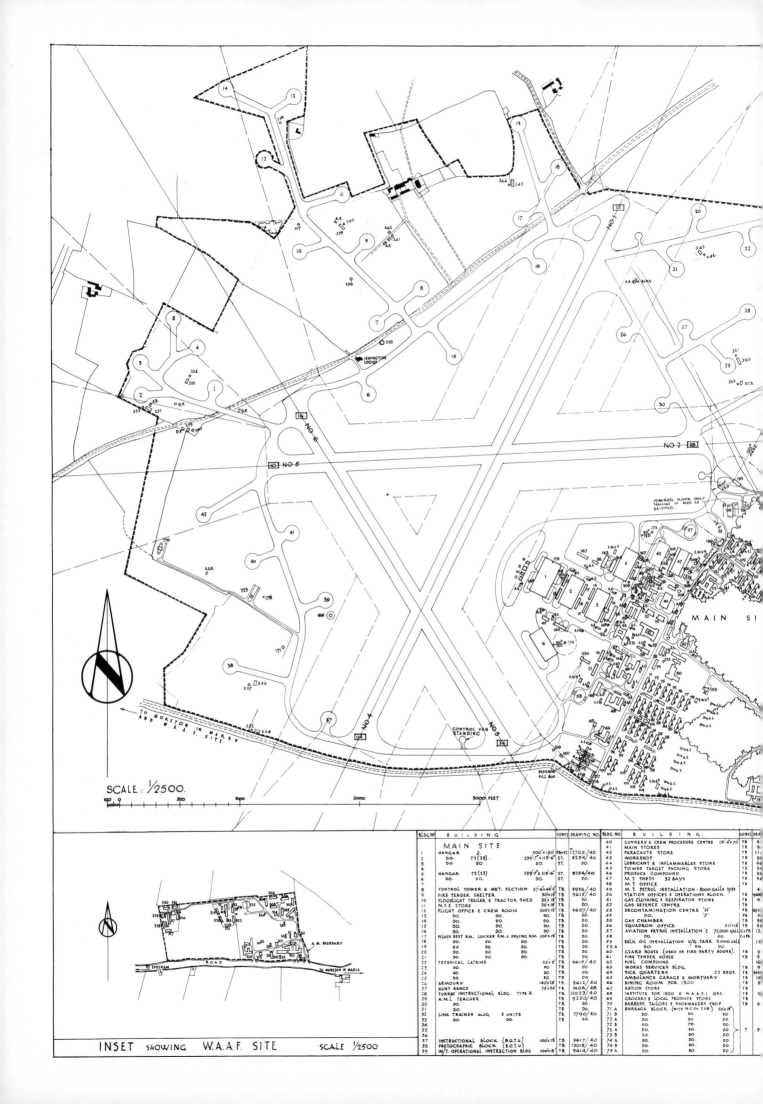

INSET SHOWING W.A.A.F. SITE   SCALE 1/2500

SCALE : 1/2500

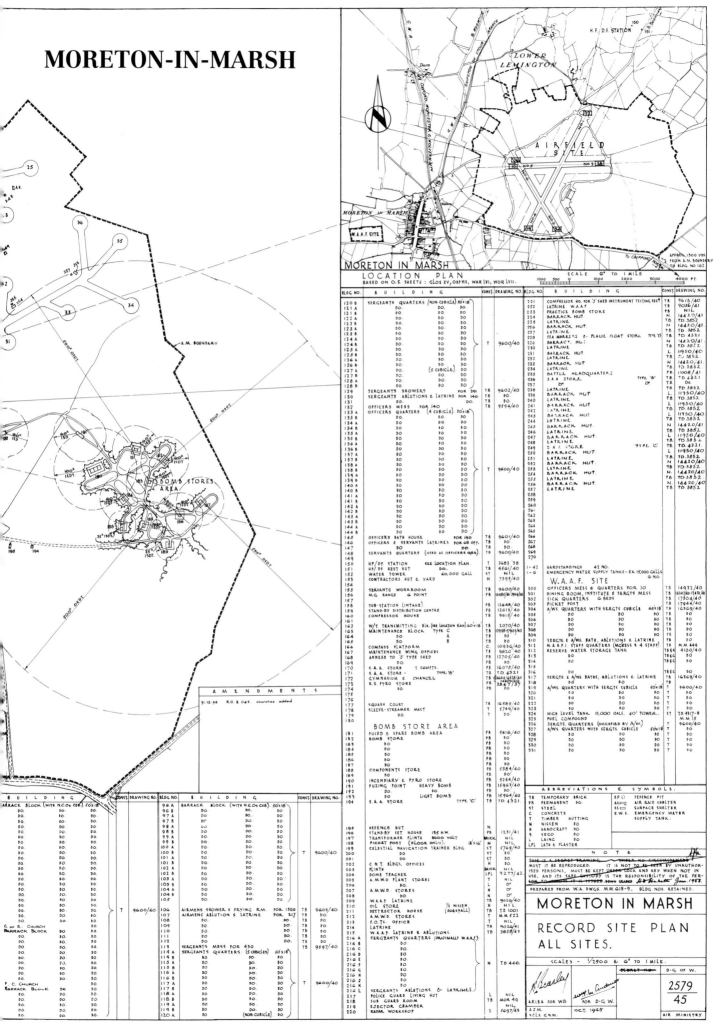

MORETON-IN-MARSH

RAF Museum

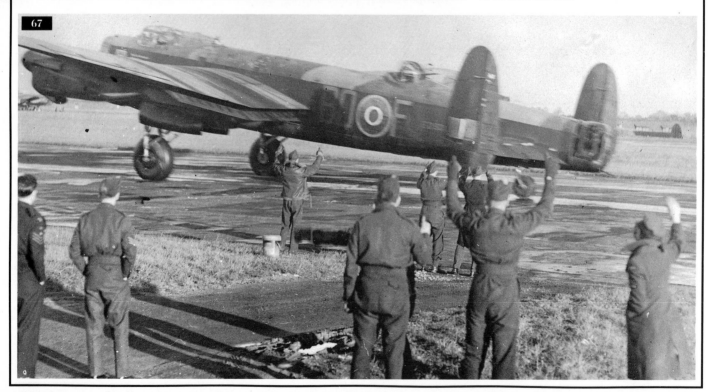

64 NORTH CREAKE
In this bleak scene during the winter of 1944-45, Stirlings of No 199 (SD) Squadron are serviced on their dispersals as the harsh wind coming in off the North Sea some 10 miles away whips up the snow.
Colin Munro via K. Merrick

65 NORTH CREAKE
North Creake viewed from the air shortly after its completion in 1944. At centre left is the control tower; extreme left one of two T2 hangars; and at top the sole B1 hangar. Most of these buildings were still standing and in use for light industrial purposes in 1992.
199 Register/SAA

66 NORTH CREAKE
An operational briefing for No 199 (SD) Squadron crews at North Creake during 1944. *199 Register/SAA*

67 NORTH KILLINGHOLME
Onlookers wish No 550 Squadron's Lancaster III ED905 'F-Fox' good luck as she takes off for Dusseldorf on her 100th sortie, 2 November 1944. One of three centenarians that served with the squadron, 'F-Fox' survived the war to be SOC on 20 August 1945. *IWM CH14188*

NORTH LUFFENHAM continued

144 Sqn (5 Gp)
17/07/41-22/04/42
Hampden

29 OTU (7/92 Gp)
25/04/42-07/43
Wellington I, III

1653 HCU (7 Gp)
27/11/44-28/10/45
Lancaster I, III; Stirling III; Beaufighter VI;
Mosquito XIX

Opened with full station status 12/40
Transferred to Flying Training Command
control 04/44
Returned to Bomber Command control
11/44 as No 73 Base HQ

NUNEATON, Leics
Opened: 02/43
Closed: 09/46
Elevation: 323ft
Pundit code: NU
Main contractor: Various
Runways: 3 concrete
Hangars: T2 (1)
User sqns/units:

18 OTU (93 Gp)
02-03/43
Wellington I, III

Opened as satellite to Bramcote 02/43
Transferred to Transport Command
control 04/43

OAKINGTON, Cambs
Opened: 01/07/40
Closed: Currently in use by Army Air
Corps
Elevation: 40ft
Pundit code: OA
Main contractor: Various
Runways: 3 concrete/tar
Hangars: B1 (1), J Type (2), T2 (2)
User sqns/units:

101 Sqn (3 Gp)
06/07/41-11/02/42
Wellington I

218 Sqn (3 Gp)
14/07-25/11/40
Blenheim IV

7 Sqn (3/8 Gp)
29/10/40-24/07/45
Stirling I, III; Lancaster I, III

3 PRU
16/11/40-07/41
Spitfire; Wellington

Navigation Training Unit (NTU)
03-06/43
Lancaster I, III

OAKINGTON continued

1409 Met Flt
01/04/43-08/01/44
Mosquito IV, IX

627 Sqn (LNSF) (8 Gp)
12/11/43-15/04/44
Mosquito IV

571 Sqn (LNSF) (8 Gp)
24/04/44-29/07/45
Mosquito XVI

Opened with full station status 01/07/40

OAKLEY, Bucks
Opened: 27/05/42
Closed: 08/45
Elevation: 233ft
Pundit code: OY
Main contractor: John Laing & Son Ltd
Runways: 3 concrete
Hangars: B1 (1), T2 (1)
User sqns/units:

11 OTU (92 Gp)
08/42-08/45
Wellington I, III, X

Opened as satellite to Bicester 27/05/42
Became satellite to Westcott 08/42

OSSINGTON, Notts
Opened: 01/42
Closed: 08/46
Elevation: 180ft
Pundit code: ON
Main contractor: Various
Runways: 3 concrete
Hangars: T2 (4)
User sqns/units:

82 OTU (93 Gp)
01/06/43-09/01/45
Wellington III, X

Opened with full station status under
Bomber Command control 01/42
Transferred to Flying Training Command
control 01/42
Command control 01/42
Returned to Bomber Command control
05/43

OULTON, Norfolk
Opened: 31/07/40
Closed: 11/47
Elevation: 157ft
Pundit code: OU
Main contractor: Various
Runways: 3 concrete
Hangars: T2 (4)
User sqns/units:

114 Sqn (2 Gp)
10/08/40-02/03/41
Blenheim IV

OULTON continued

18 Sqn (2 Gp)
03/04-13/07/41;
05/11-05/12/41
Blenheim IV

139 Sqn (2 Gp)
13/07-23/10/41;
09/12/41-01/42
Blenheim IV; Hudson II

88 Sqn (2 Gp)
29/09/42-30/03/43
Boston III, IIIa

21 Sqn (2 Gp)
01/04-19/08/43
Ventura I, II; Mitchell

214 Sqn (100 Gp)
16/05/44-27/07/45
Fortress II, III

1699 CU (100 Gp)
05/44-07/45
Fortress II, III; Liberator IV

223 Sqn (100 Gp)
23/08/44-29/07/45
Liberator IV, VI; Fortress II, III

Opened as satellite to Horsham St Faith
07/40
Became satellite to Swanton Morley 09/42
Became satellite to Foulsham 09/43

PEPLOW, Salop
Opened: 07/43
Closed: 12/49
Elevation: 230ft
Pundit code: CE
Main contractor: Various
Runways: 3 concrete
Hangars: B1 (1), T2 (4)
User sqns/units:

83 OTU
07/43-28/10/44
Wellington III, X

Used as RLG for Tern Hill in Flying
Training Command, 1941
Opened in Bomber Command with full
station status, 07/43
To Flying Training Command, 01/45

PERSHORE, Worcs
Opened: 02/41
Closed: 1978
Elevation: 123ft
Pundit code: PR
Main contractor: Various
Runways: 3 concrete/asphalt
Hangars: J Type (1), T2 (4)
User sqns/units:

23 OTU (6/91 Gp)
01/04/41-15/03/44
Wellington I, III

Opened with full station status 02/41
Transferred to Ferry Command control
03/44

POCKLINGTON, Yorks

Opened: 06/41
Closed: 09/46
Elevation: 84ft
Pundit code: PO
Main contractor: Various
Runways: 3 concrete/tarmac
Hangars: B1 (1), J Type (1), T2 (4)
User sqns/units:

405 Sqn (4 Gp)
20/06/41-07/08/42
Wellington II; Halifax II

102 Sqn (4 Gp)
07/08/42-08/09/45
Halifax II, III, VI

Opened with full station status 06/41
Became No 42 Base HQ 1943

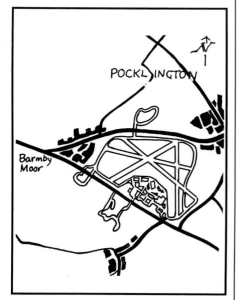

POLEBROOK, Northants

Opened: 05/41
Closed: 01/67
Elevation: 234ft
Pundit code: PK
Main contractor: Various
Hangars: J Type (1), T2 (1)
User sqns/units:

17 OTU (7 Gp)
12/40-09/41
Blenheim I, IV

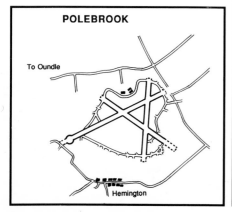

POLEBROOK continued

90 Sqn (3 Gp)
30/08/41-10/02/42
Fortress I; Blenheim IV

1653 HCU (3 Gp)
01-06/42
Liberator II

Used as satellite for Upwood 12/40
Achieved full station status 05/41

RICCALL, Yorks

Opened: 09/42
Closed: 1946
Elevation: 35ft
Pundit code: RC
Main contractor: Various
Runways: 3 concrete/asphalt
Hangars: B1 (1); T2 (6)
User sqns/units:

1658 HCU (4/7 Gp)
07/10/42-13/04/45
Halifax II, III

Opened as satellite to Marston Moor
09/42
Became No 41 Base substation 09/43
Became No 74 Base substation 11/44
Transferred to Transport Command
control 04/45

RIDGEWELL, Essex

Opened: 12/42
Closed: 03/57
Elevation: 260ft
Pundit code: RD
Main contractor: Various
Runways: 3 concrete
Hangars: T2 (2)
User sqns/units:

90 Sqn (3 Gp)
29/12/42-31/05/43
Stirling I, III

Opened as satellite to Stradishall 12/42
Transferred to USAAF control 05/43

RUFFORTH, Yorks

Opened: 11/42
Closed: 1954
Elevation: 64ft
Pundit code: RU
Main contractor: John Laing & Son Ltd
Runways: 3 tarmac
Hangars: B1 (1), T2 (2)
User sqns/units:

158 Sqn (4 Gp)
06/11/42-28/02/43
Halifax II

RUFFORTH continued

1663 HCU (4/7 Gp)
01/03/43-28/05/45
Halifax II, III, V

Opened as satellite to Marston Moor
11/42
Became No 41 Base substation 09/43
Became No 74 Base substation 11/43

SALTBY, Leics

Opened: 08/41
Closed: 09/55
Elevation: 479ft
Pundit code: SY
Main contractor: Various
Runways: 3 tarmac
Hangars: B1 (1), T2 (4)
User sqns/units:

14 OTU (7/92 Gp)
08/41-08/43
Hampden; Wellington

Opened as satellite to Cottesmore 08/41
Closed for runway building 08/43
Transferred to USAAF control 02/44

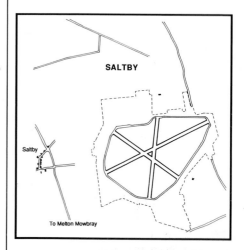

SANDTOFT, Lincs

Opened: 02/44
Closed: 11/45
Elevation: 8ft
Pundit code: SF
Main contractor: Various
Runways: 3 concrete/tarmac
Hangars: B1 (1), T2 (2)
User sqns/units:

1667 HCU (1/7 Gp)
20/02/44-10/11/45
Halifax II, V; Lancaster I, III

Opened as No 11 Base substation 02/44
Became No 71 Base substation 11/44

68 OAKINGTON

No 7 Squadron was the first to be equipped with the Short Stirling, the RAF's first four-engined heavy bomber to enter service. The squadron moved to Oakington from Leeming on 29 October 1940 from where it operated the Stirling I and III with No 3 Group. Transferred to No 8 (PFF) Group in August 1942, No 7 Squadron flew the Stirling in the Pathfinder role until it was replaced by the Lancaster in August 1943, remaining at Oakington until the end of the war. Pictured outside a J Type hangar at Oakington, N6086:L is an early Mk I fitted with the Frazer-Nash FN7 mid-upper turret. She went on to serve with No 218 Squadron and then No 1657 HCU before finally crashing at Stradishall on 11 May 1944. *via Chaz Bowyer*

69 POCKLINGTON

Halifax II crews of No 405 (Vancouver) Squadron parade for the camera during 1942. The squadron was based here under No 4 Group control from 20 June 1941 until 7 August 1942. *via Jonathan Falconer*

70 POLEBROOK

Re-formed in No 2 Group on 7 May 1941, No 90 Squadron flew the Boeing B-17C Fortress I on daylight bombing operations from Polebrook between 30 August 1941 until the squadron was disbanded on 10 February 1942. The Fortress proved unsuitable in RAF service and the type was phased out by the end of 1941. B-17C, AM928, later re-serialled AN528, served as WP-B with No 90 Squadron until it was destroyed in a ground fire at Polebrook. *via Chaz Bowyer*

71 RUFFORTH

Air and groundcrews turn-to and dig Halifax III OO-M of No 1663 HCU out of the snow on its dispersal at Rufforth early in 1944. *IWM CH12431*

SCAMPTON, Lincs

Opened: 08/36
Closed: Currently in use by RAF
Elevation: 195ft
Pundit code: SA
Main contractor: Various
Runways: 3 concrete/tarmac
Hangars: C2 Type (4), T1 (1)
User sqns/units:

49 Sqn (5 Gp)
14/03/38-02/01/43
Hampden; Manchester; Lancaster I, III

83 Sqn (5 Gp)
14/03/38-15/08/42
Hampden; Manchester; Lancaster I, III

98 Sqn (2 Gp)
02-19/03/40
Battle

57 Sqn (5 Gp)
04/09/42-28/08/43
Lancaster I, III

1661 HCU (5 Gp)
11-12/42
Halifax I, II

467 Sqn (5 Gp)
07-22/11/42
Lancaster I

617 Sqn (5 Gp)
21/03-30/08/43
Lancaster I, I(Special), III

153 Sqn (1 Gp)
15/10/44-28/09/45
Lancaster I, III

625 Sqn (1 Gp)
05/04-07/10/45
Lancaster I, III

Opened with full station status 08/36
Became No 52 Base HQ 01/43
Became No 15 Base HQ 11/44
*Flt Lt R. A. B. Learoyd, 49 Sqn, awarded VC, Dortmund-Ems Canal 12-13/08/40
*Sgt J Hannah, 83 Sqn, awarded VC, Antwerp 15-16/09/40
*Wg Cdr G. P. Gibson DSO,DFC, 617 Sqn, awarded VC, Dams raid, 16-17/05/43

SCULTHORPE, Norfolk

Opened: 01/43
Closed: Currently in use by USAF
Elevation: 219ft
Pundit code: SP
Main contractor: John Laing & Son Ltd
Runways: 3 concrete
Hangars: B1 (1), T2 (4)
User sqns/units:

342 Sqn (2 Gp/140 Wing 2 TAF)
15/05-19/07/43
Boston III; Havoc

SCULTHORPE continued

464 Sqn (2 Gp/140 Wing 2 TAF)
21/07-31/12/43
Ventura I, II; Mosquito IV

487 Sqn (2 Gp/140 Wing 2 TAF)
20/07-31/12/43
Ventura II; Mosquito IV

21 Sqn (2 Gp/140 Wing 2 TAF)
27/09-31/12/43
Mosquito VI

214 Sqn (100 Gp)
16/01-16/05/44
Fortress II

Opened as satellite to West Raynham 01/43
Achieved full station status 05/43
Closed for conversion to VHB station standard 05/44

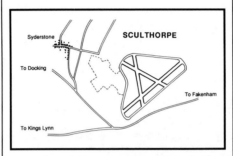

SEIGHFORD, Staffs

Opened: 01/43
Closed: 01/66
Elevation: 308ft
Pundit code: YD
Main contractor: Various
Runways: 3 concrete
Hangars: B1(1), T2(2)
User sqns/units:

30 OTU (93 Gp)
01/43-28/10/44
Wellington I, III

Opened as satellite to Hixon 01/43

SILVERSTONE, Northants

Opened: 03/43
Closed: 11/46
Elevation: 506ft
Pundit code: SV
Main contractor: J. Mowlem & Co Ltd
Runways: 3 concrete
Hangars: B1 (1), T2 (4)
User sqns/units:

17 OTU (92 Gp)
10/04/43-11/46
Wellington I, III, X

Opened with full station status 03/43

SKELLINGTHORPE, Lincs

Opened: 10/41
Closed: 1952
Elevation: 60ft
Pundit code: SG
Main contractor: Various
Runways: 3 concrete/tarmac
Hangars: B1 (1), T2 (2)
User sqns/units:

50 Sqn (5 Gp)
26/11/41-20/06/42;
17/10/42-15/06/45
Hampden; Manchester; Lancaster I, III

61 Sqn (5 Gp)
16/11/43-12/01/44;
15/04/44-16/06/45
Lancaster I, III

Opened as satellite for Swinderby 10/41
Became No 53 Base substation 11/42
*Flg Off L. T. Manser, 50 Sqn, awarded posthumous VC, Cologne 30-31/05/42

SKIPTON-ON-SWALE, Yorks

Opened: 08/42
Closed: 10/45
Elevation: 90ft
Pundit code: SK
Main contractor: Various
Runways: 3 tarmac
Hangars: B1 (1), T2 (2)
User sqns/units:

420 Sqn (4 Gp)
07/08-16/10/42
Hampden; Wellington III

432 Sqn (6 Gp)
01/05-19/09/43
Wellington X

433 Sqn (6 Gp)
25/09/43-15/10/45
Halifax III; Lancaster I, III

424 Sqn (6 Gp)
06/11/43-15/10/45
Halifax III; Lancaster I, III

Opened as satellite to Leeming 08/42
Became No 63 Base substation 05/44

SNAITH, Yorks

Opened: 07/41
Closed: 04/46
Elevation: 33ft
Pundit code: SX
Main contractor: Various
Runways: 3 tarmac
Hangars: J Type (1), T2 (2)

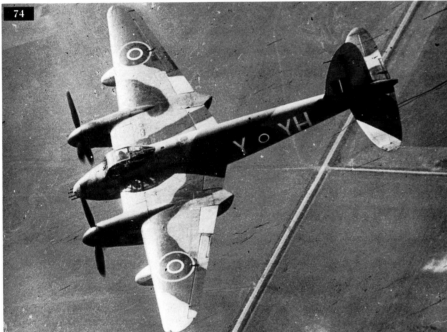

73 SCAMPTON
Sqn Ldr David Drakes and his No 49
Squadron crew failed to return from a
shipping strike off the Frisian Islands in
Hampden AE224:Z on 1 November 1941,
probably lost to flak. From left to right are:
Plt Off W. H. Cheetham, air gunner;
Plt Off V. D. Beaney, navigator/bomb-aimer;
Sqn Ldr David Drakes, pilot;
Flt Sgt W. A. Watson, air gunner.
L. Williamson

74 SCULTHORPE
No 21 Squadron operated the Mosquito FBVI
from Sculthorpe between September and
December 1943, before moving to Hunsdon
with 2 TAF. This photograph shows FBVI
PZ306:Y flying over France on 18 March
1945. *A. Carlisle via Chaz Bowyer*

75 SKELLINGTHORPE
Once the nerve centre of a busy airfield
housing the Lancasters of Nos 50 and 61
Squadrons, Skellingthorpe's watch tower is
pictured here in 1967, a gaunt and forlorn
shadow of its former self. It has since been
demolished and the site overrun by a housing
estate. *via Chaz Bowyer*

72 SCAMPTON

Popularly known as the airfield from where No 617 Squadron, 'The Dambusters', flew on the epic Dams raid of 16-17 May 1943, Scampton was also the wartime home to eight other squadrons and units.

When still a grass airfield, No 49 Squadron's Hampden P1333:F is bombed up with 250lb and 500lb GP bombs at Scampton in July 1940. P1333 crash-landed in Holland on 16-17 August 1940 whilst on ops to Meuseburg and the crew of four became PoWs. *IWM CH272*

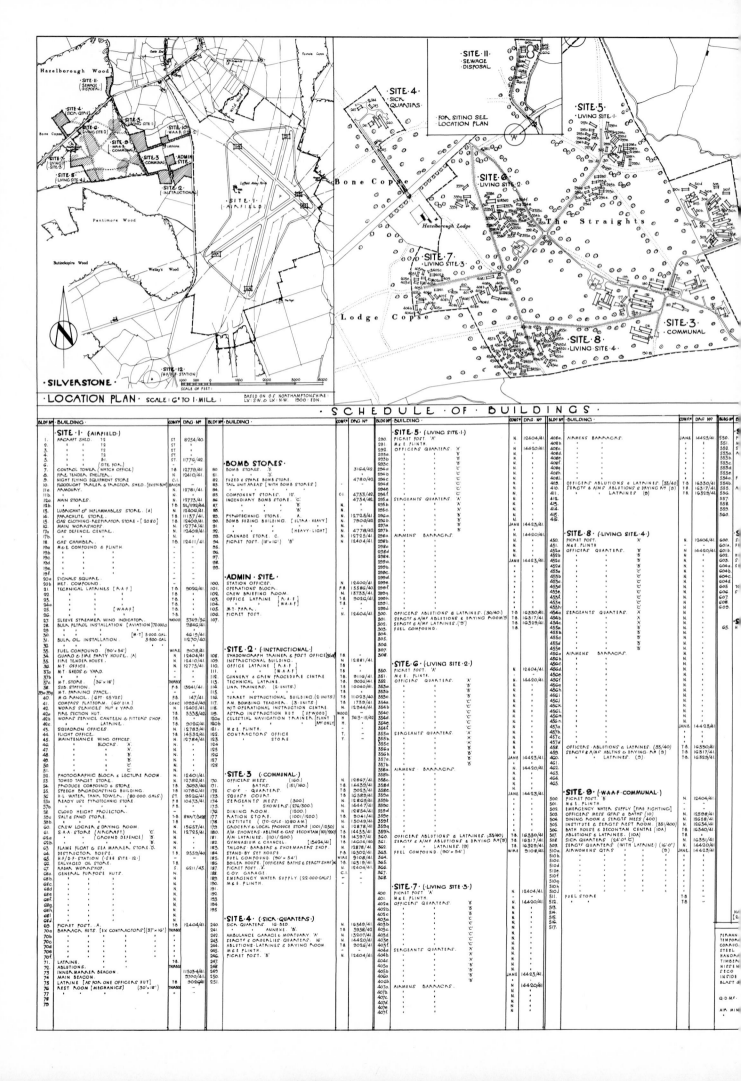

· SILVERSTONE ·

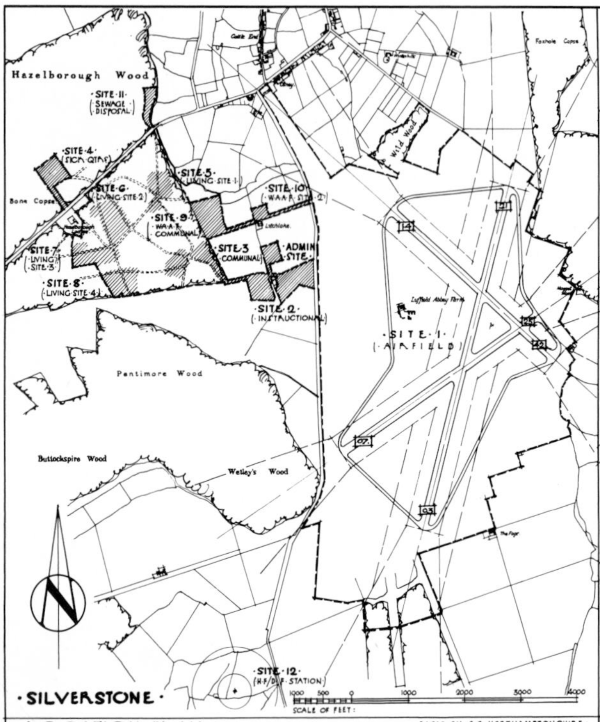

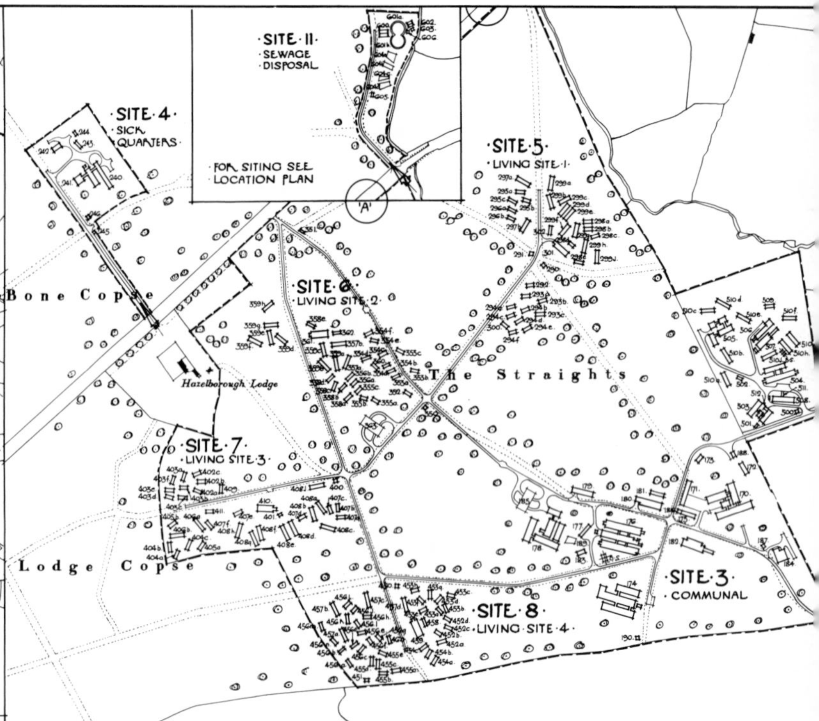

· LOCATION PLAN · SCALE: 6" TO 1 MILE ·

BASED ON O.S. NORTHAMPTONSHIRE.
LX. S.W. & LX. N.W. 1:500 EDN.

· SCHEDULE OF BUILDINGS ·

SITE·1· (AIRFIELD·)

BLDG Nº	BUILDING	CONSTR	DRG Nº
1.	AIRCRAFT SHED. T.2	ST.	8254/40
2.	" " T.2	ST.	
3.	" " T.2	ST.	
4.	" " T.2	ST.	1776/42
5.	" " B.I.	ST.	
6.	" (SITE FOR.)		
7.	CONTROL TOWER. (WATCH OFFICE.)	T.B.	12778/41
8.	FIRE TENDER SHELTER.	N.	12410/41
9.	NIGHT FLYING EQUIPMENT STORE	C.I.	
10.	FLOODLIGHT TRAILER & TRACTOR SHED. [EXISTG BLDG]	BRICK	
11a.	ARMOURY	N.	12781/41
11b.	"	N.	
12a.	MAIN STORES.	N.	12773/41
12b.	"	N.	SL/1192/41
13.	LUBRICANT & INFLAMMABLES STORE. (A)	N.	12406/41
14.	PARACHUTE STORE.	N.	11137/41
15.	GAS CLOTHING·RESPIRATOR STORE · [2080]	T.B.	12409/41
16.	MAIN WORKSHOPS.	N.	12774/41
17a.	GAS DEFENCE CENTRE.	N.	12408/41
17b.	"	N.	
18.	GAS CHAMBER.	T.B.	12411/41
19a.	M&E COMPOUND & PLINTH		
19b.	"		
19c.	"		
19d.	"		
19e.	"		
19f.	"		
20a.	SIGNALS SQUARE.		
20b.	MET. COMPOUND.		
21.	TECHNICAL LATRINES [R.A.F.]	T.B.	5006/41
22.	"	T.B.	
23.	"	T.B.	
24a.	"	T.B.	
25.	" [W.A.A.F.]	T.B.	
26.	"	T.B.	
27.	SLEEVE STREAMER WIND INDICATOR.	WOOD	5749/36
28.	BULK PETROL INSTALLATION [AVIATION] 72.000G		9846/41
29.	" [M·T] 3.000·GAL.		
30.	"		4619/41
31.	BULK OIL INSTALLATION. 3.500·GAL		11270/40
32.			
33.	FUEL COMPOUND. (90'×54')	WIRE	9108/41
34.	GUARD & FIRE PARTY HOUSE. (A)	N.	12404/41
35.	FIRE TENDER HOUSE.	N.	12410/41
36.	M.T. OFFICE	N.	12775/41
37a.	M.T. SHEDS & YARD.		
37b.	"		
38.	M.T. STORE. (36'×18')	THOMSON	
39.	SUB. STATION.	P.B.	13041/41
39a.-39b	M.T. PARKING SPACE.		
40.	H.Q. RANGE. (GPT. 25'×25')	P.B.	147/41
41.	COMPASS PLATFORM. (60' DIA)	CONC	10586/40
42.	WORKS SERVICES HUT & YARD.	T.B.	12405/41
42a.	FIRE SECTION HUT	T.B.	5538/42
42b.	WORKS SERVICE CANTEEN & FITTERS SHOP.	T.B.	
42c.	"	T.B.	9006/41
43.	SQUADRON OFFICES	N.	12783/41
44.	FLIGHT OFFICE.	T.B.	14539/41
45.	MAINTENANCE WING OFFICES.	N.	12784/41
46.	" BLOCKS. 'A'	N.	
47.	" " "	N.	
48.	" " 'B'	N.	
49.	" " "	N.	
50.	" " 'C'	N.	
51.			
52.	PHOTOGRAPHIC BLOCK & LECTURE ROOM	N.	12401/41
53.	TOWED TARGET STORE.	N.	12782/41
54.	PRODUCE COMPOUND & STORE	T.B.	
55.	SPEECH BROADCASTING BUILDING	T.B.	9278/41
56.	H.L WATER TANK TOWER. (80.000·GALS.)	ST.	9306/41
57.	READY USE PYROTECHNIC STORE.	T.B.	10473/41
57a.	"		
58.	CLOUD HEIGHT PROJECTOR.		
59a.	SALT & SAND STORE.	T·B	8WAT/5498
60.	CREW LOCKER & DRYING ROOM.	N.	15657/41
61.	S.A.A. STORE (AIRCRAFT) 'C'	N.	12725/41
62a.	" (GROUND DEFENCE)	N.	
62b.	" 'B'	N.	
63.	FLAME FLOAT & SEA MARKER STORE·'D'.		
64.	DESTRUCTOR HOUSE.	T.B.	9559/40
65.	H.F/D.F·STATION (·SEE SITE·12·)		
66.	SALVAGED OIL STORE.	S.	6211/43
67.	RADAR WORKSHOP.		
68.	GENERAL PURPOSE HUTS.		
68a.	"		
68b.	"		
68c.	"		
68d.	"		
68e.	"		
68f.	"		
68g.	"		
69.	PICKET POST. A.	N.	12404/41
70a.	BARRACK HUTS [EX CONTRACTORS][37'×16']	THOMSON	
70b.	"		
70c.	"		
70d.	"		
70e.	"		
70f.	"		
71.	LATRINES.	T.B.	
72.	ABLUTIONS.	THOMSON	
73.	INNER MARKER BEACON.		11503-4/41
74.	MAIN BEACON.		5700/40
75.	LATRINE [AS FOR ONE OFFICERS HUT]	THOMSON	9008/41
76.	REST ROOM [MECHANICS] (30'×18')		
77.			
78.			
79.			

BOMB STORES.

BLDG Nº	BUILDING	CONSTR	DRG Nº
80.	BOMB STORES. 'B'.		3164/42
81.	" " 'B'.		
82.	FUZED & SPARE BOMB STORE.		4780/42
83.	TAIL UNIT AREAS. [WITH BOMB STORES]		
84.	COMPONENT STORES. 12".	C.I	4733/42
85.	INCENDIARY BOMB STORE. 'C'.		4734/42
86.	" " 'B'	N.	
87.	" " 'B'		
88.	" " 'A'.		1272.5/42
89.	PYROTECHNIC STORE. 'A'.	N.	
90.	BOMB FUZING BUILDING. [ULTRA·HEAVY]	N.	7900/42
91.	" " [HEAVY·LIGHT]	N.	4778/42
92.	" " [HEAVY·LIGHT]	N.	12725/42
93.	GRENADE STORE. C.	N.	
94.	PICKET POST. (18'×16') 'B'	N.	12404/41
95.			
96.			
97.			
98.			
99.			

ADMIN·SITE·

BLDG Nº	BUILDING	CONSTR	DRG Nº
100.	STATION OFFICES.	N.	12400/41
101.	OPERATIONS BLOCK.	P.B.	15586/40
102.	CREW BRIEFING ROOM.	N.	13733/41
103.	OFFICE LATRINE [R.A.F.]	T.B.	9006/41
104.	" [WA·AF]	T.B.	
105.	M.T. PARK.		
106.	PICKET POST.	N.	12404/41
107.			

SITE·2· (·INSTRUCTIONAL·)

BLDG Nº	BUILDING	CONSTR	DRG Nº
108.	SHADOWGRAPH TRAINER & POST OFFICE 15641	T.B.	
109.	INSTRUCTIONAL BUILDING.	T.B.	19881/41
110.	OFFICE LATRINE [R.A.F]	T.B.	
111.	" [W.A.A.F]	T.B.	9006/41
112.	GUNNERY & CREW PROCEDURE CENTRE	T.B.	811G/41
113.	TECHNICAL LATRINE.	T.B.	9006/41
114.	LINK TRAINERS. (2 UNITS)	T.B.	10040/41
115.	"	T.B.	
116.	TURRET INSTRUCTIONAL BUILDING.[2·UNITS]	N.	11023/40
117.	A.M. BOMBING TEACHER. (3 UNITS)	T.B.	1759/41
118.	W/T OPERATIONAL INSTRUCTION CENTRE	N.	11240/41
119.	ASTRO INSTRUCTION HUT [UPWOOD]	WOOD	
120a.	CELESTIAL NAVIGATION TRAINER (PLANT)		7413-15/42
120b.	" [AF ONLY]		
121.	M & E PLINTH.		
122.	CONTRACTORS OFFICE	T.	
123.	" STORE	T.	
124.			
125.			
126.			
127.			

SITE·3· (·COMMUNAL·)

BLDG Nº	BUILDING	CONSTR	DRG Nº
170.	OFFICERS MESS. (160.)	N.	12867/41
171.	" BATHS. (151/160.)	T.B.	14459/41
172.	C.O'S QUARTERS.	T.B.	5023/41
173.	SQUASH COURT.	T.B.	16589/41
174.	SERGEANTS MESS. (300.)	N.	12868/41
175.	" SHOWERS. [276/300.]	N.	1447/41
176.	DINING ROOM. (1200.)	T.B.	12854/41
177.	RATION STORE. (1001/1200)	T.B.	9041/41
178.	INSTITUTE. (70·OFS·1080 A.M.)	N.	13049/41
179.	GROCERY & LOCAL PRODUCE STORE (1001/1250)	T.B.	12878/41
180.	A/M SHOWERS·ABLTNS & GAS DECONTAM (1101/1200)	T.B.	14453/41
181.	A/M LATRINES. (1101/1200)	N.	15404/41
182.	GYMNASIUM & CHANCEL. (15404/41)	T.B.	
183.	TAILORS·BARBERS & SHOEMAKERS SHOP.	N.	9878/41
184.	STAND·BY SET HOUSE	T.B.	16302/41
185.	FUEL COMPOUND. (90'×54')	WIRE	9108/41
186.	BOILER HOUSE. [OFFICERS BATHS & SERGTS SHR]	T.B.	16319/41
187.	PICKET POST. 'A'.	N.	
188.	C.O'S GARAGE.	C.I.	
189.	EMERGENCY WATER SUPPLY (22.000·GALS)		
190.	M&E PLINTH.		
191.			
192.			
193.			
194.			
195.			

SITE·4· (·SICK QUARTERS·)

BLDG Nº	BUILDING	CONSTR	DRG Nº
240.	SICK QUARTERS 16·BED	N.	16349/41
241.	" ANNEXE. 'B'.	T.B.	3938/42
242.	AMBULANCE GARAGE & MORTUARY. 'A'	N.	13907/41
243.	OFFICERS & ORDERLIES QUARTERS. 'C'	T.B.	13920/41
244.	ABLUTIONS·LATRINES & DRYING ROOM	T.B.	
245.	M&E PLINTH.	N.	
246.	PICKET POST. 'B'.	N.	12404/41
247.			
248.			
249.			
250.			
251.			

SITE·5· (·LIVING SITE·1·)

BLDG Nº	BUILDING	CONSTR	DRG Nº
290.	PICKET POST 'A'.	N.	12404/41
291.	M & E PLINTH	N.	14420/41
292.	OFFICERS QUARTERS. 'A'	N.	
293a.	" 'B'	N.	
293b.	" "	N.	
294a.	" 'C'	N.	
294b.	" "	N.	
294c.	" "	N.	
294d.	" "	N.	
294e.	" "	N.	
294f.	" "	N.	
295a.	SERGEANTS QUARTERS. 'A'	N.	
295b.	" "	N.	
295c.	" "	N.	
296a.	" 'B'	N.	
296b.	" "	N.	
297a.	" "	N.	
297b.	" "	JANE	14423/41
298a.	AIRMENS BARRACKS.	N.	14420/41
298b.	"	N.	
298c.	"	N.	
298d.	"	N.	
298e.	"	N.	
299a.	"	JANE	14423/41
299b.	"	N.	
299c.	"	N.	
299d.	"	N.	
300.	OFFICERS ABLUTIONS & LATRINES. (30/40.)	T·B	16330/41
301.	SERGTS & A/MS ABLTNS & DRYING ROOM'S	T.B.	16317/41
302.	SERGTS & A/MS LATRINES. (9)	T.B.	16329/41
303.	FUEL COMPOUND.		
304.			
305.			
306.			
307.			
308.			

SITE·6· (·LIVING SITE·2·)

BLDG Nº	BUILDING	CONSTR	DRG Nº
350.	PICKET POST 'A'	N.	12404/41
351.	M.C.E. PLINTH.	N.	14420/41
352.	OFFICERS QUARTERS. 'A'	N.	
353a.	" 'B'	N.	
353b.	" "	N.	
353c.	" 'C'	N.	
354a.	" "	N.	
354b.	" "	N.	
354c.	" "	N.	
354d.	" "	N.	
354e.	" "	N.	
354f.	" "	N.	
355a.	SERGEANTS QUARTERS. 'A'	N.	
355b.	" "	N.	
356a.	" 'B'	N.	
356b.	" "	N.	
357a.	" "	N.	
357b.	" "	JANE	14423/41
358a.	AIRMENS BARRACKS.	N.	14420/41
358b.	"	N.	
358c.	"	N.	
358d.	"	N.	
359a.	"	JANE	14423/41
359b.	"	N.	
359c.	"	N.	
359d.	"	N.	
360.	OFFICERS ABLUTIONS & LATRINES. (33/40.)	T·B	16330/41
361.	SERGTS & A/M'S ABLTNS & DRYING R·M (9)	T.B.	16317/41
362.	" LATRINES. (9)	T·B	16329/41
363.	FUEL COMPOUND. (90'×54')	WIRE	9108/41
364.			
365.			
366.			
367.			
368.			

SITE·7· (·LIVING SITE·3·)

BLDG Nº	BUILDING	CONSTR	DRG Nº
400.	PICKET POST 'A'	N.	12404/41
401.	M & E PLINTH.	N.	14420/41
402a.	OFFICERS QUARTERS. 'B'	N.	
402b.	" "	N.	
402c.	" "	N.	
403a.	" 'C'	N.	
403b.	" "	N.	
403c.	" "	N.	
403d.	" "	N.	
403e.	" "	N.	
404a.	SERGEANTS QUARTERS. 'A'	N.	
404b.	" "	N.	
405a.	" "	N.	
405b.	" "	JANE	14423/41
406.			
407a.	AIRMENS BARRACKS.	N.	14420/41
407b.	"	N.	
407c.	"	N.	
407d.	"	N.	
407e.	"	N.	
407f.	"	N.	

BLDG Nº	BUILDING	CONSTR	DRG Nº
408a.	AIRMENS BARRACKS.	JANE	14423/41
408b.	"	N.	
408c.	"	N.	
408d.	"	N.	
408e.	"	N.	
409.	OFFICERS ABLUTIONS & LATRINES. (33/40)	T·B	16330/41
410.	SERGTS & A/M ABLUTIONS & DRYING RM (9)	T.B.	16317/41
411.	" LATRINES (9)	T·B	16329/41
412.			
413.			
414.			
415.			

SITE·8· (·LIVING SITE·4·)

BLDG Nº	BUILDING	CONSTR	DRG Nº
450.	PICKET POST. 'A'	N.	12404/41
451.	M.&.E. PLINTH.	N.	14420/41
452a.	OFFICERS QUARTERS.	N.	
452b.	" 'B'	N.	
452c.	" "	N.	
453a.	" 'C'	N.	
453b.	" "	N.	
453c.	" "	N.	
453d.	" "	N.	
453e.	" "	N.	
454a.	SERGEANTS QUARTERS.	N.	
454b.	" 'A'	N.	
455a.	" 'B'	N.	
455b.	" "	N.	
455c.	" "	N.	
456a.	AIRMENS BARRACKS.	N.	
456b.	"	N.	
456c.	"	N.	
456d.	"	N.	
456e.	"	N.	
456f.	"	N.	
456g.	"	N.	
456h.	"	N.	
456i.	"	N.	
456j.	"	N.	
456k.	"	N.	
456l.	"	N.	
456m.	"	N.	
457a.	"	JANE	14423/41
457b.	"	N.	
457c.	"	N.	
458.	OFFICERS ABLUTIONS & LATRINES. (33/40)	T·B	16330/41
459.	SERGTS & A/M'S ABLTNS & DRYING R·M (9)	T.B.	16317/41
460.	" LATRINES. (9)	T·B	16329/41
461.			
462.			
463.			
464.			
465.			

SITE·9· (·W.A.A.F. COMMUNAL·)

BLDG Nº	BUILDING	CONSTR	DRG Nº
500.	PICKET POST 'B'	N.	12404/41
501.	M & E PLINTH.		
502.	EMERGENCY WATER SUPPLY [FIRE FIGHTING]		
503.	OFFICERS MESS QTRS & BATHS (10)	N.	12588/41
504.	DINING ROOM & SERGTS MESS (400)	N.	12588/41
505.	INSTITUTE & SERGTS REST ROOM. (351/400)	N.	12634/41
506.	BATH HOUSE & DECONTAM CENTRE (10A)	N.	12340/41
507.	ABLUTIONS & LATRINES. (10A)	N.	
508.	SICK QUARTERS (24·O·T·C')	T.B.	12351/41
509.	SERGTS QUARTERS (WITH LATRINE) (16'O')	N.	14420/41
510a.	AIRWOMENS QTRS. (9)	JANE	14423/41
510b.	"	N.	
510c.	"	N.	
510d.	"	N.	
510e.	"	N.	
510f.	"	N.	
510g.	"	N.	
510h.	"	N.	
510j.	"	N.	
511.	FUEL STORE	T.B.	
512.			
513.			
514.			
515.			
516.			
517.			

(far right column — partial)

BLDG Nº		
550.		
551.		
552.		
553a.		
553b.		
553c.		
554a.		
554b.		
555.		
557.		
559.		
560.		

BLDG Nº		
600.		
601a.		
601b.		
602.		
604a.		
604b.		
604c.		
604d.		
605.		
606.		
607.		
608.		
609.		

| 65. | | |

PERMAN
TEMPOR...
CONC...G...
STEEL
HANDRA...
TIMBER...
NISSEN
SECO...
INSIDE...
BLAST...

Q.D.M...

AIR MIN...

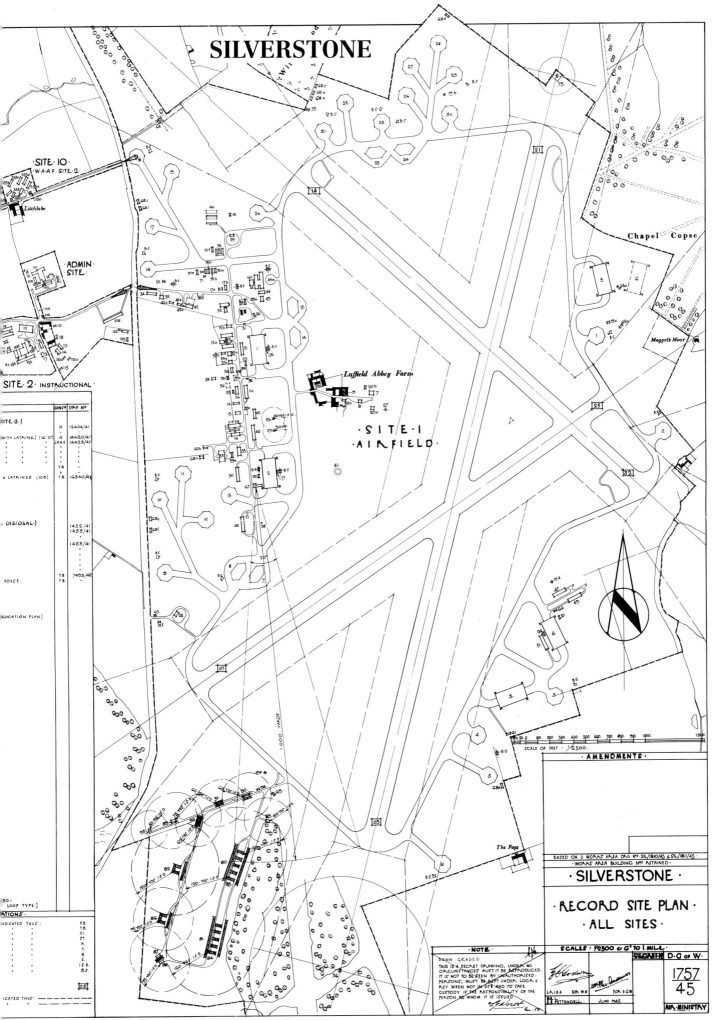

SILVERSTONE

· SITE · 1
· AIRFIELD ·

Luffield Abbey Farm

SITE·10
· W·A·A·F SITE·2 ·

Litchlake

ADMIN·
SITE·

SITE·2 INSTRUCTIONAL·

Chapel Copse

Maggot's Moor

The Fogs

N

1,000 YARDS

SCALE OF FEET : 1/2500

· AMENDMENTS ·

BASED ON II WORKS AREA DRG Nos SIL/1810/45 & SIL/1811/45.
· WORKS AREA BUILDING Nos RETAINED ·

· SILVERSTONE ·

· RECORD SITE PLAN ·

· ALL SITES ·

· NOTE ·

DOWN GRADED

THIS IS A SECRET DRAWING, UNDER NO
CIRCUMSTANCES MUST IT BE REPRODUCED.
IT IS NOT TO BE SEEN BY UNAUTHORISED
PERSONS, MUST BE KEPT UNDER LOCK &
KEY WHEN NOT IN USE AND ITS SAFE
CUSTODY IS THE RESPONSIBILITY OF THE
PERSON TO WHOM IT IS ISSUED.

SCALES : 1/2500 & 6" TO 1 MILE ·

SECRET. D·O of W·

1757
45

LNISA   FOR W5
PITTENGELL   FOR I·G·W
JUNE 1945.

AIR·MINISTRY

RAF Museum

76 SKIPTON-ON-SWALE
With revs climbing, the four Hercules engines of No 424 (Tiger) Squadron's Halifax III MZ986 'O-Oscar', are run up at dispersal before taxying out to the duty runway at Skipton. 'Oscar' failed to return from Bochum on 5 November 1944.
via Chaz Bowyer

78 SPILSBY
Pictured here in 1966, the watch tower at Spilsby has since been demolished along with most of the other buildings, runways and perimeter track. *via Chaz Bowyer*

77 SNAITH
Down but not out: No 51 Squadron's Halifax III, HR868:B, made its base although badly damaged by a nightfighter attack in a raid on Frankfurt, 20 December 1943. The port elevator was completely shattered, trim tab controls sheared, the rudder controls and rear fuselage riddled with bullet holes. Two cannon shells burst in the port engine nacelle and extensive structural damage was sustained to the main spar. A cannon shell had also burst in the nose, another had passed through the bomb doors, firing the incendiary load, the bomb door hydraulic pipeline was severed and the aircraft's petrol supply was also affected. After all of this, the pilot still managed to land the Halifax safely at Snaith, despite a burst port mainwheel tyre. Miraculously, JB911 went on to serve with No 1658 HCU at Riccall before she was finally SOC on 1 November 1946. *IWM CE114*

79 STRADISHALL
No 214 Squadron's Wellington Ic T2470:K is towed into a hangar for essential maintenance during 1940. In the background can be seen two of the station's five C Type (Hipped) hangars. *IWM CH1415*

80 STRADISHALL
Groundcrews of No 214 Squadron gather in front of a newly delivered Stirling I for a group photograph at Stradishall during the summer of 1942. *J. Hardman*

SNAITH continued

User sqns/units:

150 Sqn (1 Gp)
10/07/41-10/42
Wellington I, III

51 Sqn (4 Gp)
27/10/42-20/04/45
Whitley V; Halifax II, III

578 Sqn (4 Gp)
14/01-06/02/44
Halifax III

Opened with full station status 07/41
Became No 42 Base substation 1943

SPILSBY, Lincs
Opened: 09/43
Closed: 03/58
Elevation: 27ft
Pundit code: SL
Main contractor: Various
Runways: 3 concrete
Hangars: B1 (1), T2 (2)
User sqns/units:

207 Sqn (5 Gp)
12/10/43-21/07/45
Lancaster I, III

44 Sqn (5 Gp)
30/09/44-21/07/45
Lancaster I, III

Opened as No 55 Base substation 09/43

STANTON HARCOURT, Oxon
Opened: 03/09/40
Closed: 15/01/46
Elevation: 230ft
Pundit code: ST
Main contractor: George Wimpey & Co Ltd
Runways: 3 tarmac
Hangars: B1 (1), T2 (1)
User sqns/units:

10 OTU (6/91 Gp)
03/09/40-01/45
Whitley V; Wellington X

Opened as satellite to Abingdon 03/09/40

STEEPLE MORDEN, Cambs
Opened: 09/40
Closed: 01/09/46
Elevation: 160ft
Pundit code: KR
Main contractor: Various
Runways: 3 concrete
Hangars: T2 (1)

STEEPLE MORDEN continued

User sqns/units:

11 OTU (7/92 Gp)
09/40-09/42
Wellington I

17 OTU (92 Gp)
13/01-04/05/43
Blenheim I, IV

Opened as satellite to Bassingbourn 09/40
Transferred to USAAF control 07/43

STRADISHALL, Suffolk
Opened: 03/02/38
Closed: 27/08/70
Elevation: 382ft
Pundit: NX
Main contractor: Various
Runways: 3 concrete
Hangars: C Type (5), T2 (3)
User sqns/units:

75 Sqn (3 Gp)
13/07-14/09/39
Wellington I

148 Sqn (3 Gp)
30/04-20/05/40
Wellington I

150 Sqn (1 Gp)
18/06-03/07/40
Battle

214 Sqn (3 Gp)
14/02/40-01/10/42
Wellington I, II; Stirling I

138 Sqn (3 Gp)
16/12/41-11/03/42
Lysander IIIa; Whitley V; Halifax II

215 Sqn (3 Gp)
05/01-12/02/42
Wellington I

109 Sqn (2 Gp)
06/04-06/08/42
Wellington I, IV, VI; Mosquito IV

101 Sqn (1 Gp)
11/08-29/09/42
Wellington III

1657 HCU (3/7 Gp)
10/42-15/12/44
Stirling I

186 Sqn (3 Gp)
17/12/44-17/07/45
Lancaster I, II, III

Opened with full station status 02/38
Became No 31 Base HQ 05/43

STRATFORD, Warks
Opened: 12/07/41
Closed: 11/45
Elevation: 185ft
Pundit code: NF
Main contractor: Various
Runways: 3 tarmac
Hangars: B1 (1), T2 (1)
User sqns/units:

22 OTU (6/91 Gp)
14/09/41-15/11/42;
07/03-15/12/44
Wellington I, III, X

23 OTU (91 Gp)
11/42-03/44
Wellington III, X

Opened as satellite to Wellesbourne
Mountford 12/07/41
Became satellite to Pershore 11/42
Reverted to satellite to Wellesbourne
Mountford 03/44

STRUBBY, Lincs
Opened: 04/44
Closed: 09/72
Elevation: 35ft
Pundit code: NY
Main contractor: Various
Runways: 3 concrete/tarmac
Hangars: B1 (1), T2 (2)
User sqns/units:

619 Sqn (5 Gp)
28/09/44-30/06/45
Lancaster I, III

227 Sqn (5 Gp)
05/04-08/06/45
Lancaster I, III

Transferred to Bomber Command control
as No 55 Base substation 07/44

STURGATE, Lincs
Opened: 09/44
Closed: 1964
Elevation: 55ft
Pundit code: US
Main contractor: Various
Runways: 3 concrete/asphalt
Hangars: B1 (1), T2 (2)
User sqns/units:

No operational squadrons until 6/45

Opened as No 71 Base substation 09/44

SWANNINGTON, Norfolk

Opened: 01/04/44
Closed: 11/47
Elevation: 135ft
Pundit code: NG
Main contractor: Various
Runways: 3 concrete
Hangars: B1 (1), T2 (2)
User sqns/units:

85 Sqn (100 Gp)
01/05-21/04/44;
29/08/44-27/06/45
Mosquito XII, XVII, XXX

157 Sqn (100 Gp)
07/05-21/07/44;
29/08/44-16/08/45
Mosquito XIX, XXX

Opened with full station status 04/44

SWANTON MORLEY, Norfolk

Opened: 09/40
Closed: Currently in use by RAF
Elevation: 150ft
Pundit code: SM
Main contractor: Richard Costain Ltd
Runways: 3 grass
Hangars: Blister (4), J Type (1), T2 (4)
User sqns/units:

88 Sqn (2 Gp)
08/07-01/08/41;
30/03-19/08/43
Blenheim I, V; Boston IIIa

105 Sqn (2 Gp)
31/10/40-09/12/41
Blenheim IV; Mosquito IV

226 Sqn (2 Gp)
09/12/41-13/02/44
Boston II, IIIa; Mitchell II

98 Sqn (2 Gp)
18/08/43-18/10/44
Mitchell II

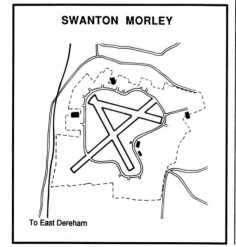

SWANTON MORLEY continued

305 Sqn (1 Gp)
04/09-18/11/43
Mitchell II

2 Group Support Unit (GSU)
04-12/44
Mosquito III; Hurricane

BSDU (100 Gp)
11/44-05/45
Lancaster I, III; Mosquito IX, XVI, XX;
Beaufighter I; Spitfire V; Proctor; Anson

Opened with full station status 09/40
*Wg Cdr H. I. Edwards DFC, 105 Sqn,
awarded VC, Bremen 04/07/41

SWINDERBY, Lincs

Opened: 08/40
Closed: Currently in use by RAF
Elevation: 69ft
Pundit code: NR
Main contractor: John Laing & Son Ltd
Runways: 3 concrete
Hangars: J Type (3), T2 (3)
User sqns/units:

300 Sqn (1 Gp)
22/08/40-11/07/41
Battle; Wellington I

301 Sqn (1 Gp)
29/08/40-18/07/41
Battle; Wellington I

455 Sqn (5 Gp)
06/06/41-08/02/42
Hampden

50 Sqn (5 Gp)
20/07-26/11/41;
20/06-16/10/42
Hampden; Lancaster I, III

1660 HCU (5/7 Gp)
10/42-11/46
Manchester; Halifax; Stirling I, III;
Lancaster I, III

1654 HCU (5 Gp)
05-15/06/43
Stirling I, III

Opened as satellite to Winthorpe 08/40
Became No 51 Base HQ 03/43
Became No 75 Base HQ 11/44

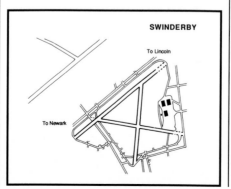

SYERSTON, Notts

Opened: 01/12/40
Closed: Currently in use by RAF
Elevation: 224ft
Pundit code: YN
Main contractor: John Laing & Son Ltd
Runways: 3 concrete
Hangars: B1 (1), J Type (2), T2 (6)
User sqns/units:

304 Sqn (1 Gp)
02/12/40-19/07/41
Wellington I

305 Sqn (1 Gp)
02/12/40-20/07/41
Wellington I

408 Sqn (5 Gp)
20/07-08/12/41
Manchester; Lancaster I

61 Sqn (5 Gp)
05/05/42-16/11/43
Manchester; Lancaster I, II, III

106 Sqn (5 Gp)
01/10/42-11/11/43
Lancaster I, III

49 Sqn (5 Gp)
22/04-28/09/45
Lancaster I, III

Opened with full station status 01/12/40
Became No 56 Base HQ 10/44
*Flt Lt W. Reid, 61 Sqn, awarded VC,
Dusseldorf 03-04/11/43

TATENHILL, Staffs

Opened: 11/41
Closed: 01/47
Elevation: 450ft
Pundit code: VL
Main contractor: Various
Runways: 3 concrete
Hangars: T2 (1)
User sqns/units:

27 OTU (7/93 Gp)
02/11/41-08/42
Wellington I

Opened as satellite to Lichfield 11/41
Transferred to Flying Training Command
control 11/42

TEMPSFORD, Beds

Opened: 1941
Closed: 02/63
elevation: 63ft
Pundit code: TE/TQ
Main contractor: John Laing & Son Ltd
Runways: 3 concrete
Hangars: B1 (1), T2 (6)

81 STRUBBY

The Lancasters of No 619 Squadron joined those of No 227 Squadron at Strubby on 28 September 1944, both units remaining for the duration of the war. Here, erks of 'A' Flight give 'D-Dumbo' its DI during the winter of 1944-45. *F. Slater via Chaz Bowyer*

82 SWINDERBY

With Berlin at a safe distance, No 50 Squadron aircrew at Swinderby enjoy a joke around the station's signpost, probably during 1942. None survived the war.

WO D. J. Penfold (left), posted to No 97 Squadron, was killed when his Lancaster III crashed at Graveley in fog, returning from Berlin on 16-17 December 1943; Plt Off H. Gilleland (centre), still with No 50 Squadron, failed to return from Soltau on 17-18 December 1942; Flt Lt Bob Hay DFC, RAAF, joined No 617 Squadron as the squadron's bombing leader, flying with Flt Lt Mickey Martin on the Dams raid. He was killed on 12 February 1944, attacking the Antheor Viaduct. *via Chaz Bowyer*

83 SWINDERBY

Returning from a gardening sortie on 18/19 September 1942, No 50 Squadron's Lancaster I, R5689:N, crashed on landing at Thurlby, Lincs, killing its skipper Flg Off G. Harrison and three other crew members.
via Jonathan Falconer

84 SYERSTON

On a balmy evening in August 1941, No 408 (Goose) Squadron's Hampden AE196:M is prepared for the coming night's operations to Hannover and Magdeburg. Transferred to No 44 Squadron, AE196 was lost in action over Brest on 13 December 1941, skippered by Wg Cdr S. T. Misselbrook DSO.
Public Archives of Canada PL4544 via Chaz Bowyer

WOODBURY
LODGE FARM

BIGGINGWOOD
SPINNEY

EVERTON
CROSSING

GIBRALTAR
FARM

CHANCE LIGHT
STANDING

CHANCE LIGHT
STANDING

CHANCE LIGHT STANDING

CHANCE LIGHT STANDING

RUNWAY Nᵒ 3

RUNWAY Nᵒ 2

RUNWAY Nᵒ 1

44

43

43

46

47

48

114

142

AIR MINISTRY BOUNDARY SHEWN

SCALE R.F. 1/2500   SCALE OF FEET

TEMPSFORD

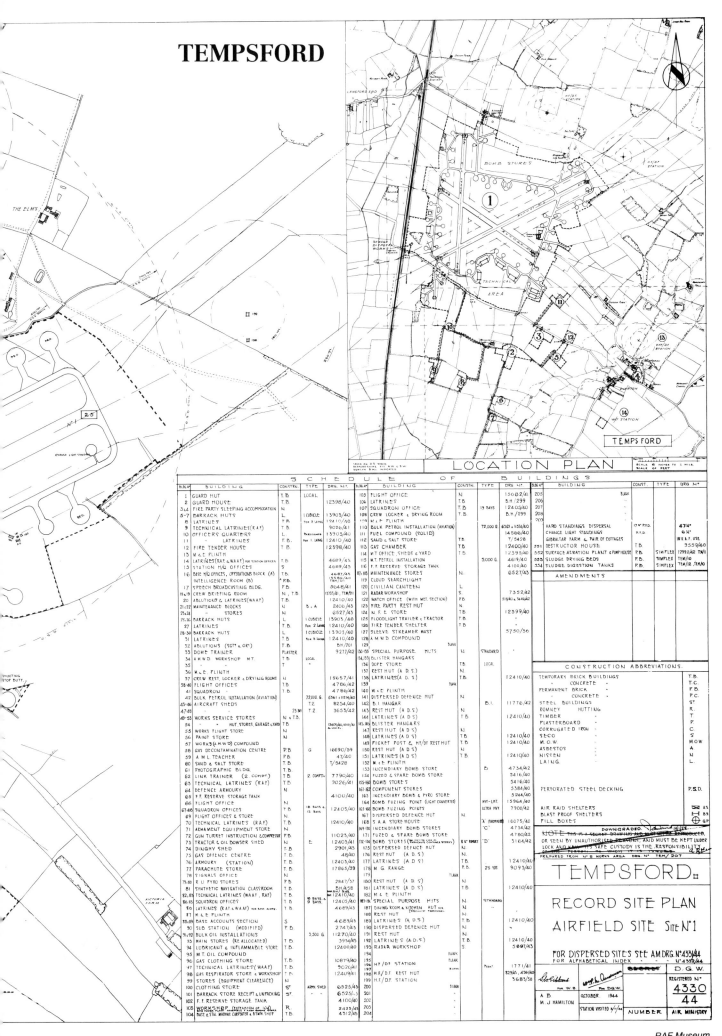

User sqns/units:

11 OTU (7/92 Gp)
16/12/41-04/42
Wellington I

109 Sqn (3 Gp)
19/01-04/42
Wellington I, VI

1418 Flt (3 Gp)
03-04/42
Wellington III

138 Sqn (3 Gp)
14/03/42-09/03/45
Whitley V; Halifax II, V; Stirling IV

161 Sqn (3 Gp)
Whitley V; Halifax II, V; Stirling IV;
Lysander IIIa; Hudson I
Opened with full station status 1941

THIRSK, Yorks
Opened: —
Closed: —
Elevation: 85ft
Pundit code: None
Main contractor: Not known
Hangars: None
User sqns/units:

226 Sqn (2 Gp)
18-27/06/40
Battle

Used occasionally as emergency landing ground for Topcliffe and Skipton

THOLTHORPE, Yorks
Opened: 08/40
Closed: 09/45
Elevation: 60ft
Pundit code: TH
Main contractor: Henry Boot Ltd
Runways: 3 concrete/tarmac
Hangars: B1 (1), T2 (2)
User sqns/units:

77 Sqn (4 Gp)
08-12/40
Whitley V

434 Sqn (6 Gp)
15/06-11/12/43
Halifax V

431 Sqn (6 Gp)
15/07-10/12/43
Wellington X; Halifax V

420 Sqn (6 Gp)
12/12/43-12/06/45
Halifax III; Lancaster X

425 Sqn (6 Gp)
10/12/43-13/06/45
Halifax III; Lancaster X

Opened as satellite to Linton-on-Ouse 08/40
Closed for rebuilding and runway laying 12/40
Reopened as No 62 Base substation 07/43

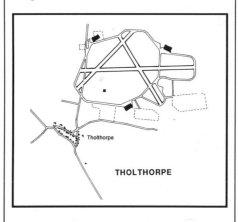

TILSTOCK, Salop
Opened: 01/08/42
Closed: 03/46
Elevation: 308ft
Pundit code: OK
Main contractor: Sir Alfred McAlpine
Runways: 3 concrete
Hangars: T2 (4)
User sqns/units:

81 OTU (92 Gp)
09/42-01/01/44
Whitley; Wellington

Opened as satellite to Hixon 08/42
Transferred to No 38 (Airborne Forces)
Group under Fighter Command control 01/44

TOPCLIFFE, Yorks
Opened: 09/40
Closed: Currently in use by Army Air Corps and RAF
Elevation: 81ft
Pundit code: TP
Main contractor: Various
Runways: 3 concrete
Hangars: C Type (5)
User sqns/units:

77 Sqn (4 Gp)
05/10/40-05/09/41
Whitley V

102 Sqn (4 Gp)
15/11/40-15/11/41
Whitley V

405 Sqn (4 Gp)
07/08-25/10/42;
01-06/03/43
Halifax II

419 Sqn (4 Gp)
18/08-01/10/42
Wellington II, III

424 Sqn (4/6 Gp)
15/10/42-08/04/43
Wellington III, X

1659 HCU (7 Gp)
03/43-09/45
Halifax III; Lancaster X

Opened with full station status 09/40
Closed for rebuilding 11/41
Reopened 06/42
Became No 6 (RCAF) Training Base HQ 01/43
Became No 61 (RCAF) Training Base HQ 09/43
Became No 76 (RCAF) Training Base HQ 11/44

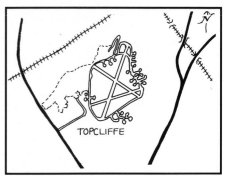

TUDDENHAM, Suffolk
Opened: 10/43
Closed: 07/63
Elevation: 75ft
Pundit code: TD
Main contractor: Various
Runways: 3 concrete
Hangars: B1 (1), T2 (2)
User sqns/units:

90 Sqn (3 Gp)
13/10/43-11/11/46
Stirling III; Lancaster I, III

186 Sqn (3 Gp)
05/10-17/12/44
Lancaster I, III

138 Sqn (3 Gp)
09/03/45-12/11/46
Lancaster I, III

Opened as No 32 Base substation 10/43

TURWESTON, Bucks
Opened: 23/11/42
Closed: 23/09/45
Elevation: 448ft
Pundit code: TW
Main contractor: Various
Runways: 3 concrete
Hangars: T2 (1)
User sqns/units:

12 OTU (92 Gp)
23/11/42-04/43
Wellington I

85 TEMPSFORD

Tempsford was home during World War 2 to the RAF's two 'cloak and dagger' squadrons under the operational control of No 3 Group. Nos 138 and 161 Squadrons undertook supply operations to the continental resistance groups as well as the dropping and collection of agents. Pictured here early in 1945, No 138 Squadron's Stirling IV LK149 'D-Dog', stands on its dispersal with its air and ground crew. Little more than 100yds away was the barn where agents received their final checks before boarding the waiting aircraft.
H. Shaw via K. Merrick

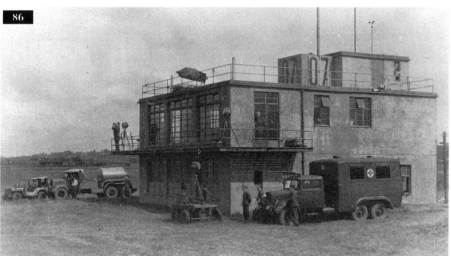

86 TEMPSFORD

Tempsford's watch tower was photographed in 1945 with the station's emergency vehicles arrayed outside. The '07' on the roof denotes the runway currently in use.
C. Annis via K. Merrick

87 TEMPSFORD

The ops board is updated by a WAAF in Tempsford watch tower's Flying Control Room in April 1944. *C. Annis via K. Merrick*

88 TEMPSFORD

VE Day celebrations at Tempsford, May 1945.
C. Annis via K. Merrick

89 THOLTHORPE

A scene at dispersal during 1944 of three No 425 (Alouette) Squadron Halifax IIIs. In the left foreground, the two air gunners of this French-Canadian squadron are wearing bright yellow electrically-heated Taylor suits with built-in buoyancy collars. KW-S MZ454 was fated to crash at Little Ouseburn, Yorks, after losing control due to icing on 5 March 1945; KW-U LL596 passed to No 1664 HCU at Dishforth before being SOC on 13 December 1946 — note the Preston-Green ventral gun turret on this aircraft.
Public Archives of Canada PL40185 via K. Merrick

90 TUDDENHAM

In March 1945, No 138 Squadron gave up its Special Duties role and became a Main Force bomber squadron operating Lancasters, still in No 3 Group. During its bomber role from March to May 1945, the squadron took part in nine raids for the loss of one aircraft. In this photograph, WO Jack Dyer and his crew pose for a photograph in front of the squadron's Lancaster III HK606:D early in the spring of 1945. From left to right: Flt Sgt Jack Robinson, gunner; Flt Sgt Don Brigham, bomb-aimer; Flt Sgt Les Vowles, flight engineer; WO Jack Dyer, pilot; Flt Sgt Ivan Smith, wireless op; Flt Sgt D. Truss, gunner; Flt Lt Freddie Woods, navigator.
D. Truss via K. Merrick

91 UPPER HEYFORD

Hampdens and a handful of Herefords equipped No 16 OTU at Upper Heyford from April 1940 until July 1942. AE148:Y later served with No 408 (Goose) Squadron and failed to return from Kiel on the night of 29-30 September 1941. Skippered by Plt Off W.F.Hull RCAF, the aircraft came down 5km southwest of Odense, Denmark, killing the crew of four. *via Chaz Bowyer*

92 UPWOOD

One of four 'C' Type Hipped hangars at Upwood, 1945. *via Jonathan Falconer*

93 UPWOOD

Airmen's quarters and Mess at Upwood, pictured at the end of the war.
via Jonathan Falconer

13 OTU (92 Gp)
30/04-08/43
Mitchell

17 OTU (92 Gp)
08/43-07/45
Wellington III, X

Opened as satellite to Chipping Warden
23/11/42
Became satellite to Silverstone 03/07/43

UPPER HEYFORD, Oxon

Opened: 10/27
Closed: Currently in use by USAF
Elevation: 421ft
Pundit code: UH
Main contractor: John Laing & Son Ltd
Runways: 3 concrete
Hangars: A Type (6)
User sqns/units:

18 Sqn (6 Gp)
20/10/31-24/09/39
Hart; Hind; Blenheim I

57 Sqn (6 Gp)
05/09/32-24/09/39
Hart; Hind; Blenheim I

7 Sqn (6 Gp)
23/09/39-22/04/40
Hampden

76 Sqn (6 Gp)
23/09/39-22/04/40
Hampden

16 OTU (6/92 Gp)
22/04/40-03/46
Hampden; Hereford; Anson; Oxford;
Wellington I, III, X

1473 Flt (92 Gp)
10/07/42-01/43
Defiant; Lysander; Mosquito III, IV, VI,
XX, XXV

Opened with full station status 10/27

UPWOOD, Hunts

Opened: 01/37
Closed: Currently in use by RAF
Elevation: 76ft
Pundit code: UD
Main contractor: Various
Runways: 3 concrete/tarmac
Hangars: C Type (4)
User sqns/units:

90 Sqn (6 Gp)
16/09/39-06/04/40
Blenheim I, IV

35 Sqn (6 Gp)
01/02-08/04/40
Blenheim I, IV

17 OTU (6/92 Gp)
04/40-04/43
Blenheim; Wellington

PFF Navigation Training Unit (NTU)
06/43-03/44
Lancaster I, III

139 Sqn (8 Gp)
01/02/44-04/02/46
Mosquito IX, XVI, XX, XXV

156 Sqn (8 Gp)
05/03/44-27/06/45
Lancaster I, III

Opened with full station status 01/37

WADDINGTON, Lincs

Opened: 11/16
Closed: Currently in use by RAF
Elevation: 235ft
Pundit code: WA
Main contractor: Various
Runways: 3 concrete/tarmac
Hangars: C Type (5)
User sqns/units:

44 Sqn (5 Gp)
16/06/37-31/05/43
Hind; Blenheim I; Anson I; Hampden;
Lancaster I, III

50 Sqn (5 Gp)
03/05/37-10/07/40
Hind; Hampden

142 Sqn (1 Gp)
15/06-03/07/40
Battle

207 Sqn (5 Gp)
01/11/40-17/11/41
Manchester

97 Sqn (5 Gp)
25/02-10/03/41
Manchester

420 Sqn (5 Gp)
19/12/41-07/08/42
Hampden

9 Sqn (5 Gp)
08/08/42-14/04/43
Lancaster I, III

467 Sqn (5 Gp)
13/11/43-15/06/45
Lancaster I, III

463 Sqn (5 Gp)
25/11/43-03/07/45
Lancaster I, III

Opened as RFC Flying Training station
11/16
Rebuilt to Expansion Scheme standard
and reopened with full station status
05/37

Became No 53 Base HQ 11/43
*Sqn Ldr J. D. Nettleton, 44 Sqn, awarded
VC, Augsburg 17/04/42
*Avro Lancaster introduced into frontline
service by 44 Sqn from Waddington

WARBOYS, Hunts

Opened: 09/41
Closed: 1963
Elevation: 90ft
Pundit code: WB
Main contractor: Various
Runways: 3 tarmac
Hangars: B1 (1), T2 (2)
User sqns/units:

156 Sqn (3/8 Gp)
15/08/42-05/03/44
Wellington III; Lancaster I, III

1655 MCU (8 Gp)
03/44-12/44
Mosquito IV, XX; Oxford

PFF NTU (8 Gp)
03/44-06/45
Halifax II; Lancaster I, III; Mosquito IV,
XVI, XX, XXV

Opened as satellite to Wyton 09/41
Achieved full station status 01/43

WATERBEACH, Cambs

Opened: 11/01/41
Closed: Currently in use by Army
Elevation: 17ft
Pundit code: WJ
Main contractor: Various
Runways: 3 concrete/tarmac
Hangars: B1 (1), J Type (2), T2 (3)
User sqns/units:

99 Sqn (3 Gp)
19/03/41-12/02/42
Wellngton I, II

1651 HCU (3 Gp)
02/01/42-21/11/43
Stirling I, III

514 Sqn (3 Gp)
23/11/43-22/08/45
Lancaster I, II, III

1678 CF (3 Gp)
11/43-12/06/44
Lancaster II

Bomber Command Film Unit
09/44-06/45
Lancaster I, III

Opened with full station status 11/01/41
Became No 33 Base HQ 09/43

94 WADDINGTON
Despite a heavy fall of snow, ops are still on for the Lancasters and their crews of No 463 (Australian) Squadron. The target for tonight, 1 March 1943, is Stuttgart, which will be attacked by a mixed force of 557 Lancasters, Halifaxes and Mosquitoes. Formed at Waddington from 'C' Flight, No 467 (Australian) Squadron on 25 November 1943, No 463 Squadron flew Lancasters from Waddington until the end of the war, often carrying cameramen of the RAF Film Unit on raids. *via Chaz Bowyer*

95 WADDINGTON
Inspecting Waddington's most famous son, Lancaster I R5868 'S-Sugar', on the occasion of completing its 100th op in June 1944 are (left to right): AVM Wrigley RAAF; Gp Capt Bonham-Carter, Station Commander; the Duke of Gloucester; and Wg Cdr W. Brill DSO,DFC, Officer Commanding No 467 (Australian) Squadron. *via Chaz Bowyer*

"NO ENEMY PLANE WILL FLY OVER THE REICH TERRITORY"
HERMAN GOERING

96 WATERBEACH
Sgts Cook DFM (left), George Mackie (second right) and Howard (extreme right) walk to debriefing after instructing on a training sortie in a No 1651 HCU Stirling I from Waterbeach during 1942. *G. Mackie*

WATTISHAM, Suffolk

Opened: 03/39
Closed: Currently in use by RAF
Elevation: 290ft
Pundit code: WT
Main contractor: Various
Runways: 3 concrete/tarmac
Hangars: L Type (4), T2 (4)
User sqns/units:

107 Sqn (2 Gp)
03/05/39-11/05/41
Blenheim IV

110 Sqn (2 Gp)
11/05/39-17/03/42
Blenheim I, IV

114 Sqn (2 Gp)
31/05-10/06/40
Blenheim IV

226 Sqn (2 Gp)
27/05-09/12/41
Blenheim IV

18 Sqn (2 Gp)
09/12/41-24/08/42

Opened with full station status 03/39
Transferred to USAAF control 09/42

WATTON, Suffolk

Opened: 01/39
Closed: Currently in use as HM Prison
Elevation: 190ft
Pundit code: WN
Main contractor: John Laing & Son Ltd
Runways: 3 concrete
Hangars: B1 (2), Type C4 (4), T2 (3)
User sqns/units:

21 Sqn (2 Gp)
02/03/39-24/06/40;
30/10/40-25/12/41
Blenheim I, IV

82 Sqn (2 Gp)
22/08/39-21/03/42
Blenheim I, IV

18 Sqn (2 Gp)
21-26/05/40
Blenheim I, IV

105 Sqn (2 Gp)
10/07-31/10/40
Blenheim IV

90 Sqn (3 Gp)
03-15/05/41
Fortress I

Opened with full station status 01/39
Passed to USAAF control 05/43

WELLESBOURNE MOUNTFORD, Warks

Opened: 04/41
Closed: 1964
Elevation: 154ft
Pundit code: WM
Main contractor: John Laing & Son Ltd
Runways: 3 concrete/tarmac
Hangars: J Type (1), T2 (4)
User sqns/units:

22 OTU (6/91 Gp)
14/04/41-01/07/45
Wellington I, III, X

Opened with full station status 04/41

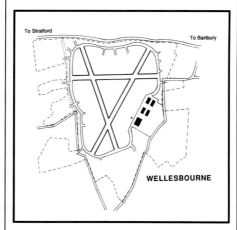

WESTCOTT, Bucks

Opened: 09/42
Closed: Currently in use by MOD
Elevation: 263ft
Pundit code: WX
Main contractor: Various
Runways: 3 concrete
Hangars: B1 (1), T2 (4)
User sqns/units:

11 OTU (92/91 Gp)
28/09/42-03/08/45
Wellington I, III, X

Opened with full station status 09/42

WESTON-ON-THE-GREEN, Oxon

Opened: 07/18
Closed: Currently in use by RAF
Elevation: 260ft
Pundit code: WG
Main contractor: Various
Runways: 3 steel matting
Hangars: Bessoneau (4), Blister (10), T2 (1)
User sqns/units:

104 Sqn (6 Gp)
09/39-04/40
Blenheim I, IV

WESTON-ON-THE- GREEN continued

108 Sqn (6 Gp)
09/39-04/40
Blenheim I, IV

13 OTU (6/7 Gp)
04-10/40
Blenheim I, IV

Used as satellite to Brize Norton 09/39
Became satellite to Bicester 10/40
Transferred to Flying Training Command control 11/40

WEST RAYNHAM, Norfolk

Opened: 05/39
Closed: Currently in use by RAF
Elevation: 262ft
Pundit code: WR
Main contractor: Various
Runways: 2 concrete/tarmac
Hangars: C Type (4)
User sqns/units:

101 Sqn (2 Gp)
09/05/39-06/07/41
Blenheim I, IV; Wellington I

90 Sqn (6 Gp)
11-14/09/39;
15/05-30/08/41
Blenheim IV; Fortress I

76 Sqn (2 Gp)
30/04-20/05/40
Anson; Hampden

139 Sqn (2 Gp)
30/05-10/06/40
Blenheim IV

18 Sqn (2 Gp)
12/06-09/09/40;
24/08-11/11/42
Blenheim IV, V

114 Sqn (2 Gp)
06/07/41-13/11/42
Blenheim IV, V

98 Sqn (2 Gp)
12/09-15/10/42
Mitchell II

180 Sqn (2 Gp)
13/09-19/10/42
Mitchell II

342 Sqn (2 Gp)
07/04-15/05/43
Boston IIIa

141 Sqn (100 Gp)
04/12/43-03/07/45
Mosquito II, VI, XXX

239 Sqn (100 Gp)
10/12/43-10/07/45
Mosquito II, VI, XXX; Beaufighter If

Opened with full station status 05/39

97 WATERBEACH

The crash tender crew at Waterbeach parade in front of their vehicle during 1943. Being a training station for much of the war, there were plenty of incidents both major and minor, involving sprog crews, to keep them busy. *H. Evans*

98 WATTISHAM

Here, in the summer of 1940, No 110 Squadron's Blenheim IV R3600 is refuelled and bombed up. R3600 joined No 110 Squadron on 26 May 1940 and flew 48 sorties before it failed to return from an anti-shipping sweep on 6 May 1941. *via Jonathan Falconer*

99 WATTON

No 82 Squadron's Blenheim IVs lined up at Watton early in 1940. The nearest aircraft, P6915:A, was lost on 7 June 1940. *RAF Museum P-3974 via Chaz Bowyer*

100 WELLESBOURNE MOUNTFORD

Tour-expired, Sqn Ldr W.A.Smith sits in the 'office' of a well-used Wellington of No 22 OTU during mid-1942. Smith returned to ops as a Pathfinder with No 7 Squadron in 1943 only to be killed in action on 3-4 July in Stirling BK724 over Cologne. *R. Smith via Chaz Bowyer*

101 WICKENBY

Wickenby opened as a satellite to Ludford Magna in No 1 Group in September 1942, under whose control it remained until the end of the war. No 12 Squadron, which arrived from Binbrook on 25 September 1942, shared the station with No 626 Squadron until after the war. No 12 Squadron's Lancaster III LM321:H2 is seen here at dispersal in the summer of 1943. Of interest is the application of the individual identity letter forward of the tailplane and the serial number above it. LM321 was eventually transferred to No 100 Squadron at Grimsby and failed to return from Acheres on 10-11 June 1944. *via Chaz Bowyer*

102 WICKENBY

Wickenby's watchtower, photographed in 1979, is happily still in use today by Wickenby Flying Club. *via Chaz Bowyer*

103 WIGSLEY

Sadly, Wigsley's fine watchtower has been allowed to fall into disrepair since the war and until recently was being used by the local farmer to store straw. It is pictured here in 1978. *via Chaz Bowyer*

104 WING

Wellington X LR132:V was used by Wing's sole occupant, No 26 OTU, resident here from January 1942 until March 1946 under the control of No 92 Group. *IWM HU1976*

WICKENBY, Lincs

Opened: 09/42
Closed: 1956
Elevation: 86ft
Pundit code: UI
Main contractor: John Laing & Son Ltd
Runways: 3 concrete
Hangars: B1 (1), T2 (2)
User sqns/units:

12 Sqn (1 Gp)
25/09/42-24/09/45
Wellington II, III; Lancaster I, III

626 Sqn (1 Gp)
07/11/43-14/10/45
Lancaster I, III

Opened as satellite to Ludford Magna
09/42
Became No 14 Base substation 12/43

WIGSLEY, Notts

Opened: 02/42
Closed: 07/58
Elevation: 23ft
Pundit code: UG
Main contractor: Various
Runways: 3 concrete
Hangars: B1 (1), T2 (2)
User sqns/units:

455 Sqn (5 Gp)
08/02-28/04/42
Hampden

1654 HCU (5/7 Gp)
15/06/42-08/45
Manchester; Halifax; Stirling; Lancaster

Opened as satellite for Swinderby 02/42
Became No 75 Base substation 11/44

WING, Bucks

Opened: 17/11/41
Closed: 04/60
Elevation: 450ft
Pundit code: UX
Main contractor: Various
Runways: 3 concrete
Hangars: B1 (1), T2 (4)
User sqns/units:

26 OTU (7/92 Gp)
15/01/42-04/03/46
Wellington I, III, X

Opened with full station status 17/11/41

WINTHORPE, Notts

Opened: 09/40
Closed: 07/59
Elevation: 54ft
Pundit code: WE
Main contractor: Various
Runways: 3 concrete

WINTHORPE continued

Hangars: B1 (1), T2 (2)
User sqns/units:

1661 HCU (5/7 Gp)
01/43-08/08/45
Manchester; Halifax; Stirling III;
Lancaster I, III

Opened as satellite to Swinderby 09/40
Became satellite to Ossington 11/41
Became satellite to Syerston 02/42
Became No 51 Base substation 01/43
Became No 75 Base substation 11/44

WITCHFORD, Cambs

Opened: 06/43
Closed: 03/46
Elevation: 47ft
Pundit code: EL
Main contractor: Various
Runways: 3 concrete
Hangars: B1 (1), T2 (2)
User sqns/units:

196 Sqn (3 Gp)
19/07-18/11/43
Wellington X; Stirling III

513 Sqn (3 Gp)
15/09-21/11/43
Stirling III

115 Sqn (3 Gp)
26/11/43-28/09/45
Lancaster I, II, III

195 Sqn (3 Gp)
01/10-13/11/44
Lancaster I, III

Opened as No 33 Base substation 06/43

WOMBLETON, Yorks

Opened: 10/43
Closed: 1949
Elevation: 120ft
Pundit code: UN
Main contractor: Various
Runways: 3 concrete
Hangars: B1 (1), T2 (2)
User sqns/units:

1666 HCU (6/7 Gp)
21/10/43-03/08/45
Halifax II; Lancaster I, II, III

1679 HCU (6 Gp)
13/12/43-27/01/44
Lancaster II

Opened as No 61 (RCAF) Training Base
substation 10/43
Became No 76 (RCAF) Training Base
substation 11/44

WOODBRIDGE, Suffolk

Opened: 15/11/43
Closed: Currently in use by USAF
Elevation: 70ft
Pundit code: OZ
Main contractor: Various
Runways: 1 bitumen/sand. 3,000yd x
250yd with undershoots and overshoots
of 500yd each.
Hangars: Blister (1), B1 (1)
User sqns/units:

None. FIDO-equipped Emergency
Diversion Runway.

Between 15 November 1943 and
30 June 1945, 4,120 emergency
landings had been made at
Woodbridge. The following brief
account, from official sources, is typical
of the many dramatic incidents which
were concluded at the airfield during
the war years. It involves Lancaster
ND763:W of No 15 Squadron from
nearby Mildenhall, skippered by Plt Off
O. Brooks RNZAF, which suffered
extensive damage from heavy flak and a
nightfighter over Dusseldorf on
23-24 April 1944:

'The aircraft was hit by heavy flak and
cannon shells from a nightfighter as the
bombs left the aircraft, causing fatal
injuries to both the bomb-aimer, WO
R. Gerrard, and the wireless operator,
Flt Sgt Bob Barnes. Gerrard died within
a few minutes and Barnes about half-
an-hour before landing.
  'The port inner engine was U/S, bomb
doors failed to close, flaps,
undercarriage, rear and mid-upper
turrets were all U/S, as was also the
elevator and rudder trim. Height was
lost from 22,000ft over the target to
4,000ft over the enemy coast. A fire
started in the rear of the aircraft and
was extinguished by the mid-upper
gunner, Sgt R. Wilson. Guns and other
equipment were jettisoned to enable
height to be maintained to reach the
English coast, which was eventually
crossed at 500ft. The navigator, Flt Sgt
K. Pincott, acted as wireless operator,
and Flt Lt J. Fabian DFC, the "Y"
Operator, rendered first aid to the
injured men and assisted with the
navigation.
  'A crash-landing was effected at
Woodbridge at 0355hrs.'

WOODHALL SPA, Lincs

Opened: 02/42
Closed: 1964
Elevation: 45ft
Pundit code: WS
Main contractor: Various
Runways: 3 concrete
Hangars: B1 (1), T2 (2)

105

105 WINTHORPE
No 1661 HCU operated a mixed bag of
Manchesters, Halifaxes, Stirlings and
Lancasters at Winthorpe from January 1943
until the unit was disbanded in August 1945.
Illustrated during 1943 is Lancaster I
W4113:J. *via Chaz Bowyer*

106 WOODBRIDGE
One of three emergency diversion airfields
down the east coast of England, Woodbridge
saw a huge number of Allied aircraft,
damaged or short of fuel, using its single
3,000yd-long runway during the closing
years of the war.
    Beneath the wing of this damaged
Lancaster under repair can be seen two
Lancaster IIs, a Lancaster I/III and a Halifax
III awaiting repair, refuelling and ferrying
back to their home bases. *via Chaz Bowyer*

107 WOODHALL SPA
No 627 Squadron was transferred from No 8
Group's LNSF to No 5 Group on 5 April 1944
to join that group's marker force, and flew
from Woodhall Spa in this role until after the
war. Here is the squadron's BXXV KB416
'P-Pat' pictured during late 1944.
D. Garton via Chaz Bowyer

108 WOODHALL SPA
Armourers at Woodhall Spa feed belted
.303in machine gun ammunition into the
nose turret of No 617 Squadron's Lancaster
III ED763 during 1944. *IWM 18175*

106

107

108

WOODHALL SPA continued

User sqns/units:

97 Sqn (5 Gp)
02/03/42-18/04/43
Lancaster I, III

619 Sqn (5 Gp)
18/04/43-09/01/44
Lancaster I, III

617 Sqn (5 Gp)
10/01/44-17/06/45
Lancaster I, III

627 Sqn (5 Gp)
15/04/44-30/09/45
Mosquito IV, XVI, XX, XXV

Opened as satellite to Coningsby 02/42
Became No 54 Base substation 08/43
*Wg Cdr G. L. Cheshire DSO,DFC, 617
Sqn, awarded VC for numerous acts of
courage on four tours of operations,
08/09/44

WOOLFOX LODGE, Rutland

Opened: 12/40
Closed: 01/66
Elevation: 344ft
Pundit code: WL
Main contractor: Various
Runways: 3 tarmac
Hangars: B1 (1), T2 (4)
User sqns/units:

14 OTU (7 Gp)
13/12/40-08/41
Hampden; Wellington

61 Sqn (5 Gp)
09/41-05/05/42
Manchester; Lancaster I, III

*1429 (Czech) Operational Training Flight
(OTF) (7 Gp)*
01/07-31/08/42
Wellington

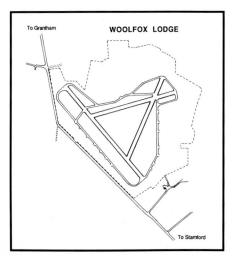

WOOLFOX LODGE
To Grantham
To Stamford

WOOLFOX LODGE continued

1665 HCU (3 Gp)
06/43-29/01/44
Stirling I, III

218 Sqn (3 Gp)
07/03-04/08/44
Stirling III; Lancaster I, III

1651 HCU (7 Gp)
10/11/44-07/45
Lancaster I, III

Opened as RLG for Cottesmore 12/40
Became satellite to North Luffenham
10/41
Achieved full station status 06/43
Transferred to USAAF control 09/44
Returned to RAF control as No 73 Base
substation 10/44

WORKSOP, Notts

Opened: 11/43
Closed: 12/60
Elevation: 195ft
Pundit code: WP
Main contractor: Wimpey & Carmichael
Runways: 3 concrete
Hangars: T2 (2)
User sqns/units:

18 OTU (91 Gp)
11/11/43-01/45
Wellington III, X

Opened as satellite to Finningley 11/43

WRATTING COMMON, Cambs

Opened: 05/43
Closed: 04/46
Elevation: 390ft
Pundit code: WW
Main contractor: Various
Runways: 3 concrete
Hangars: B1 (1), T2 (4)
User sqns/units:

90 Sqn (3 Gp)
31/05-13/10/43
Stirling III; Lancaster I, III

1651 HCU (3/7 Gp)
21/11/43-10/11/44
Stirling I, III

195 Sqn (3 Gp)
12/11/44-14/08/45
Lancaster I, III

Opened as West Wickham, No 31 Base
substation 05/43
Renamed Wratting Common 08/43

WYMESWOLD, Leics

Opened: 05/42
Closed: 1957
Elevation: 272ft
Pundit code: WD
Main contractor: Various
Runways: 3 concrete
Hangars: B1 (1), T2 (4)
User sqns/units:

28 OTU (7/93 Gp)
05/42-10/44
Wellington III, X; Lancaster; Halifax;
Stirling

Opened as satellite to Castle Donington
05/42
Transferred to Transport Command
control 15/10/44

WYTON, Hunts

Opened: 07/36
Closed: Currently in use by RAF
Elevation: 132ft
Pundit code: WY
Main contractor: Various
Runways: 3 concrete
Hangars: C Type (4)
User sqns/units:

114 Sqn (2 Gp)
01/12/36-09/12/39
Hind; Audax; Blenheim I, IV

139 Sqn (2 Gp)
03/09/36-01/12/39
Hind; Blenheim I

40 Sqn (2 Gp)
03/12/39-02/02/41
Battle; Blenheim IV; Wellington I

15 Sqn (2/3 Gp)
10/12/39-14/04/40;
15/05/40-13/08/42
Battle; Blenheim IV; Wellington I;
Stirling I

57 Sqn (2/3 Gp)
22-29/05; 11-23/06;
06-20/11/40
Blenheim IV; Wellington I

109 Sqn (8 Gp)
06/08/42-04/07/43
Lancaster I; Mosquito IV, IX

83 Sqn (8 Gp)
15/08/42-18/04/44
Lancaster I, III

1409 Met Rec Flt (8 Gp)
01/44-05/45
Mosquito

128 Sqn (LNSF) (8 Gp)
15/09/44-05/45
Mosquito XVI

163 Sqn (LNSF) (8 Gp)
25/01-19/08/45
Mosquito XVI, XXV

Opened with full station status 07/36

109 WOOLFOX LODGE
Some six frontline squadrons and training units saw service from Woolfox Lodge during World War 2, including No 1651 HCU, whose groundcrew are seen here during 1945 in front of one of the unit's Lancasters.
J. Hardman

110 WRATTING COMMON
No 90 Squadron's Stirlings line up at Wratting Common before the Berlin raid of 31 August 1943. The squadron lost one aircraft that night. Known originally as West Wickham, the station was renamed Wratting Common in August 1943 to avoid confusion with another similarly named airfield.
IWM CH10902

111 WYTON
No 139 Squadron air and groundcrews are pictured here at Wyton in August 1939 in front of a squadron Blenheim IV. *O. Baum*

112 WYTON
Mosquito PRIX ML987 'D-Dorothy', of Bomber Command's No 1409 Meteorological Flight, flew some 161 sorties in advance of Bomber Command and US 8th AF raids over Germany from Wyton. *Via Chaz Bowyer*

Airfield Locations in England and Scotland

1	Abingdon, Berks	72	Horsham St Faith, Norfolk	87	Little Horwood, Bucks
2	Alconbury, Cambs	73	Husbands Bosworth, Leics	88	Little Snoring, Norfolk
3	Attlebridge, Norfolk	74	Ingham, Lincs	89	Little Staughton, Hunts
4	Balderton, Notts	75	Kelstern, Lincs	90	Long Marston, Gloucs
5	Bardney, Lincs	76	Kimbolton, Cambs	91	Lossiemouth, Moray
6	Barford St John, Oxon	77	Kinloss, Moray	92	Ludford Magna, Lincs
7	Bassingbourn, Cambs	78	Kirmington, Lincs	93	Marham, Norfolk
8	Benson, Oxon	79	Lakenheath, Suffolk	94	Market Harborough, Leics
9	Bicester, Oxon	80	Langar, Notts	95	Marston Moor, Yorks
10	Binbrook, Lincs	81	Leconfield, Yorks	96	Melbourne, Yorks
11	Bircotes, Notts	82	Leeming, Yorks	97	Mepal, Cambs
12	Bitteswell, Leics	83	Lichfield, Staffs	98	Metheringham, Lincs
13	Blyton, Lincs	84	Lindholme, Yorks	99	Methwold, Suffolk
14	Bodney, Norfolk	85	Linton-on-Ouse, Yorks	100	Middleton St George, Co Durham
15	Bottesford, Lincs	86	Lissett, Yorks	101	Mildenhall, Suffolk
16	Bourn, Cambs				
17	Bramcote, Warks				
18	Breighton, Yorks				
19	Bruntingthorpe, Leics				
20	Burn, Yorks				
21	Carnaby, Yorks				
22	Castle Donington, Leics				
23	Chedburgh, Suffolk				
24	Cheddington, Bucks				
25	Chipping Warden, Oxon				
26	Church Broughton, Derby				
27	Coningsby, Lincs				
28	Cottesmore, Rutland				
29	Cranfield, Beds				
30	Croft, Yorks				
31	Croughton, Northants				
32	Dalton, Yorks				
33	Desborough, Northants				
34	Dishforth, Yorks				
35	Doncaster, Yorks				
36	Downham Market, Norfolk				
37	Driffield, Yorks				
38	Dunholme Lodge, Lincs				
39	East Kirkby, Lincs				
40	East Moor, Yorks				
41	East Wretham, Norfolk				
42	Edgehill, Warks				
43	Elgin, Moray				
44	Elsham Wolds, Lincs				
45	Elvington, Yorks				
46	Enstone, Oxon				
47	Faldingworth, Lincs				
48	Feltwell, Norfolk				
49	Finmere, Bucks				
50	Finningley, Yorks				
51	Fiskerton, Lincs				
52	Forres, Moray				
53	Foulsham, Norfolk				
54	Fulbeck, Lincs				
55	Full Sutton, Yorks				
56	Gamston, Notts				
57	Gaydon, Warks				
58	Gransden Lodge, Beds				
59	Graveley, Hunts				
60	Great Massingham, Norfolk				
61	Grimsby/Waltham, Lincs				
62	Hampstead Norris, Berks				
63	Harrington, Northants				
64	Harwell, Oxon				
65	Hemswell, Lincs				
66	Hinton-in-the-Hedges, Northants				
67	Hixon, Staffs				
68	Holme-on-Spalding Moor, Yorks				
69	Honeybourne, Worcs				
70	Honiley, Warks				
71	Honington, Suffolk				

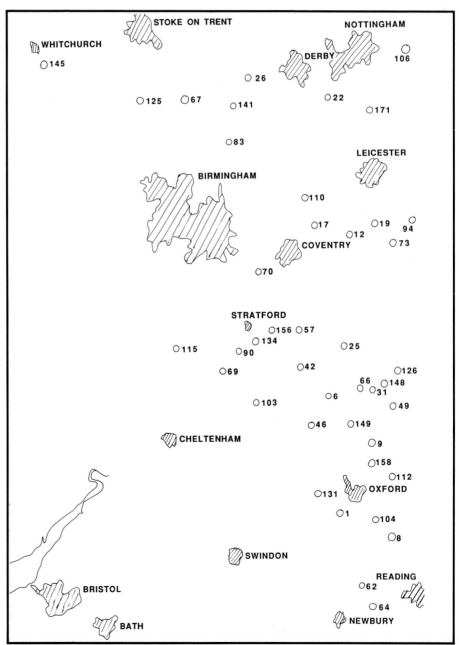

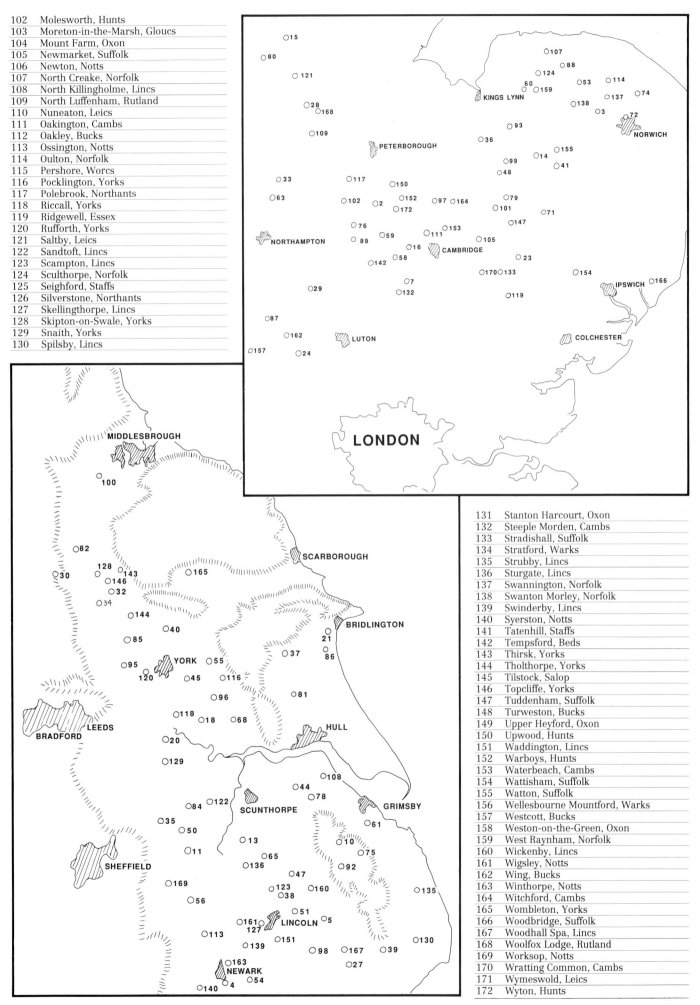

Evasion in France

After joining No 57 Squadron at East Kirkby from 1660 HCU, Swinderby, in June 1944, Len Manning's wartime career as a Lancaster rear gunner was cut dangerously short on his third op. Flying in Lancaster III JB318:O, he and his crew skippered by Flt Lt John Bulcraig DFM fell victim over northeastern France to the lethal upward-firing *Schräge Musik* 30mm cannon of a Messerschmitt Bf110G-4 piloted by Oberfeldwebel Herbert Altner. Altner was serving with 8./NJG5, a Luftwaffe nightfighter unit operating from Laon/ Athies 40 miles northwest of Reims. On the night of 18/19 July in the space of just 30 minutes he was responsible for downing five of the 27 Lancasters lost that night. Len Manning continues:

'At the end of June 1944 my crew joined No 57 Squadron at East Kirkby in Lincolnshire where we did several training flights on Lancasters before our first op on 15 July. This was a night attack on the railway yards at Nevers in central France.

On the 18th we took part in the huge daylight raid on Caen by 942 bombers — Operation "Goodwood". As we turned for home I had a grandstand view from the rear turret; the whole area was covered in dust and smoke. It was simply amazing to see so many planes in the sky at one time. We had taken off for this raid at 4am and on our return to East Kirkby we were

Right:
Sgt Len Manning (centre) was on only his third op as an air gunner with No 57 Squadron when his Lancaster was shot down over northeastern France on 18-19 July 1944 by a Messerschmitt Bf110 nightfighter of *8.NJG/5*, piloted by *Oberfeldwebel (Ofw)* Herbert Altner. Manning is pictured here with Sgt Tom Loughlin who, sadly, lost his life following the incident. *L. Manning*

Below:
On the Rue St Honoré in central Paris, the remains of an unidentified Lancaster are cleared from the city streets where they fell. Bomber Command lost 27 Lancasters alone on the Revigny raid of 18-19 July.
via Jonathan Falconer

ADVICE TO THE RELATIVE OF A MAN WHO IS MISSING

In view of the official notification that your relative is missing, you will naturally wish to hear what is being done to trace him.

The Service Departments make every endeavour to discover the fate of missing men, and draw upon all likely sources of information about them.

A man who is missing after an engagement may possibly be a prisoner of war. Continuous efforts are made to speed up the machinery whereby the names and camp addresses of prisoners of war can reach this country. The official means is by lists of names prepared by the enemy Government. These lists take some time to compile, especially if there is a long journey from the place of capture to a prisoners of war camp. Consequently "capture cards" filled in by the prisoners themselves soon after capture and sent home to their relatives are often the first news received in this country that a man is a prisoner of war. That is why you are asked in the accompanying letter to forward at once any card or letter you may receive, if it is the first news you have had.

Even if no news is received that a missing man is a prisoner of war, endeavours to trace him do not cease. Enquiries are pursued not only among those who were serving with him, but also through diplomatic channels and the International Red Cross Committee at Geneva.

The moment reliable news is obtained from any of these sources it is sent to the Service Department concerned. They will pass the news on to you at once, if they are satisfied that it is reliable. It would be cruel to raise false hopes, such as may well be raised if you listen to one other possible channel of news, namely, the enemy's broadcasts. These are listened to by official listeners, working continuously night and day. The few names of prisoners given by enemy announcers are carefully checked. They are often misleading, and this is not surprising, for the object of the inclusion of prisoners' names in these broadcasts is not to help the relatives of prisoners, but to induce British listeners to hear some tale which otherwise they could not be made to hear. The only advantage of listening to these broadcasts is an advantage to the enemy.

The official listeners can never miss any name included in an enemy broadcast. They pass every name on to the Service Department concerned. There every name is checked, and in every case where a name can be verified, the news is sent direct to the relatives.

There is, therefore, a complete official service designed to secure for you and to tell you all discoverable news about your relative. This official service is also a very human service, which well understands the anxiety of relatives and will spare no effort to relieve it.

(18997) 20217/M.595 20,000 7/43 K.H.K. Gp. 8/8

Left:
The dreaded Post Office telegram that brought tidings of such great sorrow to so many families during the war years, opened with the heart-stopping line 'Deeply regret to inform you...'. L. Manning

Bottom left:
Following the telegram came the official letter from the squadron commander. The letter gave brief details of the circumstances of the loss, and came with a short leaflet which told the next-of-kin what was being done to trace their missing relative. In reality there was little hope, borne out by the stark fact that more than 47,000 aircrew of Bomber Command lost their lives on operations during World War 2.
via Jonathan Falconer

told, after debriefing, that we were to be on again that same night. This was to become my third and last op.

'On the evening of 18 July we took off for Revigny in northern France, which lies some 50 miles southeast of Reims. After crossing the French coast we were picked up by searchlights and during our evasive action we lost the protection of the bomber stream which made us vulnerable to attack by enemy fighters. Having lost the searchlights we set a new course for the target.

'Soon after this there was an enormous explosion in the port wing: we had been hit by cannon fire from an enemy nightfighter. Immediately, flames streamed past my turret which by now had seized up. This was because the hydraulic power it needed to function was drawn from the port engine which had stopped working after the attack. I centralised the turret by hand, opened the rear doors and clambered back into the fuselage. Fred Taylor was already out of his mid-upper turret and clipping his chute on to his harness. He struggled to open the rear crew door, but once this was done he jumped out into the night.

'By this time the aircraft was in a steep dive and the fuselage a mass of flame and molten metal. My chute which was stowed on the port side had started to smoulder. I pulled it from its stowage and battled against the strong "G" forces to clip it on to my harness. With a supreme effort I just managed to fix the chute on to one of the clips, but the second clip eluded me. With everything about me burning I thought to myself "It's now or never" and leapt through the open door.

'As I fell, I pulled the rip cord and hoped the chute would open. It did with a crack, but I found myself hanging to one side. I felt something brush past my face. It was the intercom cord attached to my flying helmet which had been whipped off as the chute opened, becoming entangled in the silken shroud lines of my chute. I grabbed the cord and hung on. This probably saved my life as it helped to take my weight (I should have removed the flying helmet before jumping).

'When I looked up I could see the canopy smouldering and I hoped that I would reach the ground before it fell apart. On

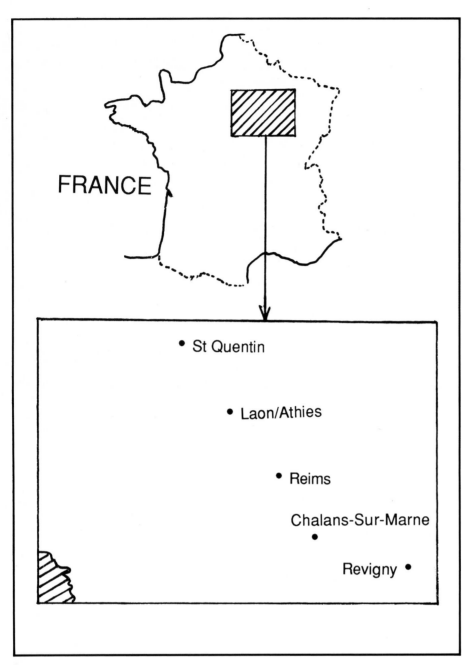

FRANCE

• St Quentin

• Laon/Athies

• Reims

Chalans-Sur-Marne
•

Revigny •

Above:
Map showing where the events of 18-19 July 1944 took place.

Right:
A Messerschmitt Bf110G, similar to the one piloted by *Ofw* Herbert Altner, which shot down Len Manning's Lancaster and four others, all within the space of 30 minutes. This particular example, *werke nummer 180850*, was captured by the RAF and used for evaluation purposes.
via Jonathan Falconer

the way down I saw a terrific explosion which was the Lanc blowing up as it hit the ground with a full bomb-load.

'I hit the ground flat on my back which winded me. My chute had started to burn so I quickly smothered the flames and gathered it up, pushing it into a hedge before staggering off into the darkness. I lurched on for about eight miles before I collapsed exhausted into the doorway of a farmhouse. The farmer must have heard me moaning for by now the burns on my face were giving me great pain. He took me in and with the help of his wife put me to bed.

'The following morning I was given civilian clothes to replace my burnt flying suit and boots, and then moved to another farm in the same village, Sablonniere. I was again put to bed. Then to my amazement I was interrogated by members of

the Resistance to ensure that I was not a German spy. This was all pretty frightening but, having convinced them I was English, they gave me a Sten gun which I kept under the bed. Later, a doctor arrived to treat my burns which he dusted with a white powder.

'The Germans came looking for me at the farm but the farmer convinced them that I had not been seen. In view of this the farmer decided to move me again. A member of the Resistance came for me and we travelled cross-country to dodge German patrols. At one stage my guide indicated that he was lost and would have to call at a house to ask the way. He pushed a Luger pistol into my hand and hid me in a hedge, telling me to shoot if I encountered any trouble at the house. He returned shortly with directions and we continued on our way until we reached a small café in the village of La Tretoir. The café was owned by two elderly ladies, Louisette Beaujard and her mother. Although neither spoke English I

was made very welcome and given a room in their hotel across the courtyard. If the Germans came into the village I would have to move into the ladies' room over the café, I was told, because German officers used the hotel when in the village.

'Two young men, Albert Bertin and Jacque Gaignard, were also staying with the ladies at the hotel. They were on the run from the Germans who wanted to conscript them for forced labour in Germany. Later, another chap appeared named Maurice Leterne, and from time to time a young lady, Madeleine Foley-Godard, would bring us cigarettes and money from the Resistance.

'I had the run of the orchard behind the hotel, but the café was strictly out of bounds. I was warned to make myself scarce when the postman was about because he was suspected of being a collaborator. There was also a lot of furtive coming and going by members of the Resistance.

'One evening a group of Germans came into the café for drinks while we were having our evening meal in the back room. Madame Beaujard came in to fetch some change and one of the Germans followed her. He stood by the door and looked around the room at the four of us. Madame gave him his change and he turned and left the room without a word, much to our relief.

'Some days later we were told that German tanks were coming towards the village and once again I moved into the ladies' room over the café. The next morning I was roused by the noise of the tanks. Looking down from the window I saw that the courtyard was full of German tanks; soldiers were standing about holding machine guns and some had grenades stuck inside the tops of their belts. This was another worrying time for me but later that day the soldiers and their tanks moved out and this was the last time that I saw any Germans.

'After a few more weeks some jubilant young Resistance men arrived riding a captured German motorcycle combination. They told us that the Americans had arrived outside the village and were setting up a field hospital. The following day I went down and found an officer who offered me a lift to Paris. He gave me a good supply of coffee and tinned food for my French friends. That night there was a big party to celebrate the liberation and all the good wines were brought out of hiding. My charred battle dress also reappeared, darned and pressed.

'After three months in France, the next day I returned to the American camp and was driven to the Hotel Maurice in Paris

where the RAF had set up a reception centre for evaders. The following day I was flown to England, arriving at RAF Hendon in north London, where I was interrogated once again to make sure I was not a German spy. I was then taken to a hotel at Marylebone where I made a full report to Bomber Command Intelligence. Telegrams were then sent home

Below:
One of the five 'kill' certificates awarded to *Ofw* **Altner, confirming his victories against** *'britischen viermotorigen Kampfflugzeuges'* **on the night of 18-19 July 1944.**
via L. Manning

and I was sent on leave. Living as I did in London, I arrived home before the telegram so it was quite a shock for my parents to find me at the front door, having heard nothing of me since I was reported missing some three months earlier.'

Two other members of Len Manning's crew survived being shot down; Fred Taylor, the mid-upper gunner, also evaded capture, and 'Rusty' Ruston, the navigator, became a PoW. The rest of the crew were killed when their Lancaster crashed and exploded near the small village of Basseville, 39 miles northeast of Melun and some five or so miles from La Tretoir. They were Flt Lt John Bulcraig DFM, the

pilot, a second tourist, who had flown his first tour early in the war as a navigator with No 50 Squadron on Hampdens; Flg Off Edward 'Robby' Robson, bombaimer; Sgt Tom Loughlin, wireless operator; and Flt Sgt Norman Gale DFM, flight engineer. The four men are buried side-by-side at Basseville's small communal cemetery where, with four dead from World War 1, they are the only British burials.

Below:
A grateful Len Manning poses for the camera with his 'rescuers', Louisette Beaujard and her mother, at La Tretoir, France. *L. Manning*

How to Bend a Lanc

Warrant Officer (WO) Ron Clark from Cumberland had joined No 100 Squadron at Grimsby from No 1651 HCU at Lindholme in May 1943 where the regular mount for him and his crew was Lancaster EE139;R, nicknamed *The Phantom of the Ruhr*. In the following account Ron Clark relates the terrifying ordeal suffered by him and his crew when they were coned by searchlights over the target, badly shot up by flak and then finally left for dead after being mauled by a nightfighter.

'It was now September and the nights were getting longer. On the 23rd I felt a tingle inside at the briefing as the target was revealed: Mannheim and Ludwigshafen in southern Germany. We knew it was a tough proposition from our previous visit.

'There was no cancellation and out at the dispersal EE139 was bombed up and waiting. "Ben" Bennett, my flight engineer had long since painted her name below the cockpit window, *The Phantom of the Ruhr*, a ghoulish figure hurling down a thousand-pounder from each bony fist. There was also a neat row of miniature bombs including three red ones for the "Big City" and two yellow ice cream cornets for trips to Milan and Turin.

'Being "top of the bill" we taxied out and took off first. We were soon overhead the bungalows in Waltham and climbing into the darkness. They never complained about the noise. There was not much conversation on the intercom except the odd irreverent remark from Geoff in the rear turret. He often addressed Doug the bomb-aimer by his surname to counter the Londoner's banter. Judging by the silence, Les in the mid-upper turret was now feeling even older than his 29 years. He sometimes got his fingers caught in the trigger guards of his twin .303in Brownings and we were quick to dub him "Trigger".

'Unserviceability of equipment at this point could be very inconvenient. With an engine out one would have to decide whether or not to go on to a nearby target like the Ruhr, or to drop the bomb load over the sea and return to base as would probably be the case with a distant target.

'We were now heading deep into Germany and by now we could judge our position by the areas of flak activity; there was always something going on. We checked the intercom regularly and kept a good look-out. As we approached the abrupt turning-in point to the target there were one or two radar-controlled searchlights probing purposefully. Far below,

the River Neckar glinted from the light. By now the flak guns would be following our movements, our speed and height noted.

'We turned in towards the target and Doug tended his bomb-sight with the parachute pack under his belly as usual. I slid the heavy goggles over my face whilst Ben was mentally running through the engine fire drill. The barrage had started and everything the flak crews had was hurled up at us: weird scare flares, high explosive and illuminations. The nightfighters were high up above with their navigation lights on, waiting for us to be silhouetted against the coming fires beneath.

'Suddenly a searchlight latched on to us and immediately all the others followed. A sharp evasive turn was not sufficient to escape their attentions. I called up Doug on the intercom to ask if he had seen the markers. There was no reply. He had been blinded by the monstrous glare and he knew like the rest of us that we were in mortal peril.

'It took about 15 seconds for the shells to reach us. Their fuses would probably be a little inaccurate as by now we had lost some height and increased our speed. There was a crunch behind me as a shell tore through the bomb bay and out through the roof to explode somewhere above us. We were hit again and the aircraft went into a steep spiralling turn.

'The searchlights were staring through the roof perspex at times and the speed became excessive as we plunged towards the centre of Mannheim. Ben throttled the engines back and helped me wrench the aileron control free. This immediately set up a severe vibration but I was able to straighten her up and ease out of the dive, having by then lost about 10,000ft in altitude. We decided to jettison the bomb-load as a 15-second straight-and-level sequence seemed to be inappropriate under the circumstances. When the bombs went the Lancaster and the rest of us felt easier.

'We were now at 8,000ft, down from 19,000ft, where the searchlights seemed

Left:
With WO Ron Clark at the controls, No 100 Squadron's Lancaster III, EE139:R *Phantom of the Ruhr*, survived flak and nightfighter damage to return home safely after the raid on Mannheim-Ludwigshafen, 23-24 September 1943. *H. Bennett DFM*

Above:
Ron Clark, skipper of *Phantom of the Ruhr*, pictured as a pilot officer, DFC, with No 625 Squadron, Kelstern, with whom he finished his first tour. *R. Clark DFC*

to be just outside the windscreen. But then my blood froze as I saw several streams of tracer fire pass very close and underneath us to meet at a point ahead like a series of tram lines. The spider had struck at us in its fatal web.

'Evasive action was imperative and I swung the suffering Lanc back into a steep diving turn. My mouth by then was so dry that I could only croak "Fighter!" into the intercom at the same time as

Below:
Flak damage to the starboard horizontal stabiliser and elevator was sustained over the target. *R. Clark DFC*

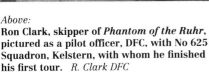

"Lish" Easby the wireless op, who was standing in the astrodome, shouted "Corkscrew!" We came back to straight and level and the aircraft was shaking like a leaf. As I couldn't focus my eyes on the vibrating instrument panel I shouted to Jim Siddell to tell me from the repeater compass at the navigator's position when I was on the outbound track. We were now well below the other bombers and flying through their falling bomb-loads. We found later that part of an incendiary bomb had lodged in one of the engine exhaust manifolds.

'I then realised that Ben was saying something to me. "The aileron control has been severed by the shell," he said.

'"What's that Ben?" Trimming wires were still attached to the tab on the aileron, I realised. It suddenly flashed

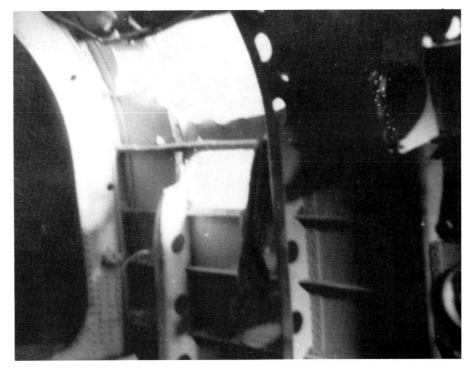

Above:
Lucky escape: over Mannheim a flak shell tore up through the *Phantom's* bomb bay and out through the fuselage roof, missing Sgt Lish Easby the wireless operator by mere inches, to explode harmlessly in the sky above. *R. Clark DFC*

through my mind that Ben had been coolly assessing the technical aspects of our predicament and was preparing to cut the trimming wires. I hurriedly told him to do as he thought best since the situation was desperate and there was no time for discussion.

'He got down by the throttle pedestal and somehow identified the trim wires to the starboard aileron which he then cut with his penknife. Inspiration was followed by a miracle and the aircraft immediately stopped shaking and became quite controllable with the half aileron control left to us. We were still very vulnerable to attack and the searchlights grimly hung on to us as we edged off the grotesque stage and into the enfolding darkness of the wings.

'The target began to recede and the searchlight beams seemed almost parallel to the ground as though the spotlights were lingering to welcome us back for an encore. We now had to take stock and gain some altitude. Miraculously no one was injured, the engines kept going and the systems seemed okay. Of course, we were uncertain about the extent of damage to the airframe and the possibility of fuel or engine coolant leaks. A voice asked me if I thought we'd make the coast to which I replied with some confidence "We're on our way home".

'Ben's superb coolness under fire and his airmanship coupled with his technical expertise had made a safe return to base a good possibility. He was to be awarded a well-deserved DFM.

'We flew back to Grimsby without further incident. I believe we were not

Above:
Inside a T2 hangar at Grimsby/Waltham on the morning after the raid, the *Phantom* receives a damage assessment from the station's engineering staff and experts from Avro. *R. Clark DFC*

attacked again because of our low altitude and our assailants probably assumed that we were a write-off. As we flew around the faint lights of the wartime Drem system at Grimsby we started the landing checks, but as 10 degrees of flap caused some vibration and rolling, I decided on a flapless landing. We didn't want a hydraulic leak at this stage and it was important to get the landing gear down. We were soon on the approach to the runway with the gear down and thankfully three green lights on the panel; no burst tyres we thought. It was difficult to keep the speed down without flaps but a little extra might be a good thing tonight, I

thought. The runway loomed up and the *Phantom* was home again, rolling smoothly down the runway with brake pressure normal.

'Later that day, after we had got up, we went over to see our kite in the big hangar. Apart from the extensive damage caused by the direct hit, the flak damage on the tailplane and the nightfighter cannonfire damage to the starboard wing flap, there had been distortion of the main

Below:
Ron Clark with his crew pose for the camera in August 1943 with two ladies from Waltham village whose bungalow lay just over the hedge from the *Phantom's* dispersal. From left to right: Sgt Geoff Green, rear gunner; WO Ron Clark, pilot; Sgt 'Trigger' Simpson, mid-upper gunner; Sgt 'Ben' Bennett, flight engineer; Sgt 'Lish' Easby, wireless operator. Not present in this group are Sgt Jim Siddell, navigator, and Sgt Doug Wheeler, bomb aimer. *R. Clark DFC*

wing structure. I took a photograph of "Lish" looking out of the shell hole and that was the end of our association with the *Phantom of the Ruhr*. It was a long time before she was nursed back to health and other hands were to guide her to her total of 120 operations. For me, it was business as usual. We were assigned a new aircraft and one week later we topped the bill once again on operations to Hagen.'

For their skill in getting the *Phantom* and its crew safely home against all the odds, WO Ron Clark was awarded the DFC, and the flight engineer, Sgt 'Ben' Bennett, the DFM.

Another alarming fact about this episode was discovered after the crew had inspected the *Phantom* in the hangar. Normally, when the aircraft stood on the ground the outer mainplanes had a slight dihedral, but now they noticed a pronounced anhedral. A working party from Avro (Woodford) confirmed on investigation that the wing root fittings had been subjected to abnormal stress loadings, resulting from the uncontrollable high-speed dive over the target and the subsequent pull-out. The Avro experts were astonished at what had happened and told an equally chastened crew they were extremely lucky not to have shed the wings completely.

Ron Clark and all but one of his original No 100 Squadron crew survived the war. Sadly, Sgt Jim Siddell, the navigator, went missing one night in October 1944 whilst flying as a navigator in a No 613 Squadron Mosquito FBVI. He is buried at Barneveld near Arnhem.

Daylight over France

The German defensive positions in the vicinity of the French Channel port of Calais were repeatedly attacked in heavy raids by Bomber Command after D-Day: six times in just eight days towards the end of September when over 3,260 sorties were flown by the RAF for the loss of 12 aircraft — 11 Lancasters and one Halifax. The one and only Halifax to be lost was a No 6 (RCAF) Group Mk III, LW136:Z of No 429 Squadron, Leeming, skippered by a 21 year-old Canadian, Plt Off George 'Nobby' Clarke, from Windsor, Ontario. He and his crew were part of a force of 188 aircraft despatched to attack German troop positions on the afternoon of 24 September 1944.

Briefing was at 1400hrs and they took off from Leeming in the pouring rain at 1652hrs. Thirty-one Halifaxes of No 6 Group formed part of the force and were timed to make their attack between 1849 and 1855hrs. However, when they reached the target they found it to be covered completely at 2,000ft by stratocumulus cloud, so only 126 aircraft actually bombed. Many of the attacking aircraft came down below the cloud base to bomb visually — instead of on the Pathfinders' Oboe-aimed sky markers — where the visibility was better. Clarke took Z-Zebra down to 1,800ft to release his bombs at 1850hrs. The light flak at this height was deadly and very accurate.

The following excerpt is taken from the personal diary of 20 year-old Flt Sgt Leslie Fry, Clarke's flight engineer, who records the alarming events of that day:

'Paul [the bomb-aimer] had just said "bombs gone" when a shell hit the kite, by the side of my seat. Several bits of shell hit me, four bits stayed in and had to be taken out in hospital.'

The Halifax had sustained very severe damage to both the mid-upper and rear turrets; miraculously the two gunners, 18 year-old Sgt 'Scotty' Ogilvie and 19 year-old Sgt Bob Nimmo, escaped serious injury. The rudder and aileron trim controls, the DR compass, port outer mainplane and all four engines were badly damaged by the light flak. With the Halifax crippled and losing height fast, Clarke headed south into France and over the Allied lines. He gave the order to abandon the aircraft as it passed over a valley near the small village of Clerques:

'I left my position, then Gerry [the wireless operator] started to dress my wounds. He had just started when he told me to put my 'chute on as we were going to jump.

'While Gerry went up to the nose for his 'chute, I dressed myself as best I could.

Gerry, after seeing that I would be OK, went to the rear exit. I went and had a look at my flight engineer's panel and while I was there I saw that the front escape hatch was open. Shorty [the navigator] was sitting on the floor ready to jump and Paul [the bomb-aimer] was pointing down at the deck.'

Plt Off 'Shorty' Short (21) and Flt Sgt Paul Roy (22) dropped feet-first through the open hatch into the rushing air of the slipstream and down towards the ground. Then Nobby told the remaining crew to wait as the aircraft very soon found itself over rising ground again and the starboard inner was now showing signs of packing up altogether.

'I then went back to the rear exit: Gerry and Scotty were there, but as the plane

was too low for us to jump I went back to see Nobby. He asked me which engines were U/S [unserviceable]. I told him but the engines would not feather. The two outer engines were U/S and the starboard inner went duff. Nobby shouted "We're going down!" but I did not need telling as I could see for myself. We had only just passed over one hill; I thought we would hit the next.

'Before we hit I looked out of the astrodome and saw a large hole in the port wing about three feet round. We crashed in a wood. After we came to a stop I got up and had a look at Nobby. The port inner was still turning over (without any props) so I pulled the cutouts and she stopped, but was on fire.

'I climbed out through the second pilot's exit, back along the top of the fuselage. The kite had broken her back just in front of the front spar, and by this time the port inner was burning like hell. I went inside the aircraft again and said to Nobby, "Let's get the hell away from here!" and we did.

'I dumped my 'chute about 25 feet from the burning plane. As we started running again, a petrol tank went up. We came

Below:
Sgt Les Fry from Ramsgate, Kent, was a flight engineer with No 429 (RCAF) Squadron, based at Leeming from August to November 1944. *via Jonathan Falconer*

Below:
Paul Roy, the 22 year-old French-Canadian bomb-aimer from Montmagny Station, Quebec, was killed baling out over Calais on 24 September 1944. *via Jonathan Falconer*

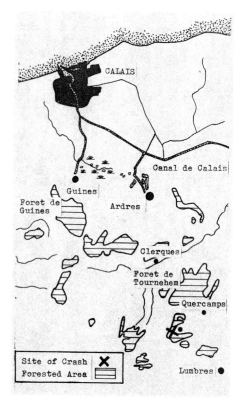

Left:
Paul Roy was buried in the secluded Canadian War Cemetery between Calais and Boulogne, high on a hill and surrounded by pine trees. *Jonathan Falconer*

from Calais. Still onboard was a 1,000lb bomb which had hung up while they were over the target. Fortunately it did not explode when the aircraft crashed and caught fire, completely burning itself out.

Of all the crew, Sgt Les Fry was the most badly injured with shrapnel wounds from the flak to his left arm and buttocks which eventually required surgery. Nobby and Sgt Bob Nimmo were uninjured, and Plt Off 'Shorty' Short the navigator found walking painful because he had strained ligaments in his leg as a result of the parachute jump to safety. Twenty-three year-old Flt Sgt Gerry Pare, the wireless op/AG, had suffered several cuts to his scalp and Sgt 'Scotty' Ogilvie had bruised his shoulder.

The whereabouts of French-Canadian Flt Sgt Paul Roy, who had jumped at the same time as 'Shorty', remained a mystery. Not until a few weeks later did his fellow crew members learn that he had been killed baling out. Paul had been found by Allied troops but was declared dead on arrival at a field dressing station. Although his parachute was seen to open, it is likely that it failed to open sufficiently to slow his descent and he fell to his death, thus not surviving to take up his promotion to Plt Off which was effective from 25 September. A new bomb-aimer, Plt Off Frank Manchip (24), soon joined them.

Above:
No 429 Squadron's Halifax III LW136 crashed on the edge of the Foret de Tournehem, near the village of Quercamps.

Below:
The retrospective secret Intelligence Broadcast of Bomber Command activity for 24 September 1944 which records the loss of 'Nobby' Clarke's Halifax III over Calais.
via B. Robertson

upon Scotty, Gerry and Bob. Scotty could not walk very well so we started to carry him, but not far as he wanted to walk.'

A little over 10min after releasing his bombs over Calais, Clarke had successfully crash-landed his crippled Halifax amongst the trees at the edge of the Foret de Tournehem about two miles southwest of Quer Camp and some 18 miles inland

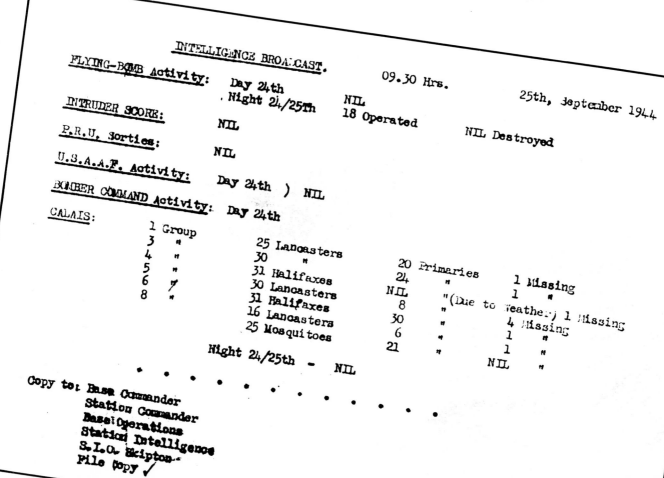

A One-Way Ticket to Duisberg

We have already met Flg Off 'Nobby' Clarke and his No 429 Squadron crew from Leeming when they were shot down over Calais on 24 September 1944 (see page 97). Returning to operations in October after a spell of leave followed by a period of inactivity due to poor weather, Clarke's crew flew a number of ops against oil and area targets in Germany before flying what amounted to their 17th and final op on 30 November, to Duisberg in the Ruhr. The precise chain of events on that fateful day and night will never be known for sure, but what follows is a reconstruction based on detailed primary research by the author.

Sometime before noon, briefing was announced for 1400hrs. For those whose churning stomachs could take it, a light lunch in the mess preceded a repeat of the performance earlier that morning before the station had been stood down.

With the formalities of briefing finally over, there was much scraping of benches on the concrete floor as the crews hurried to the locker rooms to change into flying kit. Valuables were handed in and 'chutes and escape kits collected. Amidst the usual babble of conversation and the jumble of parachutes, helmets and flying boots, 'Nobby' Clarke and his crew struggled into their unwieldy flying gear. Sandwiches and flasks of coffee for the return journey together with slabs of Fry's Sandwich chocolate and barley sugar sweets were handed out to each crew member from wrappings of newspaper.

Right:
Flg Off 'Nobby' Clarke from Windsor, Ontario, skipper of Les Fry's crew.
via Jonathan Falconer

Below:
An unidentified Halifax III, similar to the one flown by 'Nobby' Clarke and his crew on the night of 30 November/1 December 1944.
Public Archives of Canada PL41623
via K. Merrick

Outside the locker room the buses arrived to take the crews on the bumpy ride to their aircraft, dispersed around the perimeter of the airfield like huge crouching birds. A corporal stood at the open door shouting out the letters by which each aircraft was known. As space became available on a bus for that aircraft's crew, they climbed on board and were gone in to the night. Some crews sat around the dusty floor waiting. Others slouched against the wall, alone with their thoughts. Some paced up and down like caged tigers, unable to relax.

Because they were flying in Halifax III MZ314 W-Whisky once again, Nobby and his crew had to wait for transport until most of the other crews had left the locker room. When at last the bus came for them they clambered aboard, the rear door slammed shut after they had seated themselves on the slatted wooden seats, and with a thoughtful silence they rumbled of to dispersal.

Some 576 aircraft from four bomber groups were detailed for the night's raid on the German industrial city of Duisberg. These were as follows:

No 1 Group 16 Lancasters
No 4 Group 234 Halifaxes
No 6 Group 52 Lancasters; 191 Halifaxes
No 8 Group 25 Mosquitoes; 58 Lancasters

The target was to be marked by a mixed force of 83 Mosquitoes and Lancasters of the Pathfinder Force, and an airborne 'Mandrel' screen (electronic countermeasures) was also to be flown by 88 Stirlings, Halifaxes and Liberators of No 100 (SD) Group and the US 8th Air Force. Also a diversionary force of 53 Mosquitoes was to attack Hamburg. From the total of 576 despatched, 553 aircraft attacked the primary target, but 15 crews aborted over enemy territory *en route*, and eight over friendly territory.

The bus drew up beneath one of the huge black wings of 'Whisky' and the seven boys piled out on to the concrete dispersal pan. A cool breeze ruffled their hair and made their eyes smart after the smoky atmosphere of the locker room and crew bus.

The last streaks of sunlight had all but vanished from the western sky. Now, from around the vastness of the airfield, the sound of revving aero engines drifted across to them on the dusky air. The first aircraft were taxiing out to the take-off point. Bobby and Scotty were now ensconced in their turrets checking on the movements of their guns. 'Shorty' the navigator was tucked away at his snug station in the nose of the aircraft beneath Nobby's position. At this point in the aircraft the fuselage was some 9ft deep. Having checked their guns, Bobby and Scotty climbed back out of the aircraft for a last-minute cigarette and a leak in the grass at the edge of the dispersal.

Nobby looked at his watch. He completed the formalities of signing the Form 700 for the groundcrew corporal after a careful check of the control surfaces, wheel tyres and undercarriage oleo legs. Then they all climbed into the aft belly hatch of the aircraft: Les, Nobby, Frank Manchip (the bomb-aimer) and Jerry Pare (the wireless op) made their way up the fuselage to the nose, Bobby and Scotty to their turrets. Nobby stowed his 'chute and strapped himself into his seat. Outside, on the cold dark dispersal pan, the groundcrew were moving the starter trolley into position under the port wing.

Les checked to see that all the fuel cocks below his instrument panel were in their correct positions, then he leant forward to Nobby and declared 'Ready for start-up, skip'.

'Okay, Les, see if they're ready outside.' Les looked out of the cockpit window and down to the ground beneath. He called

back that the groundcrew were ready to start the port inner and Nobby switched on the ignition.

'Contact!' yelled the fitter from down beneath the wing. Les pressed one of the four black starter buttons on his panel and the first of four Bristol Hercules radial engines coughed, spluttered and finally roared into life. The same procedure was repeated until all four engines were running. Nobby checked the intercom, opened up the engines to 1,000rpm and then allowed them to warm up to operating temperature.

Taxiing times for each individual aircraft had been set at briefing and 'Whisky's' time to taxi out for take-off had now arrived. Les was standing behind Nobby, keeping watch on the array of dials on his engineer's panel. Frank came up the two steps from the nose to assist Nobby at take-off.

With the wheel chocks pulled away, Nobby gently opened the throttles and the great Halifax trundled and swayed forward, following the aircraft in front around the perimeter track in a stately procession towards the duty runway for the night. Nobby went through his final cockpit check. A green Aldis light from the control van winked through the darkness. 'Okay, boys, here we go!' called Nobby over the intercom.

At first the engines were opened up to 1,400rpm then up to the gate as the machine accelerated down the runway. Seven men and 8,000lb of bombs headed skywards between the two lines of yellow flare-path lights and away into the night.

Although the throttles were almost fully open, Nobby held 'Whisky's' nose down as she strained to leave the ground in order to build up as much speed as possible. Frank eased the throttles through the gate for full take-off power and slammed the clamp on to keep them from slipping back at the crucial moment through vibration. With both hands firmly grasping the control column, Nobby eased it back and the engine note changed as the big black bird clawed its way into the sky at 110mph, leaving the runway to slip away beneath. The wheelbrake lever was nipped to stop the wheels turning before the main gear and tailwheel were retracted with a clunk. The red and green indicator lights went out on Nobby's

Left:
Flg Off Vincent Mathias RNZAF and his No 578 Squadron crew, pictured at Burn during September 1944. Left to right: Robert Brown, wireless operator; Basil Hudspeth, mid-upper gunner; Roy Harvey, navigator; Vincent Mathias, pilot; Geoff Lovegrove, bomb-aimer; Oswald Parry, flight engineer; David Evans, rear gunner.
via Jonathan Falconer

Above right:
Bomber Command Air Operations over NW Europe, 30 November/1 December 1944.

Right:
Map showing the location of the crash site near Altweerterheide, Holland.

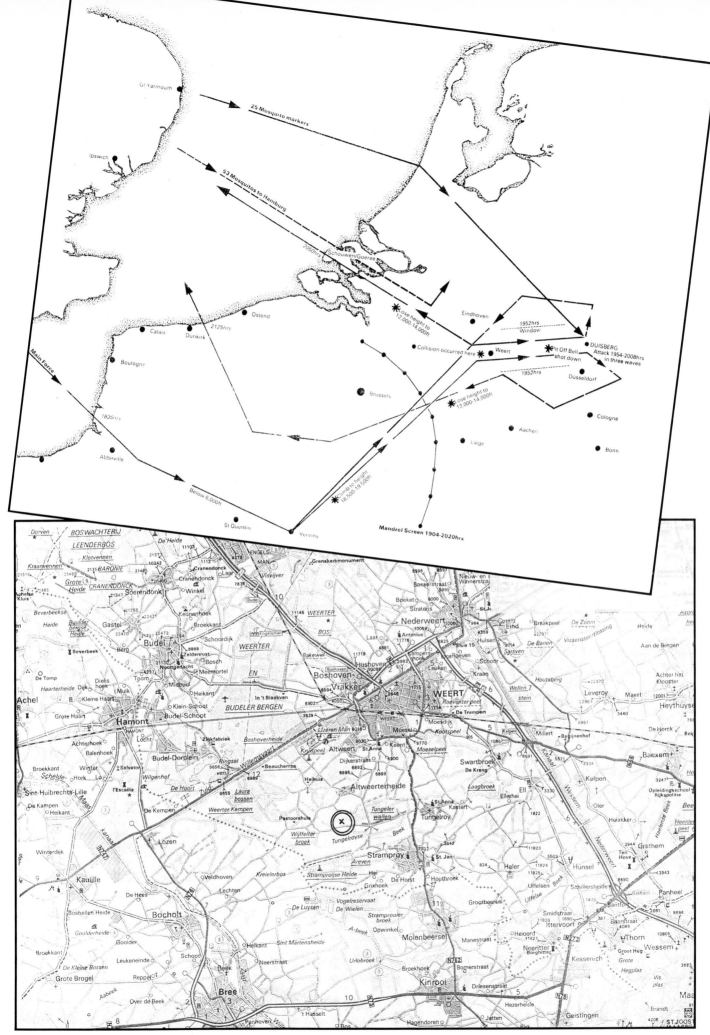

instrument panel. W-Whisky was airborne at 1643hrs.

The No 4 Group station at Burn, just over 40 miles south of Leeming, reverberated to the sound of its resident Halifax squadron, No 578, getting airborne. It, too, would be one of the No 4 Group's squadrons accompanying the Lancaster crews of No 1 Group and the Canadians of No 6 Group to bomb Duisberg.

At 1710hrs Halifax III NR193:V was eased off the runway by her pilot, a 28-year-old New Zealander called Vincent Mathias, and was soon lost in the blackness of the night. For Plt Off Mathias and his British crew this was their 16th op since joining the squadron from No 1652 HCU at Marston Moor on 18 August.

Meanwhile, Nobby continued in a shallow climb until the airspeed had built sufficiently for him to adjust the fuel mixture and engine revolutions to normal. Les eased the throttles back as the heavy bomber continued to climb. The flaps were now fully retracted and the power eased off again to suit the rate of climb selected. Shorty gave Nobby a course to steer and with the reassuring glow of the red and green navigation lights of the other aircraft in the sky all around them, they flew south in the climb towards their first checkpoint over Reading.

To prevent the Germans receiving early warning of their impending arrival the crews of Nos 1, 4 and 6 Groups which comprised the main attacking force, had been briefed to stay below a height of 6,000ft until they reached the town of Vervins at 0400 degrees E over Picardy. In fact, the enemy controllers concluded that the Main Force's southeasterly course threatened the Frankfurt area so one *Gruppe* of nightfighters was sent to a beacon in that area to await the arrival of the bombers.

The three groups made rendezvous over Reading where one by one the navigation lights were turned out as the armada of bombers droned its way southeastwards at a speed of 200mph towards Beachy Head where it left the shores of England behind. Navigating with the aid of 'Gee', landfall in France was made over the Somme estuary in the inky blackness at 1835hrs. The force headed inland for 110 miles across the bygone killing fields of the Western Front until it reached Vervins and the latitude of 0400 degrees E.

At this point the bomber stream split into two diverging courses and climbed up through the thick covering of stratocumulus, heading northeastwards across Belgium in a long slow climb over a distance of 130 miles to the bombing height of 18,500-19,500ft. The aircraft broke through the cloud into the hazy light of a full moon, with broken patches of cirrus scudding high above them. Passing

through the 10,000ft height band the order came from each aircraft's skipper for his crew members to switch on their personal oxygen supplies. In W-Whisky Les was busy keeping a log of the engine conditions and recording the state of the fuel load.

Confirmed by the strong 'Mandrel' screen, the Germans were kept guessing as to where the bombers would finally strike. By the time the two formations had crossed from Belgium into the Dutch province of Limburg, a major course change was imminent. At a point between Eindhoven and Weert the two separate formations turned eastwards onto parallel, but still separate, courses for the 50-mile run-in to the target. No 4 Group's Halifaxes were now slightly ahead of No 6 Group's.

The tactical plan was for the two Main Force formations and a special 'Window' force comprising two Mosquitoes from No 608 Squadron, Downham Market, to converge on the Ruhr from different directions. The Pathfinder Force was timed to drop its markers between 1958 and 2006hrs from a height of 16,800-18,500ft. With the Main Force attack, No 1 Group's Lancasters were timed to bomb between 2000 and 2004hrs; No 4 Group was to

ROYAL AIR FORCE.

Form 551.

PH26023

OFFICER OR AIRMAN—REPORT ON ACCIDENTAL OR SELF-INFLICTED INJURIES OR IMMEDIATE DEATH THEREFROM.

(N.B.—To be rendered in accordance with para. 2312 of K.R. and A.C.I.)

1. Surname ......**S.H.O.R.T.**...................................... Christian Names (in full)...**Clarence William**
FARRADAY

Rank ...**Pilot Officer**......... Number...**J.91067**...... Unit ...**429 Squadron, R.C.A.F.**

Date and time of accident...**App. 2000 hrs. 30-11-44**....Place of accident ......**Over Holland**

2. Short statement by injured person of the circumstances of the injury. If an aircraft accident state the type and number of the aircraft. If injury sustained in the performance of Air Force duty the particular act of duty to be specified.

Signed statements of witnesses, or of persons to whom the injured person may have mentioned his injury, to be attached.

This officer was flying on operations on 30-11-44 as navigator of Halifax III aircraft No. MZ314 and particulars of the accident are not known. According to Air Ministry Signal PC.630 dated 3rd Dec., 1944, this aircraft is believed to have collided with another of 578 Squadron in the air over Holland, killing all seven members of the crew.

3. (a) Description of injuries :—

.................................**UNKNOWN.**.................................

(b) Are the injuries (i) serious or (ii) of such a nature that they might be the exciting cause of disability later?

(i) ~~killed.~~ **killed.** ....(ii) ......

(c) Whether (i) admitted to hospital or (ii) provided with medical comforts (see para 2312 K.R. & A.C.I.)

(i) ....

MAY 28 1945 ......(ii) ......

Date:....**15.3.45.**....................Signature of Medical Officer... *Neil Gordon F/L*

Wt. 52041/O4205 155,000 2/44 W.H.& S. 668/69

(Neil Gordon F/L). [OVER

CAS.T.A26026/44/P.4/CAS/BUR.

The Director General
Graves Registration & Enquiries
The War Office (A.G.13)
32 Grosvenor Gardens, S.W.1

Halifax M.R.193

NZ426055	P/O V.W. Mathias-
1637806	Sgt Harvey, R.C.W.H.
1607117	F/S Lovegrove, G.L.
1076492	F/S Brown, R.
2203123	Sgt Farry, O.A.
1594181	Sgt Hudspeth, B.
2210016	Sgt Evans, D.

Halifax MZ.314

J91067	P/O G.W.F.	Short
J89367	P/O F.W.	Manchip
R164443	WO2 G.L.	Fare
R221522	F/S S.M.	Ogilvie-
R222102	F/S R.F.	Nimmo
J86980	F/O G.W.	Clarke-

1.   Reference your letter DC/5353/AG.13, dated 11th June, 1945.

2.   A signal received in this department states that 14 bodies were recovered from the wreckage of two aircraft which apparently collided and crashed in Holland at 2000 hrs., on 30th November, 1944. They were all buried in the British Burial Ground at Weert. Of the bodies recovered, 6 were identified as members of the crew of Halifax NR.193. Of the 14, 3 of the bodies were unidentified and it has been assumed by the Air Ministry that one of these three unknown's is F/Sgt. Brown, the only one not accounted for in his crew.

3.   From the information contained in these reports, and in your above referenced letter, it is known that the two aircraft involved were Halifax NR.193 and Halifax MZ.314, and that the two personnel for whom there has been no burial information, P/O Nimmo and P/O Short, must be the ones buried as unknown in Graves G.13 and G.14.

(J.S. Harris) Wing Commander,
for Air Officer Commanding-in-Chief,
R.C.A.F., Overseas.

WLC/YS

104

concentrate its aircraft over the target area in 3min waves between 2000 and 2006hrs; No 6 Group similarly between 2006 and 2012hrs. The whole raid was timed to last just 14min with 553 bombers being streamed over the target during this time.

At about 2000hrs over the Dutch town of Weert, Nobby had almost certainly just turned on to the final leg that ran into the target when something went very badly wrong. Frank the bomb-aimer had gone down into the nose to check his bomb sight and fusing panel; Les had gone aft beyond the cockpit bulkhead to check the master fuel cocks. Nobby called up the gunners for them to keep their eyes peeled for enemy fighters. Shorty's voice came over the intercom giving Nobby the ETA on target. Each member of the crew was busy at his station as the procession of aircraft in each formation began to converge for the final run-in to the target.

In the blacked-out towns and villages that dotted the flat Limburg countryside far below, the war-weary inhabitants were settling down for the evening. Two miles from the Belgian border in the tiny village of Altweerterheide the Blok family, tired after a hard day's work on their farm, were settling down for a well-earned rest in their farmhouse kitchen having just put their youngest children to bed.

High over Weert disaster struck. Two fully-loaded bombers collided. Nobby and his crew were in one of them, Vincent Mathias and his crew in the other. Violent explosions and gunfire in the night were sounds that the Bloks were all too familiar with, living as they did in a corner of Europe that for five years had witnessed the nightly procession of Allied bombers droning their way east towards the Ruhr. The gut-wrenching sound of rending metal high in the sky that night was nothing out of the ordinary for them. Not, that is, until shards of razor sharp metal, heavy engines, iron bombs and the pitiful remains of what moments before had been two four-engined bombers and 14 men, rained down about their farm in the meadow.

The two fatally damaged aircraft had become locked together by the force of the impact and had fallen 18,000ft to hit the ground two miles south of Weert, near Altweerterheide. Wreckage from the two aircraft and the bodies of the 14 crew crashed to earth in a meadow bounded by three farms, close to a road leading towards the small town of Bocholt over the Belgian border nearby. It was a miracle indeed that the inhabitants of the village escaped injury since pieces of the falling aircraft narrowly missed smashing through the roof of the Blok's farmhouse where the youngest members of the family lay sleeping. For some reason the wreckage did not catch fire despite the presence of a volatile cocktail of high octane fuel, bombs, ammunition and pressurised oxygen cylinders. But there were no survivors amongst the two crews.

The collision must have been severe enough to prevent all 14 men from baling out. With the terrific pressures exerted on their bodies by 'G' forces as both aircraft tumbled out of control, even if they had been struggling to reach the emergency hatches the effects of positive 'G' would have pinned them to the insides of the fuselages, rendering them completely helpless.

Meanwhile, up above, the rest of the bomber force droned its way inexorably eastwards towards Duisberg, some 40 miles distant, oblivious of the fate which had befallen the two crews. Most of No 429 Squadron's aircraft had returned safely home by 2300hrs, the last aircraft touching down on Leeming's runway at 2318hrs. The attack on Duisberg had not been concentrated but, nevertheless, much fresh damage had been caused to the city. Fires were visible from up to 60 miles away by homeward-bound crews. Some 528 houses were destroyed and 805 seriously damaged. Contemporary reports do not mention any damage to industrial premises, but 246 people were killed including 55 foreign workers and 12 prisoners of war.

Altweerterheide was already in Allied hands at the time of the crash and had been so since the beginning of November. On the day after the crash, Friday 1 December 1944, British military authorities arrived at the scene to examine the wreckage and to collect the bodies of the 14 crew before their eventual burial in the nearby Cemetery Keent at Nederweert. One year later, the bodies of all 14 men were exhumed and reburied in the newly opened Canadian War Cemetery at Groesbeek near Nijmegen.

We shall never know for certain the precise chain of events which led these two bombers to collide over Holland with such tragic consequences. The spectre of mid-air collision was forever in the backs of the minds of the bomber crews and the raid planners at Bomber Command HQ, particularly during the huge massed raids that marked the culmination of the strategic air offensive from mid-1944 until the war's end. But, with many other factors more likely to pluck them from the skies, such as flak, fighters, the elements and fatigue, mid-air collision was just another part of the calculated risk of operational flying, particularly at night. Bomber Command lost approximately 112 aircraft through collision between July 1942 and May 1945, 2,278 to German fighters, 1,345 to flak, and 2,072 to unknown causes (probably one, or a combination of each of the former).

Proverbs of a Pilot

These humorous 'proverbs' for pupil pilots were written by Sgt Jim Bowler on 31 July 1940, during his operational training as a bomber pilot at Lossiemouth with No 20 Operational Training Unit (OTU).

1. My sons, hear the advice of my great-grandfather and forsake not the laws of those that fly safely.

2. For the days of thy life are legion and I have instructed much youth of the land in the ways of an aeroplane in the air.

3. Verily, men do foolish things thoughtlessly, knowing not why, but an aeroplane doeth nought without reason.

4. Let not thy familiarity with aeroplanes breed contempt, lest thou become exceeding careless at a time when great care is necessary to thy well-being.

5. A wise pilot scenteth trouble afar off and avoideth a forced landing in waste places.

6. My sons, obey the law and observe prudence. Spin thou no lower than 1500 cubits nor stunt above thine own domicile, for the hand of the Lord is heavy and reacheth far and wide throughout the land.

7. Incur not the wrath of those in authority by breaking their rules, for he who maketh the wrong circuit shall be cast into outer darkness, and whoso flyeth low over football games shall be forever damned.

8. As the telephone operator who giveth the wrong number, so is he who extolleth his episodes in the air.

9. For I have watched him do his stuff on the ground. Lo, for an hour I have heard him talk of himself till he thinketh he is the best pilot ever.

10. He is like unto a woman who knoweth not how to say goodbye on the telephone, and the truth is not in him.

11. Though he be as honest as the day in all else, yet will he lie about his aerial adventures. His chest protrudeth and he maketh other men weary.

12. He doth enlarge upon the dangers of his adventures, but in my sleeve shall be heard the tinkling of silvery laughter.

13. Let not thy prowess in the air persuade thee that others cannot do even as thyself. For he that showeth off in public places is an abomination to his fellow pilots.

14. More praiseworthy is he that can touch tailskid and wheels together when landing than he who taxieth into another machine whilst watching the damsel who hath observed his prowess in the air.

15. Beware the man who taketh off without looking behind him, for there is no health in him. Verily, I say unto you, his days are numbered.

Below:
Sgt Jim Bowler and his crew during training at No 20 OTU Lossiemouth, July-September 1940. Left to right: Sgts 'Ginger' Dick, front gunner and second wireless op; A 'Mac' MacNab, rear gunner; Jake Linton, first wireless op; John Pascoe, first pilot; Jim Bowler, second pilot; J. E. 'Mac' Mackinley, observer. *Mrs F. Davies*

16. My son, another student pilot shall come unto thee saying 'Hearken not unto the words of your great-grandfather, for he doteth; listen to me whilst I tell thee how thou shouldst do so and so'.

17. But a little knowledge is of times of great danger, and thou knowest full well that my teachings are founded on much experience.

18. Clever men take the reproofs of their instructors in the same wise, one like unto the other with jest, confessing their dumbness and regarding themselves with humour.

19. Yet they try again, profiting by his wise counsel, and taking offence at nought that is said. For whoso hearkeneth unto his precepts shall fly safely and shall be quite free from fear of trouble.

20. Knoweth thou the pilot who criticiseth not another's flying? I say unto you that there is not one who cannot point out another's faults and advise him what he should do.

21. A reproof entereth more into a pilot of sense than one hundred compliments into a fool.

22. Better is a dancing partner with two left feet than he who laggeth behind in a formation and keepeth not his appointed place, for the leader breedeth wild thoughts.

23. As a wet dog who shaketh himself beside thee, so also is a pilot who usurpeth thy rightful place when landing in a formation.

24. Though the leader taketh thee over the city at low altitudes, having no regard for thy personal safety, yet will thou follow him closely, but on the ground thou will revile him after.

25. As a plate of soup that is cold, yea even as a kiss from one's sister, so also is a flight without objective: it lacketh kick.

26. As a postage stamp which lacketh its glue, so are the words of caution to a fool; they stick not, going in at one ear and out of the other, for there is nought to stop them.

27. Beware that thou leave not the switches 'ON' when leaving thy aeroplane, lest the mark of Cain be upon thee.

28. My son, hearken unto my teachings and forsake not the laws of prudence, for the reckless shall not inherit the earth for long. Hear instruction and be wise, and refuse it not; thus wilt thou fly safely. Length of days and peace shall be added to thee. Amen.

The Early Days

Sgt Jim Bowler was a Wellington pilot with No 99 Squadron, flying from Newmarket in Suffolk during the late summer and autumn of 1940. He was an avid letter writer to his fiancée Frances and the following excerpts are taken from the numerous letters he wrote her during his three-month period of duty with the squadron. It is interesting to note how free he is with details of the operations he flew. Despite the invasion fever that was sweeping the land in the summer of 1940, and a paranoia that fifth columnists were lurking at every street corner, there is no evidence of the censor having tampered with these letters.

Tuesday 24 September 1940
'This is just more or less to tell you of a major flying episode! No doubt you have heard on the wireless today about the biggest raid of the war upon Berlin last night. We were there, dropping 500lb bombs and a six-hour delayed one, at one o'clock this morning; we left at 9.30pm last night and landed at 5 o'clock this morning to the accompaniment of German bombs dropping round the aerodrome! So while you were asleep (presumably) darling, we were trekking 1,200 miles or more to Berlin and back. We're now working fine as a crew, we five pals and Frank. Ted the navigator took us dead on to Berlin over cloud, and Jake the wireless operator, he's only nineteen, gets us home just like a veteran on radio. I'm hoping to become captain after about five more trips, it all depends on the report Frank gives of me to the CO when he is due for his rest.

'We bombed Berlin from 13,000ft. There were flares from other kites all over the place, scores of them on the job, and coming out we were chased by two fighters, but managed to keep them off and get rid of them. The temperature was minus 10 degrees and I was thankful for my Irvin-suit — fur-lined jacket and trousers (£24 a time).

'You'll guess I'm pretty tired after only 3 hours' sleep, but I'm dossing down early tonight and everyone has all day off tomorrow. I asked if I could go home tonight for a day but it was impossible, worst luck, and I'll just have to wait for ordinary leave.'

Monday 30 September 1940
'On Saturday night we went to Hanau, near Frankfurt in the Ruhr, to bomb a munitions factory. The trip was about 900 miles. We were up from 10.30pm to 4.30am Sunday, and landed in semi-fog. I was almost too tired to eat my meal when we landed! Next trip you will be crossing off the teens, darling, and before you know it you'll be off double figures on to singles. We aren't operating so often just at present, there's no moon out.

'We may be billeted out in big houses in the town before long, we flying crews, although I'd rather be where I am for the winter.

'Frank had to make a press statement about our trip to Hanau, and though I didn't hear it I'm told it was given out on the wireless. He seems to think we're pretty good for a fairly new crew throughout, particularly as both Mac and Ginger the gunners never make a murmur when ack-ack is bursting all round us. Jake, our 19 year-old wireless operator, makes us really proud of him; he gets courses home and whatever we ask him for, like a veteran; and all the way out he listens in to German transmitters and checks up on our position. Ted (I may as well mention everyone) navigates us fine and bombs well, so we're happy all round. We were fired at all the way to Hanau and back, especially over Cologne coming back, so I had plenty of practice jinking. That was Frank's 23rd trip. He wants to stay on operations instead of going to an OTU, thinks it's an easier life!

'PS: I realised an ambition last Friday, to fly a Wimpy [Wellington] as only pilot on board. I went to Mildenhall to fetch our new aeroplane "B" for Berty, on my own. I flew back with 12 passengers on board: 4 officers and 8 airmen. Felt like an airliner pilot! Bragger!!'

Tuesday 8 October 1940
'We went to Berlin again on Friday, took 7¾hrs, and to Boulogne last night, back by 10pm for a change! At Berlin we had a very hot reception, they let us drop our bombs in the city then caught us in the searchlights and sent up everything they had all the way across the city. Next morning there were about 15 holes in the machine and we took a distinctly dim view of Berlin hospitality, you can bet. Last night it was filthy weather for the take-off, an hour and a half late, and we were the only crew on the squadron who went through to our target and dropped our bombs. (Don't think I'm not bragging, because I am!)'

Thursday 31 October 1940
'Just after I had scribbled Tuesday's note to you we had quite an exciting "welcome home to Newmarket". We were up at the house when some "Flying Pencils" [Dorniers] made a daylight attack on the aerodrome so we naturally dashed out to watch the fun and games. When we saw the German machine gunners firing tracer bullets all over the show, and heard them falling on the road, we started sheltering against a wall, dashing from one side to the other like idiots! We were down by it when one of them dropped a big stick of bombs quite close to us, so we promptly raced across a boneyard and some fields to see if we could be of any help, but luckily no-one was hurt, though two houses had very close shaves. One of the bombs

fell about 20yds from that little stone bridge we used to go to, in the middle of the road! Some of their bombs hit the aerodrome and one of the bombs made an enormous crater smack in the middle of the race course in front of the grand-stand!

'There was racing here yesterday on the other course, so we went across to watch and saw Gordon Richards win the Cesare-witch. He's a jockey, not a horse, if you've never heard of him, and he wasn't doing the running himself either (that's beaten you to it!)

'It's a queer game, the horses dash around a track miles away and all you see of them is when they come up for the finish past the stands. Mad, I call it! You should hear the bookmakers shouting one another down with the odds they're offer-ing, just like Coalville market! (Break — wardens are bawling outside about our blackout.)'

Sunday 10 November 1940
'This afternoon is a break in what has seemed like two days of rushing around getting "B" for Berty fit again after an inspection over at Mildenhall. We should have operated tonight, but apparently the weather is going to be bad and everyone has the afternoon and night off. It's very cold now and raining hard, so I'm pretty pleased we aren't going.

'Yesterday we had a little minor excite-ment after hearing Jerry overhead during the afternoon. He started dropping bombs by guess-work through the clouds, and they were quite near too, so we all bolted down the air-raid shelters for half-an-hour. He must have been scared to come

down below the clouds. When the squadron operated last Friday night they were after the beer cellar at Munich where Hitler was supposed to be having a big pow-wow. Fletcher and his crew didn't come back, but don't worry, they only ran out of petrol and went down in the sea near Hastings. Coastal Command have picked them all up safe and sound; we're expecting to see them tomorrow.*

'Hope my last letter didn't make you feel dismal, darling, I don't know what was biting me when I wrote it, I'm sure. I love you just as much as ever, but sometimes this war makes everything seem so unreal compared with peacetime days, with hardly ever seeing you at all, and when all I have to represent you are letters. I sup-pose when it's all over I shall be able to settle my mind properly once more and my life will revolve around you, instead of round you and aeroplanes and bombs as it is doing at the moment. May the time soon come when I shall have something better to do in life than destroy things, though I don't mind in the least destroy-ing what we are fighting against.

'I think I told you that now there are only Mac, Ginger and me left of the origi-nal No 2 crew from Lossiemouth. All being well, John, Ted and Jake will be by the Mediterranean sea before the week is out. Our new navigator seems like a good lad but I'm not very keen on the wireless operator. He may be OK but if he isn't we'll soon have him swapped.'

Thursday 14 November 1940
'"B" for Berty has not yet been over your place and the one you flew in never will either! Last night we went to Berlin again

for the third time. All was fine going out and on the target but coming back we ran into snow and had to fly blind. However, we found our coast OK and set course for home, still in snow and then we ran into a lot of static electricity which made the front guns and propellers glow blue and look weird and threw all the instruments haywire, finally burning the wireless set use. And we got completely lost, but even-tually came to what seemed a very big place and looked round low, hoping to see an aerodrome. To cut a long story short, we were on our last drop of petrol and all had to do the wisest thing possible, leave the machine by parachute.

'I was in the seat at the time and wanted Frank to go out first, but as captain he naturally insisted upon being last, and persuaded me to go first to set an example to the others. We all went through the bottom door by which you entered, and went out at 3,000ft into the snow clouds, and gosh what a queer sensation it was. This was at 1.10am this morning, after 8½hrs in the air. I just dived through and got clear of the machine, pulled the rip-cord and in a second or two got a terrific jolt, then was swinging down in dead silence through snow. I didn't see the ground until about 200ft up, and a few seconds later landed on my back with a terrific bang, seeing stars, and the next thing I knew I was being dragged across the field I landed in at about 20mph, help-less to stop myself. Finally, the silk hit a hedge and I just shot forward head first into it! Then I detached the silk, was vio-lently sick (shame!) and staggered into someone's back garden where I could get no answer to my knocks.

'Sorry darling, but I just can't carry on tonight. I feel ill and pretty well all-in. I'll carry on tomorrow.'

Friday 15 November 1940
'Well, I feel a lot better now after a nor-mal night's sleep. To continue the narra-tive, I staggered on a little further, knocked at another house and stood wait-ing in the snow, listening to a dog barking inside. Then a quavering female voice asked who was there. I told her and that I felt very ill and was in a shocking state, but she didn't trust me and wouldn't let me in, so I thanked her for her hospitality and staggered further on to a pill box at the side of the road where there were sol-diers. After making sure who I was, they phoned the commanding officer at Heston aerodrome half-a-mile away, and he fetched me in his car and put me to bed at the aerodrome in his pyjamas.

'So, we were in London! He was a fine fellow and took everything out of my

Left:
No 99 Squadron's Wellington Ic, R3167 B-Berty, skippered by Sgt Frank Swatton with Sgt Jim Bowler as second pilot, crashed on to houses at Hampton Court, Middx, returning from Berlin on 13-14 November 1940 after becoming lost in bad weather and running out of fuel. *Mrs F. M. Davies*

hands and within half-an-hour I knew all the others were safe, though we were spread over 10 miles. "B" for Berty had hit a house in Hampton Court and was burnt out. Two people in the house had a miraculous escape and Mac and I went to see the wreck and ruins yesterday morning.

'I've never been so pleased in my life as I was when I knew everyone was safe. Mac landed on the edge of a gravel pit full of water at Hounslow and just missed drowning; Frank landed in a garden near the house; our new wireless op landed in a road; our new navigator landed on the hospital he's in, walked off the roof and sprained his ankle! But we got the biggest laugh over Ginger: he landed in a tree in Hounslow military barracks, and hung there for two hours in the snow! He bawled out for help, a soldier thought he was a Jerry and called out the guard. First they fetched a ladder which was too short, then another too short, and next thing Ginger heard was the Fire Brigade clanging its bell; and finally they got him down a fire escape and he spent the night in the hospital there.

'We got back here last night in two staff cars sent down for us, and in the morning we're fetching a brand new "B" for Berty over and I hope she lasts a long time. I'm OK now apart from bruises and stiff neck and shoulders.

'PS: I'm not in the slightest superstitious, but it's interesting to know it was my 13th operation, on the 13th of the month!'

Tuesday 19 November 1940
'I suppose this will sound rather a tame letter after the last! Hope you were thrilled because I can assure you that I was when it all happened. We've been interviewed by quite a few of the "big boys" of the RAF, but none of them condemned what we did, they were all delighted to know we were all safe and didn't care a toss what had happened to the machine. You should see the new "B" for Berty which we have now: the other was a Ic, but this one is the very latest, a Mk Id with two extra guns just in case they're needed. We should have operated in her tonight, but the wireless isn't quite ready so our trip was scrubbed.

'You may like to tell your confederates about this. When the squadron last went to Munich, one of the crews took with them an umbrella with the words 'You wouldn't listen to reason, you b.....s, now listen to these!" painted on it. Hope they translated it and I bet that would make them say "Ach" a few times!

'Our crew are now all members of the "Caterpillar Club". There are no membership privileges: membership means that you have saved your life by parachute. We shall all have a little solid gold caterpillar brooch with our names on from the Irvin Parachute Co. The idea of a caterpillar comes from the silkworm caterpillar "whose life hangs by a silken thread", as they put it.'

Above:
After baling out over West London in the dark and in a snowstorm on 13 November 1940, Sgt 'Ginger' Dick, Jim Bowler's WOp/AG, landed in a tree at Hounslow Barracks and hung there for two hours before he was rescued. *Mrs F. M. Davies*

Above right:
Sgt Alistair Macnab, rear gunner (pictured), and Jim Bowler visited the scene of 'B-Berty's' crash at Hampton Court on the morning after. Fortunately there had been no civilian deaths as a result of the crash although two houses were destroyed and the aircraft written off. *Mrs F. M. Davies*

Sunday 24 November 1940
'We took the new Berty on his/her maiden operation on Friday night and should have gone to a place in Germany on the Rhine, but Mac had some trouble with the rear gun turret just after take-off so rather than go through enemy fighter zones we went down to Ostend and bombed the docks there. Our substitute navigator was a young pilot officer on his first trip, about 6ft 7in tall, but he did some wizard bomb-aiming and we started some glorious fires with our incendiaries. When this navigator moved past me to do his bombing I saw his head go past, looked down about two minutes later and saw his legs just moving after him! Strue!

'As a contrast to the previous trip, there was not a cloud between the earth and the moon, beyond that I can't vouch for, and everything went perfectly. Hardly half a dozen shots were fired at us, not many searchlights were out, and the moon lit up the target like daytime. I said we went on Friday night, actually we took off at 3am Saturday morning and landed at 6am.

'Frank has been selected to represent the squadron by his looks and has got to sit for an oil painting for the Air Ministry. You should hear what he has to say about it. Quite a good choice, I think, don't you?

'I'm going to write a letter to the parachute firm after this to get our little gold caterpillars I told you about. Ginger seems to be dying to get his, he really is an excitable sort of lad.

'Our navigator who was hurt has returned today. He's hopping about with a stick and has one foot and ankle in Plaster of Paris. He seemed pretty shaken, too, by his experience. He told me he was sick as a dog all over his navigation table after I had told him to put on his parachute and take off his flying helmet. Poor little blighter, no doubt he will be going on a long leave. I almost wish I had broken a leg!! Some dirty "souvenir hunters" at the hospital in which he has been have stolen half his clothes, all his money, his watch, and his flying boots.

'Well, darling, once this month is over and that won't be long, it will soon come round to Christmas. It would be marvellous if it happened, but I'm afraid it's not even worth hoping I shall be at home for it. That glorious week we had together here might have happened a year ago, so long does it seem since I last saw you. However, it should be our ordinary turn soon, and on that reassuring note I think I may as well close down for tonight. Cheerio, dearest, write as often and as much as you can.
Your ever adoring, Jim.
XXXXXXXXXXXXXXXXXXXXXXX'

On the following evening, Jim Bowler and his crew failed to return from a raid on Kiel, shot down into the North Sea by flak. Their bodies were never found.

*Sgt Fletcher and crew, No 99 Squadron, ditched Wellington I N2727 off Fairlight, Sussex. The aircraft was lost, broken up by the tides.

Wombleton-on-Mud

Bill Johnson was a groundcrew engine fitter at Wombleton, Yorkshire, a No 6 (RCAF) Group station, from late in 1943 until the end of the war.

'When I first reported to Wombleton late in 1943, the civilian contractors were still at work. No 1666 HCU was in residence, later to be joined by No 1679 HCU which moved away after a while, leaving its aircraft with 1666, so we had a mixture of Halifax IIs and Lanc IIIs, all of them throw-outs from frontline squadrons. In most cases they were fit only for the breaker's yard but, nevertheless, we were expected to keep 'em flying. This we did to the best of our ability with the tools we had got and the availability of spare parts. The most common snags we experienced on both aircraft were the everlasting glycol leaks and radiator changes, the latter caused by striking low-flying birds.

'It was only the youth of the groundstaff that enabled them to do their jobs at all. The biggest enemy was the mud; drainage was something the contractors had forgotten. The mud was still there during the summer and wellies were the order of the day. Every day. The NAAFI, Mess hall and Nissen huts all had sludge tramped in.

'We dreaded the day an aircraft would come off the runway or perimeter track and sink deep into the mud. After we had put an air bag under the wing and inflated it with the aid of a small generator pump which took hours, it meant many more hours of digging, trying to get something solid under the wheels. Then came the problem of moving the aircraft by towing with tractors or any available fuel bowser. Once the job was complete there was just the problem of getting ourselves cleaned up, usually after a long walk from the drome to our billets via the Mess hall.

'That brought the next dreadful thought: ice-cold water in the ablutions. Hot water was available for about one hour most evenings on a first-come first-served basis. Those personnel who worked regular hours were the luckiest, while the late comers off the airfield had no chance and usually ended up having to heat water on the billet stove. If it was in use. But most nights there was no coke even to provide that comfort and so cleanliness came as a luxury. That's why we occasionally took leave to get cleaned up.

'When the planes were airborne, those of us who worked out on the dispersals would spend our spare time servicing the different items used for our respective jobs: ladders, engine stands, trolley accumulators, chocks etc. We would also look for anything from which we could make some sort of shelter for ourselves, somewhere to store spares and toolboxes, and possibly make a work-bench to hold a vice. We also made quite a lot of our own tools as an improvement on those issued to us. We did anything possible to improve our lot.

'There's nowhere colder than the wide open spaces of an aerodrome. I've spent many an hour during the bitterly cold nights doing some work on an engine by the light of a torch so that the aircraft would be ready for the following morning. It's not the best of jobs in those conditions and the nearest living soul would be half-a-mile away; the only sound the dropping of a spanner from 15ft down on to the ground, with the resulting climb down from the engine stand to search for it. The torch batteries would then probably give up the ghost, just for a bonus.

'During the winter months, one of the amusing features of aerodrome life was the different sorts of clothing worn by the lads for a bit of extra warmth. All sorts of gear and, of course, the wellies. At times it caused a few laughs when one was asked by someone else — probably a desk type — if one was an airman before he could say what was on his mind. It was understandable, really, because Wombleton was an open airfield with country lanes running through it and the usual troupe of local villagers carried on their daily chores as if we weren't there. Anyone could go anywhere without question and any "Top Brass" would have to be very careful regarding saluting by airmen: it could be a farmer, or vice versa!

'Although the aircraft allocated to us were throw-outs from the squadrons, nevertheless they were used on occasions to

Right:
The 'B' Flight groundcrew of No 1666 HCU in mid-1944. Bill Johnson is second from the right. *W. Johnson*

create diversions from Main Force raids over enemy territory. The petrol loads were altered at times to try to ensure the planes had a chance to do this job. Sometimes we were told to leave certain tanks empty as a weight-saving exercise in order to make it possible for the aircraft to carry other things.

'Perhaps the best thing that happened to the lads at Wombleton was the eventual issue of bicycles, saving miles of walking and hours of time. But guess who had his bike nicked? Yours truly! I never did get it back and I had £5 deducted from my wages at 10 shillings (50p) each fortnight, which was a very painful sum to lose in those days.

'The next best thing was the issue of leather jerkins to give a bit of warmth and protection from the winds. I never did get the sleeves.

'One of the funniest things to happen to me was on one dark night at about 2 o'clock in the morning when I was wearily pedalling my way around the perimeter track after doing some work on one of the dispersals. I heard the sound of engines coming up behind me, and when I looked round I could just make out the shape of a Halifax. So I pedalled a bit faster and flashed the torch I was carrying to warn the pilot I was there. He obviously

Right:
General maintenance of aircraft was undertaken by groundcrews on the dispersal, but major overhauls meant the aircraft had to return to the hangars. *via K. Merrick*

Below:
An ex-No 5 Group Lancaster serving as ND-G with No 1666 HCU early in 1945. On the nose are recorded 28 ops. *W. Johnson*

Below:
**Halifax B Mk II Srs I (Special), ND-O, of
No 1666 HCU pictured in June 1944.**
W. Johnson

Beneath the glare of the hangar lights, groundcrew work on a Merlin XX-engined Halifax Mk V Srs Ia fitted with four-bladed Rotol propellers and Dowty undercarriage. No 6 (RCAF) Group, and Nos 77, 346 and 347 Squadrons in No 4 Group, used this mark on bomber operations for a limited period during 1943-44. This night photograph was probably taken early in 1944 at an airfield in Yorkshire. *IWM CH14222*

thought I was signalling him to follow me and increased his speed, and I mine. And so it went on, the only RAF bike to crash the sound barrier! After a few hundred yards I decided to abandon the bike and run across the mud alongside the track. The pilot eventually realised his mistake and stopped the aircraft while he sorted himself out. After all, he should have known to follow two lights and not one.

'The biggest mystery at Wombleton was when one of our Halifaxes circled the drome twice one night and prepared to land, but it never did. Instead, it flew off and away and was never seen or heard of again, although a farmer four miles away found tyre marks across his field which faded out as if the pilot had either attempted to land and changed his mind, or he didn't realise how low he was and brushed the ground by accident. Whatever the reason, that aircraft is still unaccounted for to this day.'

Below:
If an aircraft slithered off a taxiway into the mud, or bellied in after suffering damage on ops, the hard-pressed groundcrews would be called upon to dig them out. In this photograph, No 466 (Australian) Squadron's Halifax III, MZ307:B, swung on take-off at Driffield on 17 September 1944, causing the undercarriage to collapse and crushing the bomb-bay. *via K. Merrick*

Internees in Portugal

On the night of 3/4 June 1943, Flg Off Rudy Lacerbe RCAF and his No 28 OTU crew, from Wymeswold in Leicestershire, were part of a 16-strong leaflet-dropping operation flown over France by OTU aircraft and crews. Their Wellington Ic, DV613, was intercepted by one or more marauding German fighters — most probably roving Junkers Ju88-C6s of *5/KG40* based at Bordeaux — and in the running fight that ensued their aircraft was badly damaged and two of the crew wounded as they were chased far to the south over the Bay of Biscay. By the time they had shaken off their assailants the Wellington was damaged, very short of fuel and getting ever closer to neutral Portugal. Deciding there was little else that could be done to salvage the situation, Lacerbe ordered his crew to prepare to bale out over the Portuguese coastal town of Espinho. After the crew had all left the stricken aircraft, Lacerbe set the autopilot control to enable him to bale out and to prevent the aircraft from crashing on to the populated mainland; it eventually crashed into the sea off the coast near Espinho.

Following their unscheduled arrival in neutral Portugal by parachute, Lacerbe and his crew were interned by the Portuguese authorities. The following excerpts are taken from two letters written by Flg Off 'Bunny' Shaw RCAF, the navigator, from the internment camp where the crew were held in the ancient fortified town of Elvas on the Portuguese/Spanish border, to his ladyfriend 'Sandy'. They were eventually repatriated to England a few months later.

8th June 1943
'I guess a letter from me will shake you, especially coming from a neutral country! Well, lass, I fear it has happened at last, for we are all now interned after an unpleasant experience with Jerries.

'To cut a long story short (and also hoping that the Censors will not prevent the mailing of this epistle) we were badly shot up and Lloyd wounded in both legs. Everything was in a hell of a mess but I attended to his injuries myself and changed dressings frequently — by that I mean the kite was in a mess and not Lloyd. Frankly, one leg sustained a nasty cut but the other is definitely more nasty — maybe a stiff knee.

'I then decided to carry on and make Portugal which by good fortune and lady luck we did. Here we all baled out and I left the plane with Lloyd so that when we landed I shouldn't be far away. The village peasants were very kind to us all and I eventually got him to a hospital. Meanwhile, you can easily imagine the excitement surrounding the local folk — believe me, I really felt like a curio! That's if I had any feelings left! My next job was to fetch over the British Consul and he sent a cable to Molly for me, stating Lloyd was safe. You see, I thought maybe those nasty telegrams would already have been delivered by the AM.'

21st June 1943
'Just a few lines to let you know we are all OK although gradually frying to death in a temperature of some 130 degrees F in the shade! I'll have to show you my sunburn tan when I get back, so hurry up and find out about the swimming baths!

'You will be very glad to hear that Lloyd has had his operation and they removed a piece of cannon shell from the knee. It must have given him merry hell you know, and yet I received such a jolly letter from him this week in which he assures us all is well and in fact he hopes to be up and about within three weeks!

'We are actually in a town called Elvas which is in fact on the Spanish border. It is an old fortress with terrific walls around the whole town, but in its way that is most helpful for we are allowed to walk around so long as we don't wander out of the walls — what a joke!

'I have been made the CO of the Internee Camp which means I really just hand out

Left:
Flg Off Rudy Lacerbe (far right) and his No 28 OTU crew were involved in a running fight with Junkers Ju88s over the Bay of Biscay on 2-3 June 1943. With their Wellington Ic badly damaged and two crewmembers injured, Lacerbe shook off the assailants and headed for Portugal. All of the crew successfully baled out and were interned for several months before repatriation to England. Left to right: Bill Breslau (USA); Lloyd French (RCAF); 'Bunny' Shaw (RCAF); Freddie Wright (RAFVR); Rudy Lacerbe (RCAF).
Mrs J. Yeomans

Right:
Map to show the location of places and the sequence of events of 3-4 June 1943, and subsequently, mentioned in 'Bunny' Shaw's letters.

the mail (never heard of it!), pay them, give them their milk and tuck 'em in each night. Coming over?! I'm also supposed to be responsible for their behaviour, but as to that I have "mon droits".

'A major from the garrison has proved an excellent gentleman and four times weekly I roll up for sword fighting, gym and games. I'm glad I had some slight knowledge anyway of fencing, for these boys are really good and sword work with horse-riding is like eating bread and butter for them. It helps the time to pass anyway for apart from this there is absolutely nothing to do. That may sound very nice, but after a couple of days it's nothing but a curse and with the heat makes the fellows difficult to check. We have a few books and a dart board, but the main interest seems to be wine and women! Good job I'm both a teetotaller and a good lad, methinks!

'If you have time, please drop me a few lines, Sandy, I'm hungry for mail and news of England.'

On the night of the fated flight, Flg Off Rudy Lacerbe's crew comprised Flg Off B.L. 'Bunny' Shaw RCAF, navigator; Sgt Lloyd G. French RCAF, bomb-aimer; Sgt Freddie Wright RAFVR, wireless operator/air gunner; and Sgt Bill Breslau RCAF, air gunner.

Only two days before this incident, the Douglas DC-3 airliner carrying the well-known English film star Leslie Howard home to England from a lecture tour of Spain and Portugal, was intercepted and attacked by eight Junkers Ju88s of *KG40* over the Bay of Biscay. The four crew and 13 passengers were all killed when the DC-3 ploughed into the sea and no trace of the aircraft or its occupants was ever found.

Lloyd French must have thought he had a charmed life for, on 29 July 1943, he survived when the BOAC Short Sunderland III flying boat (G-AGES, ex-RAF JM661) taking him home to England from Lisbon-Portela, via Foynes in the Irish Republic, crashed in fog into Mt Brandon near Ballyquin, Co Kerry on the southwestern tip of Ireland, where it burst into flames killing 10 of the 25 passengers and crew.

The author has experienced considerable difficulty in discovering the whole story behind this episode, despite wide-ranging enquiries. If anybody reading this book knows more of these events, then the author would be pleased to hear from them.

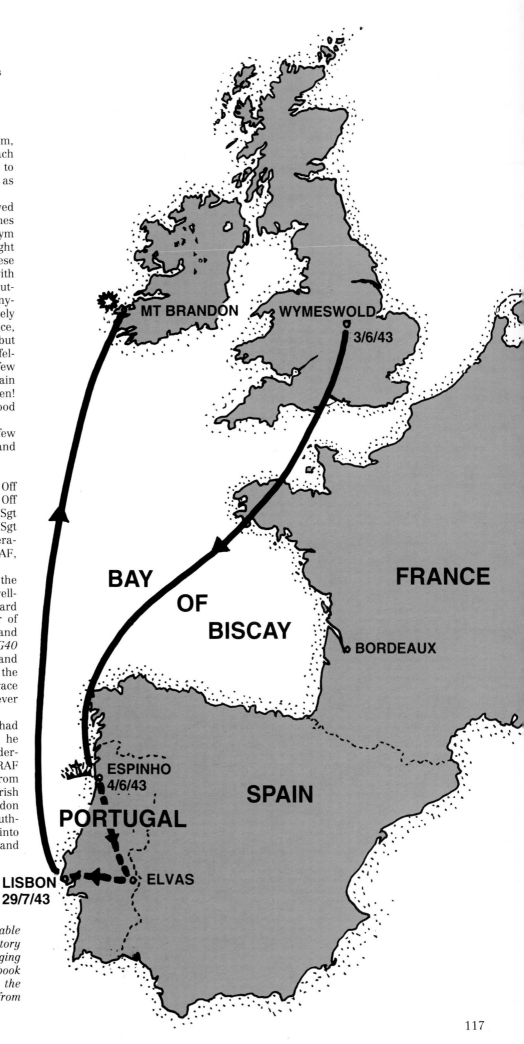

Appendix I

A Brief Résumé of the Command Structure

Policy orders devised by the Chiefs of Staff — and relevant to RAF Bomber Command and the current directives relating to bombing priorities — were, in the first instance, interpreted at Bomber Command Headquarters, High Wycombe, Bucks. Operational orders were then formulated by the Commander-in-Chief and his staff and then communicated to the individual Group Headquarters under the command of an Air Vice-Marshal who was responsible for ensuring that his squadrons complied with all of Bomber Command HQ's instructions: for example: the target for attack, numbers of aircraft to be despatched, bomb loads etc.

The next tier of command was at station level, each of which was commanded by a Group Captain or, from late in 1942 when the Base system came into existence, an Air Commodore. This situation came about as a result of the rapid growth in the number of airfields which began to put a strain on the administrative abilities of individual Group headquarters. To ease this strain and to offer greater local control to stations and their satellites, the Base system was devised. This comprised a parent station — usually one of the pre-war permanent types — which hosted the Base administrative apparatus and usually two squadrons, and a number of sub-stations of temporary wartime construction, each commanded by a Group Captain. Each Base Headquarters was identified by a two-digit code, the first digit identifying the parent Group and the second the base itself. For example, Pocklington in Yorkshire was designated as No 42 Base Headquarters and its four satellite stations — Elvington, Full Sutton, Snaith and Burn — each became known as a No 42 Base Substation. On 16 September 1943, a Bomber Command Directive stated that from henceforth all bases were to be known by number and not their geographical location. This situation pertained until the end of the war.

Stations could house either one or two squadrons and/or a number of smaller miscellaneous units, such as Beam Approach Training Flights (BAT Flt). Each individual station provided its resident squadrons with technical and domestic housing with facilities, messing facilities, flying control, emergency services and airfield security.

A squadron was normally commanded by a Wing Commander with a total complement on average of some 24 aircraft, and was responsible for its own aircraft maintenance and administration. At the sharp end, individual aircraft, aircrews and groundcrews were allocated to a particular flight, of which each squadron had three. Each flight was made up of some eight aircraft, each with its own dispersal pan on the airfield perimeter and with an aircrew of seven (generally) and its own dedicated groundcrew.

RAF Bomber Command Headquarters and Air Officer Commanders-in-Chief 1939-45

Headquarters
Formed 14/07/36 at Hillingdon House, Uxbridge, Middx
08/39-03/40 — Richings Park, Langley, Bucks
03/40-04/69 — High Wycombe, Bucks

Air Officer Commanders-in-Chief (with dates of appointment)
ACM Sir Edgar Ludlow-Hewitt — 12/09/37
AM Sir Charles Portal — 03/04/40
AM Sir Richard Peirse — 05/10/40
AVM J. E. A. Baldwin (Acting AOCinC) 09/01/42
ACM Sir Arthur Harris 22/02/42-15/09/45

Senior Air Staff Officers (with dates of appointment)
Air Cdre N. H. Bottomley — 17/11/38
AVM R. H. M. S. Saundby — 21/11/40

RAF Bomber Command Frontline and Training Groups, Headquarters and Air Officers Commanding

NO 1 GROUP HEADQUARTERS
Formed 01/05/36 at Abingdon, Berks
09/39 — Benson, Oxon
12/39 — Disbanded
06/40 — Re-formed Hucknall, Notts
07/41 — Bawtry Hall, Yorks

Air Officers Commanding (with dates of appointment)
AVM A.C. Wright — 03/09/39
Air Cdre J. J. Breen — 27/06/40
AVM R. D. Oxland — 27/11/40
AVM E. A. B. Rice — 24/02/43
AVM R. S. Blucke — 12/02/45

NO 2 GROUP HEADQUARTERS
Formed 20/03/36 at Abingdon, Berks
05/38 — Wyton, Hunts
10/39 — Castlewood House, Huntingdon
05/43 — Bylaugh Hall, East Dereham, Norfolk
01/06/43 — No 2 Group joined 2 TAF and left Bomber Command control for duration of war

Air Officers Commanding (with dates of appointment)
AVM C. T. Maclean — 16/05/38
AVM J. M. Robb — 17/04/40
AVM D. F. Stevenson — 12/02/41
AVM A. Lees — 17/12/41
AVM J. H. D'Albiac — 29/12/42
AVM B. E. Embry — 01/06/43 (2 TAF)

NO 3 GROUP HEADQUARTERS
Formed 01/05/36 at Andover, Hants
01/37 — Mildenhall, Suffolk
03/40 — Exning, Suffolk

Air Officers Commanding (with dates of appointment)
AVM J. E. A. Baldwin — 28/08/39
AVM The Hon R. A. Cochrane — 14/09/42
AVM R. Harrison — 27/02/43

NO 4 GROUP HEADQUARTERS
Formed 01/04/37 at Mildenhall, Suffolk
06/37 — Linton-on-Ouse, Yorks
04/40 — Heslington Hall, Yorks
07/05/45 — to Transport Command

Air Officers Commanding (with dates of appointment)
AVM A. Coningham — 03/07/39
AVM C. R. Carr — 26/07/41
AVM J. R. Whitley — 12/02/45

NO 5 GROUP HEADQUARTERS
Formed 01/09/37 at Mildenhall, Suffolk
10/37 — St Vincent's, Grantham, Lincs
11/43 — Moreton Hall, Swinderby, Lincs
12/45 — Disbanded

Air Officers Commanding (with dates of appointment)
Air Cdre W. B. Calloway — 17/08/37
AVM A. T. Harris — 11/09/39
AVM N. R. Bottomley — 22/11/40
AVM J. C. Slessor — 12/05/41

AVM W. A. Coryton — 25/04/42
AVM The Hon Sir R. A. Cochrane — 28/02/43
AVM H. A. Constantine — 16/02/45

NO 6 (BOMBER) GROUP HEADQUARTERS
Formed 02/09/39 at Abingdon, Berks
09/39 — Abingdon, Berks
11/05/42 — No 6 (Bomber) Group became No
   91 (OTU) Group

Air Officers Commanding (with dates of appointment)
Air Cdre W. F.McN. Foster — 02/09/39
Gp Capt H. S. P. Walmsley — 16/03/42

NO 6 (RCAF) GROUP HEADQUARTERS
Formed 25/10/42 at Allerton Park, Yorks
08/45 UK HQ disbanded

Air Officers Commanding (with dates of appointment)
AVM G. E. Brookes — 25/10/42
AVM C. M. McEwen — 29/02/44
Air Cdre J. L. Hurley — 19/06/45

NO 8 (PATHFINDER) GROUP HEADQUARTERS
Formed 15/08/42 at Wyton, Hunts, as
   'Pathfinder Force' and redesignated No 8
   (PFF) Group at Wyton on 13/01/43

08/42 — Wyton, Hunts
06/43 — Castle Hill House, Hunts
12/45 — Disbanded

Air Officers Commanding (with dates of appointment)
AVM D. C. T. Bennett — 13/01/43 (Bennett, as
   an Air Cdre, had been appointed to
   command the PFF in 08/42)
AVM J.R. Whitley — 21/05/45

NO 100 (SPECIAL DUTIES) GROUP HEADQUARTERS
Formed 23/11/43 at Radlett, Herts
23/11/43 — Radlett, Herts
03/12/43 — West Raynham, Norfolk
01/01/44 — Bylaugh Hall, East Dereham,
   Norfolk
12/45 — Disbanded

Air Officers Commanding (with dates of appointment)
AVM E. B. Addison — 18/11/43

NO 91 (OTU) GROUP HEADQUARTERS
Formed 11/05/42 at Abingdon, Berks

Air Officers Commanding (with dates of appointment)
Gp Capt H.S.P Walmsley — 16/03/42
AVM J. A. Gray — 08/02/44

NO 92 (OTU) GROUP HEADQUARTERS
Formed 14/05/42 at Winslow Hall, Bucks

Air Officers Commanding (with dates of appointment)
Gp Capt H. A. Haines — 14/05/42
AVM H. K. Thorold — 17/03/43
AVM G. S. Hodson — 23/02/45

NO 93 (OTU) GROUP HEADQUARTERS
Formed 15/06/42 at Egginton Hall, Derby

Air Officers Commanding (with dates of appointment)
Gp Capt C. E. Maitland — 15/06/42
Air Cdre A. P. Ritchie — 25/02/43
AVM O.T. Boyd — 24/02/44
AVM G.S. Hodson — 09/08/44

NO 7 (HCU) GROUP HEADQUARTERS
Formed 01/11/44 at St Vincent's, Grantham,
   Lincs

Air Officer Commanding (with date of appointment)
Unknown

Below:
**Stirling aircrew of No 75(NZ) Squadron,
Mepal, in the spring of 1944. Two of these
men were killed in action and one taken PoW
shortly after this picture was taken.**
J. McFarland

Appendix II

The Frontline Groups

At the outbreak of war in September 1939, Bomber Command's frontline force consisted of 29 home-based squadrons divided between four Groups and spread across 17 airfields. Each Group was equipped with a particular type of twin-engined bomber aircraft dedicated to a specific bombing role — light, medium or heavy.

No 2 Group was East Anglia-based and equipped with the elegant Bristol Blenheim light bomber; No 3 Group, also based in East Anglia, was equipped with Dr Barnes Wallis' 'geodetic' medium bomber, the Vickers Wellington; Yorkshire-based No 4 Group's warhorse was the slab-sided Armstrong Whitworth Whitley heavy bomber; and No 5 Group was based in Lincolnshire and equipped with the 'flying panhandle' — the Handley Page Hampden medium bomber. No 1 Group, with 10 squadrons of single-engined Fairey Battle light bombers, had moved to France on 1 September to form part of the Advanced Air Striking Force (AASF) and did not come under Bomber Command's operational control again until June 1940.

The Orders of Battle which follow show how, from comparatively small beginnings, Bomber Command grew into an awesome Leviathan capable of laying waste to Nazi Germany's cities and industrial might. In September 1939, Bomber Command could muster a daily average of 280 aircraft with crews; in the closing months of the war, Bomber Command could field a daily average of 1,069 aircraft with crews, drawn from 95 squadrons flying from more than 60 airfields and under the control of seven Groups. By now it was a predominantly heavy bomber force.

If we take a look at the disposition of its Groups in 1945, the motif of the picture is little changed from 1939; but what has changed is its sheer size and destructive power. No 1 Group operated from airfields in north Lincolnshire and was an all-Avro Lancaster force; No 2 Group's light bombers had been hived off in May 1943 to join the 2nd TAF, in preparation for the Normandy landings in June 1944; No 3 Group was based in Suffolk and Cambridgeshire and, like No 1 Group, it too was an all-Lancaster Group; No 4 Group's squadrons flew Handley Page

Halifaxes from airfields in East Yorkshire. South of the Humber Estuary, No 5 Group was predominantly an all-Lancaster force flying from Lincolnshire, although the Group did operate a number of de Havilland Mosquitoes in the Pathfinder role. No 5 Group was unique in the Command because it possessed its own target-marking element, made up of three squadrons 'on loan' from No 8 (PFF) Group. The decision to amputate a vital part of the PFF's body and transplant it elsewhere in the Command was the source of some considerable displeasure at No 8 Group's Headquarters.

Moving further north to North Yorkshire and Co Durham, the Canadian squadrons of No 6 (RCAF) Group flew a mixed force of Halifaxes and Lancasters. Bomber Command's specialist target marking force was No 8 (PFF) Group — the Pathfinders — which flew a mixed force of Lancasters and Mosquitoes from airfields around Ely in Cambridgeshire's fenlands. Finally, another specialised force existed for bomber support duties in the shape of No 100 (SD) Group, which flew electronic/radio countermeasures and intruder sorties with a mixed force of Mosquitoes, Halifaxes, Lancasters, Stirlings, Liberators and Flying Fortresses from airfields in northern Norfolk.

One point worth bearing in mind when noting the aircraft types allocated to the various squadrons concerns the changing criteria, as the war progressed and new types entered service, for the classification of light, medium and heavy bomber aircraft. In 1940, the twin-engined Armstrong Whitworth Whitley was classed as a heavy bomber. It could fly 1,630 miles with a 3,750lb bomb load at a cruising speed of 165mph; it was withdrawn from frontline service in May 1942. Yet the Avro Lancaster, undisputed queen of the new breed of four-engined heavies, which entered squadron service in January 1942, could carry a 14,000lb bomb load up to 1,660 miles at a cruising speed of 216mph. It, too, was classed as a heavy bomber. Of the same period, de Havilland's twin-engined 'Wooden Wonder' the Mosquito was classed as a light bomber, yet it was capable of carrying a 3,000lb bomb load for up to 1,620 miles at a cruising speed of 265mph. By comparison, its counterpart of 1940, the single-engined Fairey Battle, could carry a 1,420lb bomb load over 1,200 miles at a

cruising speed of little over 200mph. These comparisons only go to show how rapid was the development in bomber design under wartime conditions.

RAF Bomber Command, Homebased Frontline Unit Strengths 1939-45

27 September 1939

No 1 Group, HQ: Forming at Benson, Oxon

No 2 Group, HQ: Wyton, Cambs

21 Sqn	} 79 Wing Watton	Blenheim I. IV
82 Sqn		
114 Sqn	} 82 Wing Wyton	Blenheim I, IV
139 Sqn		
107 Sqn	} 83 Wing Wattisham	Blenheim I, IV
110 Sqn		
101 Sqn	West Raynham	Blenheim IV

No 3 Group, HQ: Mildenhall, Suffolk

9 Sqn	Honington	Wellington I
37 Sqn	Feltwell	Wellington I
38 Sqn	Marham	Wellington I
99 Sqn	Mildenhall	Wellington I
115 Sqn	Marham	Wellington I
149 Sqn	Mildenhall	Wellington I
214 Sqn	Feltwell	Wellington I
215 Sqn	Bassingbourn	Wellington I; Harrow

No 4 Group, HQ: Linton-on-Ouse, Yorks

10 Sqn	Dishforth	Whitley IV
51 Sqn	Linton-on-Ouse	Whitley II, III
58 Sqn	Linton-on-Ouse	Whitley III
77 Sqn	Driffield	Whitley III, V
78 Sqn	Dishforth	Whitley I, IV, V
102 Sqn	Driffield	Whitley III

No 5 Group, HQ: St Vincent's, Grantham, Lincs

44 Sqn	Waddington	Hampden
49 Sqn	Scampton	Hampden
50 Sqn	Waddington	Hampden
61 Sqn	Hemswell	Hampden
83 Sqn	Scampton	Hampden
106 Sqn	Cottesmore	Hampden
144 Sqn	Hemswell	Hampden
185 Sqn	Cottesmore	Hampden

February 1940

No 1 Group: in France as a part of AASF under control of HQ, AASF, Reims

No 2 Group, HQ: Castlewood House, Huntingdon

15 Sqn	Wyton	Blenheim IV
21 Sqn	Watton	Blenheim IV

40 Sqn	Wyton	Blenheim IV
82 Sqn	Watton	Blenheim IV
101 Sqn	West Raynham	Blenheim IV
107 Sqn	Wattisham	Blenheim IV
110 Sqn	Wattisham	Blenheim IV

No 3 Group, HQ: Mildenhall, Suffolk

9 Sqn	Honington	Wellington I
37 Sqn	Feltwell	Wellington I
38 Sqn	Marham	Wellington I
99 Sqn	Newmarket	Wellington I
115 Sqn	Marham	Wellington I
149 Sqn	Mildenhall	Wellington I
214 Sqn	Methwold	Wellington I

No 4 Group, HQ: Linton-on-Ouse, Yorks

10 Sqn	Dishforth	Whitley IV
51 Sqn	Dishforth	Whitley III, IV, V
58 Sqn	Linton-on-Ouse	Whitley III
77 Sqn	Driffield	Whitley V
78 Sqn	Linton-on-Ouse	Whitley IV, V
102 Sqn	Driffield	Whitley V

No 5 Group, HQ: St Vincent's, Grantham, Lincs

44 Sqn	Waddington	Hampden
49 Sqn	Scampton	Hampden
50 Sqn	Waddington	Hampden
61 Sqn	Hemswell	Hampden
83 Sqn	Scampton	Hampden
106 Sqn	Finningley	Hampden
144 Sqn	Hemswell	Hampden

No 6 Group, HQ: Abingdon, Berks

7 Sqn	Upper Heyford	Hampden; Anson
35 Sqn	Upwood	Blenheim IV; Battle; Anson
52 Sqn	Benson	Battle; Anson
63 Sqn	Benson	Battle; Anson
75 Sqn	Harwell	Wellington I
76 Sqn	Upper Heyford	Hampden; Anson
90 Sqn	Upwood	Blenheim I, IV
97 Sqn	Abingdon	Whitley II, III; Anson
104 Sqn	Bicester	Blenheim I, IV; Anson
108 Sqn	Bicester	Blenheim I, IV; Anson
148 Sqn	Harwell	Wellington I; Anson
166 Sqn	Abingdon	Whitley I, III
185 Sqn	Cottesmore	Hampden; Hereford; Anson
207 Sqn	Benson	Battle; Anson

February 1941

No 1 Group, HQ: Hucknall, Notts

12 Sqn	Binbrook	Wellington II
103 Sqn	Newton	Wellington I
142 Sqn	Binbrook	Wellington II
150 Sqn	Newton	Wellington I
300 Sqn	Swinderby	Wellington I
301 Sqn	Swinderby	Wellington I
304 Sqn	Syerston	Wellington I
305 Sqn	Syerston	Wellington I

No 2 Group, HQ: Castlewood House, Huntingdon

18 Sqn	Great Massingham	Blenheim IV
21 Sqn	Watton	Blenheim IV
82 Sqn	Watton	Blenheim IV
101 Sqn	West Raynham	Blenheim IV
105 Sqn	Swanton Morley	Blenheim IV
107 Sqn	Wattisham	Blenheim IV
110 Sqn	Wattisham	Blenheim IV
114 Sqn	Oulton	Blenheim IV
139 Sqn	Horsham St Faith	Blenheim IV

No 3 Group, HQ: Exning, Suffolk

7 Sqn	Oakington	Stirling I
9 Sqn	Honington	Wellington I
15 Sqn	Wyton	Wellington I
40 Sqn	Wyton	Wellington I
57 Sqn	Feltwell	Wellington I
75 Sqn	Feltwell	Wellington I
99 Sqn	Newmarket	Wellington I
115 Sqn	Marham	Wellington I
149 Sqn	Mildenhall	Wellington I
214 Sqn	Stradishall	Wellington I
311 Sqn	East Wretham	Wellington I

No 4 Group, HQ: Heslington Hall, Yorks

10 Sqn	Leeming	Whitley V
35 Sqn	Linton-on-Ouse	Halifax I
51 Sqn	Dishforth	Whitley V
58 Sqn	Linton-on-Ouse	Whitley V
77 Sqn	Topcliffe	Whitley V
78 Sqn	Dishforth	Whitley V
102 Sqn	Topcliffe	Whitley V

No 5 Group, HQ: St Vincent's, Grantham, Lincs

44 Sqn	Waddington	Hampden
49 Sqn	Scampton	Hampden
57 Sqn	Methwold	Wellington I
61 Sqn	Hemswell	Hampden
83 Sqn	Scampton	Hampden
97 Sqn	Waddington	Manchester
106 Sqn	Coningsby	Hampden
144 Sqn	Hemswell	Hampden
207 Sqn	Waddington	Manchester

February 1942

No 1 Group, HQ: Bawtry Hall, Yorks

12 Sqn	Binbrook	Wellington II
101 Sqn	Bourn	Wellington I, III
142 Sqn	Grimsby/Waltham	Wellington IV
150 Sqn	Snaith	Wellington I
300 Sqn	Hemswell	Wellington IV
301 Sqn	Hemswell	Wellington IV
304 Sqn	Lindholme	Wellington I
305 Sqn	Lindholme	Wellington II
460 Sqn	Breighton	Wellington IV

No 2 Group, HQ: Castlewood House, Huntingdon

18 Sqn	Wattisham	Blenheim IV
82 Sqn	Watton	Blenheim IV
88 Sqn	Attlebridge	Blenheim IV/Boston III
105 Sqn	Horsham St Faith	Mosquito IV
107 Sqn	Great Massingham	Blenheim IV/Boston III
110 Sqn	Wattisham	Blenheim IV
114 Sqn	West Raynham	Blenheim IV
139 Sqn	Oulton	Hudson III
226 Sqn	Swanton Morley	Boston III

No 3 Group, HQ: Exning, Suffolk

7 Sqn	Oakington	Stirling I
9 Sqn	Honington	Wellington III
15 Sqn	Wyton	Stirling I
40 Sqn	Alconbury	Wellington I
75 Sqn	Feltwell	Wellington III
90 Sqn	Polebrook	Fortress I/Blenheim IV
99 Sqn	Waterbeach	Wellington I
101 Sqn	Oakington	Wellington I
109 Sqn	Tempsford	Wellington I
115 Sqn	Marham	Wellington I, III
138 Sqn	Stradishall	Lysander IIIa; Whitley V; Halifax II
149 Sqn	Mildenhall	Stirling I
156 Sqn	Alconbury	Wellington I, III
161 Sqn	Newmarket	Lysander IIIa; Hudson I; Whitley V
214 Sqn	Stradishall	Wellington I
218 Sqn	Marham	Stirling I
311 Sqn	East Wretham	Wellington I
419 Sqn	Mildenhall	Wellington I, III

No 4 Group, HQ: Heslington Hall, Yorks

10 Sqn	Leeming	Halifax I, II
35 Sqn	Linton-on-Ouse	Halifax I, II
51 Sqn	Dishforth	Whitley V
58 Sqn	Linton-on-Ouse	Whitley V
76 Sqn	Middleton St George	Halifax I, II
77 Sqn	Leeming	Whitley V
102 Sqn	Dalton	Whitley V/Halifax II
104 Sqn	Driffield	Wellington II
158 Sqn	Driffield	Wellington II
405 Sqn	Pocklington	Wellington II
458 Sqn	Holme	Wellington I

No 5 Group, HQ: St Vincent's, Grantham, Lincs

44 Sqn	Waddington	Lancaster I
49 Sqn	Scampton	Hampden
50 Sqn	Skellingthorpe	Hampden
57 Sqn	Methwold	Wellington III
61 Sqn	Woolfox Lodge	Manchester
83 Sqn	Scampton	Manchester
97 Sqn	Coningsby	Manchester/Lancaster I
106 Sqn	Coningsby	Hampden/Manchester
144 Sqn	North Luffenham	Hampden
207 Sqn	Bottesford	Manchester
408 Sqn	Balderton	Hampden
420 Sqn	Waddington	Hampden
455 Sqn	Wigsley	Hampden

February 1943

No 1 Group, HQ: Bawtry Hall, Yorks

12 Sqn	Wickenby	Lancaster I, III
101 Sqn	Holme	Lancaster I, III
103 Sqn	Elsham Wolds	Lancaster I, III
166 Sqn	Kirmington	Wellington III, X
199 Sqn	Ingham	Wellington III
300 Sqn	Hemswell	Wellington III
301 Sqn	Hemswell	Wellington IV
305 Sqn	Hemswell	Wellington IV
460 Sqn	Breighton	Lancaster I, III

No 2 Group, HQ: Castlewood House, Huntingdon

21 Sqn	Methwold	Ventura I, II
88 Sqn	Oulton	Boston III
98 Sqn	Foulsham	Mitchell II
105 Sqn	Marham	Mosquito IV
107 Sqn	Great Massingham	Boston III, IIIa
139 Sqn	Marham	Mosquito IV
180 Sqn	Foulsham	Mitchell II
226 Sqn	Swanton Morley	Boston III, IIIa
464 Sqn	Feltwell	Ventura I, II
487 Sqn	Feltwell	Ventura II

No 3 Group, HQ: Exning, Suffolk

15 Sqn	Bourn	Stirling I, III
75 Sqn	Newmarket	Stirling I
90 Sqn	Ridgewell	Stirling I
115 Sqn	East Wretham	Wellington III

138 Sqn	Tempsford	Halifax II, V
149 Sqn	Lakenheath	Stirling I, III
161 Sqn	Tempsford	Lysander; Halifax; Hudson; Havoc; Albemarle
192 Sqn	Gransden Lodge	Wellington I, III, X; Mosquito IV
214 Sqn	Chedburgh	Stirling I, III
218 Sqn	Downham Market	Stirling I, III

No 4 Group, HQ: Heslington Hall, Yorks
10 Sqn	Melbourne	Halifax II
51 Sqn	Snaith	Halifax II
76 Sqn	Linton-on-Ouse	Halifax II/V
77 Sqn	Elvington	Halifax II
78 Sqn	Linton-on-Ouse	Halifax II
102 Sqn	Pocklington	Halifax II
158 Sqn	Rufforth	Halifax II
196 Sqn	Leconfield	Wellington X
429 Sqn	East Moor	Wellington III, X
466 Sqn	Leconfield	Wellington X

No 5 Group, HQ: St Vincent's, Grantham, Lincs
9 Sqn	Waddington	Lancaster I, III
44 Sqn	Waddington	Lancaster I, III
49 Sqn	Fiskerton	Lancaster I, III
50 Sqn	Skellingthorpe	Lancaster I, III
57 Sqn	Scampton	Lancaster I, III
61 Sqn	Syerston	Lancaster I, III
97 Sqn	Woodhall Spa	Lancaster I, III
106 Sqn	Syerston	Lancaster I, III
207 Sqn	Langar	Lancaster I, III
467 Sqn	Bottesford	Lancaster I, III

No 6 (RCAF) Group, HQ: Allerton Park, Yorks
405 Sqn	det Beaulieu, Hants	Halifax II
408 Sqn	Leeming	Halifax II
419 Sqn	Middleton St George	Halifax II
420 Sqn	Middleton St George	Wellington III, X
424 Sqn	Topcliffe	Wellington III, X
425 Sqn	Dishforth	Wellington III
426 Sqn	Dishforth	Wellington III
427 Sqn	Croft	Wellington III, X
428 Sqn	Dalton	Wellington III

No 8 (PFF) Group, HQ: Wyton, Hunts
7 Sqn	Oakington	Stirling I, III
35 Sqn	Graveley	Halifax II
83 Sqn	Wyton	Lancaster I, III
109 Sqn	Wyton	Mosquito IV
156 Sqn	Warboys	Wellington III; Lancaster I, III

February 1944

No 1 Group, HQ: Bawtry Hall, Yorks
12 Sqn	Wickenby	Lancaster I, III
100 Sqn	Grimsby/Waltham	Lancaster I, III
101 Sqn	Ludford Magna	Lancaster I, III

Right:
A scene at dispersal during 1944 of three No 425 (Alouette) Squadron Halifax IIIs. In the left foreground, the two air gunners of this French-Canadian squadron are wearing bright yellow electrically-heated Taylor suits with built-in buoyancy collars.
Public Archives of Canada PL40185 via K. Merrick

No 1 Group (continued)

103 Sqn	Elsham Wolds	Lancaster I, III
166 Sqn	Kirmington	Lancaster I, III
300 Sqn	Ingham	Wellington X
460 Sqn	Binbrook	Lancaster I, III
550 Sqn	North Killingholme	Lancaster I, III
576 Sqn	Elsham Wolds	Lancaster I, III
625 Sqn	Kelstern	Lancaster I, III
626 Sqn	Wickenby	Lancaster I, III

No 2 Group: under control of 2 TAF

No 3 Group, HQ: Exning, Suffolk

15 Sqn	Mildenhall	Lancaster I, III
75 Sqn	Mepal	Stirling III
90 Sqn	Tuddenham	Stirling III
115 Sqn	Witchford	Lancaster II
138 Sqn	Tempsford	Halifax II, V
149 Sqn	Lakenheath	Stirling III
161 Sqn	Tempsford	Halifax V; Hudson IIIa, V
199 Sqn	Lakenheath	Stirling III
218 Sqn	Downham Market	Stirling III
514 Sqn	Waterbeach	Lancaster II
622 Sqn	Mildenhall	Lancaster I, III

No 4 Group, HQ: Heslington Hall, Yorks

10 Sqn	Melbourne	Halifax II
51 Sqn	Snaith	Halifax III
76 Sqn	Holme	Halifax V, III
77 Sqn	Elvington	Halifax II
78 Sqn	Breighton	Halifax II
102 Sqn	Pocklington	Halifax II
158 Sqn	Lissett	Halifax III
466 Sqn	Leconfield	Halifax III
578 Sqn	Burn	Halifax III
640 Sqn	Leconfield	Halifax III

No 5 Group, HQ: Moreton Hall, Swinderby, Lincs

9 Sqn	Bardney	Lancaster I, III
44 Sqn	Dunholme Lodge	Lancaster I, III
49 Sqn	Fiskerton	Lancaster I, III
50 Sqn	Skellingthorpe	Lancaster I, III
57 Sqn	East Kirkby	Lancaster I, III
61 Sqn	Coningsby	Lancaster I, III
97 Sqn	Bourn	Lancaster I, III
106 Sqn	Metheringham	Lancaster I, III
207 Sqn	Spilsby	Lancaster I, III
463 Sqn	Waddington	Lancaster I, III
467 Sqn	Waddington	Lancaster I, III
617 Sqn	Woodhall Spa	Lancaster I, III
619 Sqn	Coningsby	Lancaster I, III
630 Sqn	East Kirkby	Lancaster I, III

No 6 (RCAF) Group, HQ: Allerton Park, Yorks

408 Sqn	Linton-on-Ouse	Lancaster II
419 Sqn	Middleton St George	Halifax II
420 Sqn	Tholthorpe	Halifax III
424 Sqn	Skipton-on-Swale	Halifax III
425 Sqn	Tholthorpe	Halifax III
426 Sqn	Linton-on-Ouse	Lancaster II
427 Sqn	Leeming	Halifax V, III
428 Sqn	Middleton St George	Halifax V, II
429 Sqn	Leeming	Halifax V
431 Sqn	Croft	Halifax V
432 Sqn	East Moor	Lancaster II/Halifax III
433 Sqn	Skipton-on-Swale	Halifax III
434 Sqn	Croft	Halifax V

No 8 (PFF) Group, HQ: Castle Hill House, Hunts

7 Sqn	Oakington	Lancaster I, III
35 Sqn	Graveley	Halifax III
83 Sqn	Wyton	Lancaster I, III
105 Sqn	Marham	Mosquito IV, IX
109 Sqn	Marham	Mosquito IV, IX
139 Sqn	Upwood	Mosquito IV, IX, XVI, XX
156 Sqn	Warboys	Lancaster I, III
405 Sqn	Gransden Lodge	Lancaster I, III
627 Sqn	Oakington	Mosquito IV
692 Sqn	Graveley	Mosquito IV

No 100 (SD) Group, HQ: Bylaugh Hall, East Dereham, Norfolk

141 Sqn	West Raynham	Mosquito II
169 Sqn	Little Snoring	Mosquito II
192 Sqn	Foulsham	Wellington X; Halifax V; Mosquito IV
214 Sqn	Sculthorpe	Stirling I; Fortress II
239 Sqn	West Raynham	Mosquito II
515 Sqn	Little Snoring	Beaufighter IIf; Mosquito II

22 March 1945

No 1 Group, HQ: Bawtry Hall, Yorks

12 Sqn	Wickenby	Lancaster I, III
100 Sqn	Grimsby	Lancaster I, III
101 Sqn	Ludford Magna	Lancaster I, III
103 Sqn	Elsham Wolds	Lancaster I, III
150 Sqn	Hemswell	Lancaster I, III
153 Sqn	Scampton	Lancaster I, III
166 Sqn	Kirmington	Lancaster I, III
170 Sqn	Hemswell	Lancaster I, III
300 Sqn	Faldingworth	Lancaster I, III
460 Sqn	Binbrook	Lancaster I, III
550 Sqn	North Killingholme	Lancaster I, III
576 Sqn	Fiskerton	Lancaster I, III
625 Sqn	Kelstern	Lancaster I, III
626 Sqn	Wickenby	Lancaster I, III

No 3 Group, HQ: Exning, Suffolk

15 Sqn	Mildenhall	Lancaster I, III
75 Sqn	Mepal	Lancaster I, III
90 Sqn	Tuddenham	Lancaster I, III
115 Sqn	Witchford	Lancaster I, III
149 Sqn	Methwold	Lancaster I, III
186 Sqn	Stradishall	Lancaster I, III
195 Sqn	Wratting Common	Lancaster I, III
218 Sqn	Chedburgh	Lancaster I, III
514 Sqn	Waterbeach	Lancaster I, III
622 Sqn	Mildenhall	Lancaster I, III

No 4 Group, HQ: Heslington Hall, Yorks

10 Sqn	Melbourne	Halifax III
51 Sqn	Snaith	Halifax III
76 Sqn	Holme	Halifax III, VI
77 Sqn	Full Sutton	Halifax III, VI
78 Sqn	Breighton	Halifax III
102 Sqn	Pocklington	Halifax III, VI
158 Sqn	Lissett	Halifax III
346 Sqn	Elvington	Halifax III, VI
347 Sqn	Elvington	Halifax III, VI
466 Sqn	Driffield	Halifax III
640 Sqn	Leconfield	Halifax III, VI

No 5 Group, HQ: Moreton Hall, Swinderby, Lincs

9 Sqn	Bardney	Lancaster I, III
44 Sqn	Spilsby	Lancaster I, III
49 Sqn	Fulbeck	Lancaster I, III
50 Sqn	Skellingthorpe	Lancaster I, III
57 Sqn	East Kirkby	Lancaster I, III
61 Sqn	Skellingthorpe	Lancaster I, III
106 Sqn	Metheringham	Lancaster I, III
189 Sqn	Fulbeck	Lancaster I, III
207 Sqn	Spilsby	Lancaster I, III
227 Sqn	Balderton	Lancaster I, III
463 Sqn	Waddington	Lancaster I, III
467 Sqn	Waddington	Lancaster I, III
617 Sqn	Woodhall Spa	Lancaster I, III; Mosquito VI
619 Sqn	Strubby	Lancaster I, III
630 Sqn	East Kirkby	Lancaster I, III

On loan from No 8 (PFF) Group

83 Sqn (PFF)	Coningsby	Lancaster I, III
97 Sqn (PFF)	Coningsby	Lancaster I, III
627 Sqn (PFF)	Woodhall Spa	Mosquito IV, IX, XVI, XX, XXV

No 6 (RCAF) Group, HQ: Allerton Park, Yorks

408 Sqn	Linton-on-Ouse	Halifax VII
415 Sqn	East Moor	Halifax III, VII
419 Sqn	Middleton St George	Lancaster X
420 Sqn	Tholthorpe	Halifax III
424 Sqn	Skipton-on-Swale	Lancaster I, III
425 Sqn	Tholthorpe	Halifax III
426 Sqn	Linton-on-Ouse	Halifax VII
427 Sqn	Leeming	Lancaster I, III; Halifax III
428 Sqn	Middleton St George	Lancaster X
431 Sqn	Croft	Lancaster X
432 Sqn	East Moor	Halifax VII
433 Sqn	Skipton-on-Swale	Lancaster I, III, Halifax III
434 Sqn	Croft	Lancaster I, III, X

No 8 (PFF) Group, HQ: Castle Hill House, Hunts

7 Sqn	Oakington	Lancaster I, III
35 Sqn	Graveley	Lancaster I, III
105 Sqn	Bourn	Mosquito IX, XVI
109 Sqn	Little Staughton	Mosquito IX, XVI
128 Sqn	Wyton	Mosquito XVI
139 Sqn	Upwood	Mosquito IX, XVI, XX, XXV
142 Sqn	Gransden Lodge	Mosquito XXV
156 Sqn	Upwood	Lancaster I, III
162 Sqn	Bourn	Mosquito XX, XXV
163 Sqn	Wyton	Mosquito XXV
405 Sqn	Gransden Lodge	Lancaster I, III
571 Sqn	Oakington	Mosquito XVI
582 Sqn	Little Staughton	Lancaster I, III
608 Sqn	Downham Market	Mosquito XX, XXV
635 Sqn	Downham Market	Lancaster I, III
692 Sqn	Graveley	Mosquito XVI

No 100 (SD) Group, HQ: Bylaugh Hall, East Dereham, Norfolk

23 Sqn	Little Snoring	Mosquito VI
85 Sqn	Swannington	Mosquito XXX
141 Sqn	West Raynham	Mosquito VI, XXX
157 Sqn	Swannington	Mosquito XIX, XXX
169 Sqn	Great Massingham	Mosquito VI, XIX
171 Sqn	North Creake	Halifax III
192 Sqn	Foulsham	Halifax III; Mosquito IV, XVI
199 Sqn	North Creake	Halifax III; Stirling III
214 Sqn	Oulton	Fortress III
223 Sqn	Oulton	Liberator IV
239 Sqn	West Raynham	Mosquito XXX
462 Sqn	Foulsham	Halifax III
515 Sqn	Little Snoring	Mosquito VI

Appendix III

The Organisation of Training Groups in Bomber Command

At the outbreak of war in 1939, Bomber Command had wisely reserved a proportion of its aircraft and crews for operational training duties. Aircraft of the same type as those in current use with the frontline squadrons were allocated to a number of squadrons — known as Group Pool Squadrons — under the control of a newly formed No 6 (Training) Group; these Group Pool Squadrons became known as Operational Training Units (OTU) from early in 1940. In July 1940 a second OTU Group, No 7, was formed to cope with the increase in demand for operational training. Nos 6 and 7 Groups were later renumbered Nos 91 and 92 Groups when a third OTU Group, No 93, was formed on 11 May 1942. On average, a single OTU could have some 50 aircraft on strength at any one time.

With the downturn in operational training requirements as the war drew to a close, No 93 Group's units were eventually absorbed into the remaining two training Groups in January 1945.

Heavy Conversion Units (HCU) were the final link in the training chain, formed to convert aircrews from the twin-engined aircraft at OTUs to the four-engined heavy types then to be found on most frontline bomber squadrons. The first HCUs were formed in late 1941/early 1942 and came under the direct control of the respective Bomber Group which they fed with converted crews. Under the Base system, the first Base in any Group, eg Marston Moor in Yorkshire, No 41 (Training) Base Headquarters, became the Group's training station, providing the Group's HCU element with the help of its substations. In November 1944, however, all HCUs were absorbed into a newly formed No 7 (HCU) Group.

RAF Bomber Command Training Unit Strengths 1939-45

September 1939

No 6 Group, HQ: Abingdon, Berks

97 Sqn ⎱ 166 Sqn ⎰	Abingdon	Whitley	(No 4 Group Pool)
104 Sqn ⎱ 108 Sqn ⎰	Bicester	Blenheim	(No 2 Group Pool)
90 Sqn	Upwood	Blenheim	(No 2 Group Pool)
52 Sqn ⎱ 63 Sqn ⎰	Benson	Battle	(No 1 Group Pool)
35 Sqn ⎱ 207 Sqn ⎰	Cranfield	Battle	(No 1 Group Pool)
98 Sqn	Hucknall	Battle	(No 1 Group Pool)
75 Sqn ⎱ 148 Sqn ⎰	Harwell	Wellington	(No 3 Group Pool)
7 Sqn ⎱ 76 Sqn ⎰	U Heyford	Hampden	(No 5 Group Pool)

June 1940

No 6 Group, HQ: Abingdon, Berks

10 OTU	Abingdon	Whitley II, III, V
11 OTU	Bassingbourn	Wellington I
12 OTU	Benson	Battle
13 OTU	Bicester / Weston-on-the-Green	Blenheim I, IV
14 OTU	Cottesmore	Hampden; Hereford
15 OTU	Harwell	Wellington I
16 OTU	Upper Heyford	Hampden; Hereford
17 OTU	Upwood	Blenheim I, IV
18 OTU	Bramcote	Wellington I, III
19 OTU	Kinloss	Whitley II, III, V
20 OTU	Lossiemouth / Elgin	Wellington I

February 1941

No 6 Group, HQ: Abingdon, Berks

10 OTU	Abingdon / Stanton Harcourt	Whitley III, V

12 OTU	Benson / Mount Farm	Wellington I
15 OTU	Harwell / Hampstead Norris	Wellington I
19 OTU	Kinloss	Whitley III, V
20 OTU	Lossiemouth / Elgin	Wellington I

No 7 Group, HQ: Bicester

11 OTU	Bassingbourn / Steeple Morden	Wellington I
13 OTU	Bicester / Hinton-in-the-Hedges	Blenheim I, IV
14 OTU	Cottesmore / Woolfox Lodge	Hampden; Hereford
16 OTU	Upper Heyford / Croughton	Hampden; Hereford
17 OTU	Upwood	Blenheim I, IV
18 OTU	Bramcote	Wellington I

February 1942

No 1 Group, HQ: Bawtry Hall, Yorks

1653 HCU	Polebrook	Liberator III

No 3 Group, HQ: Exning, Suffolk

1651 HCU	Waterbeach	Stirling I

No 4 Group, HQ: Heslington Hall, Yorks

1652 HCU	Marston Moor	Halifax

No 6 Group, HQ: Abingdon, Berks

10 OTU	Abingdon	Whitley V
12 OTU	Chipping Warden	Wellington I
15 OTU	Harwell / Hampstead Norris	Wellington I
19 OTU	Kinloss / Forres	Whitley V
20 OTU	Lossiemouth / Elgin	Wellington I
21 OTU	Moreton-in-the-Marsh / Edgehill	Wellington I

| 22 OTU | Wellesbourne Mountford Stratford | Wellington I |
| 23 OTU | Pershore | Wellington I |

No 7 Group, HQ: Bicester

11 OTU	Bassingbourn Steeple Morden	Wellington
13 OTU	Bicester Hinton-in-the-Hedges	Blenheim I, IV
14 OTU	Cottesmore Saltby	Hampden; Hereford
16 OTU	Upper Heyford Croughton	Hampden
17 OTU	Upwood	Blenheim I, IV
18 OTU	Bramcote Bitteswell	Wellington I
25 OTU	Finningley	Wellington I
26 OTU	Wing	Wellington I
27 OTU	Lichfield Tatenhill	Wellington I

February 1943

No 1 Group, HQ: Bawtry Hall, Yorks

| 1662 HCU | Blyton | Halifax I, II; Lancaster I |

No 3 Group, HQ: Exning, Suffolk

| 1651 HCU | Waterbeach | Stirling I |
| 1657 HCU | Stradishall | Stirling I |

No 4 Group, HQ: Heslington Hall, Yorks

1652 HCU	Marston Moor	Halifax I, II, V
1658 HCU	Riccall	Halifax I, II, V
1659 HCU	Leeming	Halifax I, II, V

No 5 Group, HQ: St Vincent's, Grantham, Lincs

1654 HCU	Wigsley	Manchester; Lancaster I; Halifax II, V
1656 HCU	Lindholme	Manchester; Lancaster I; Halifax V
1660 HCU	Swinderby	Manchester; Lancaster I; Halifax II,V
1661 HCU	Winthorpe	Lancaster I; Halifax I, II

No 91 Group, HQ: Abingdon, Berks

10 OTU	Abingdon Stanton Harcourt	Whitley V
15 OTU	Harwell Hampstead Norris	Wellington Ic
19 OTU	Kinloss Forres	Whitley V
20 OTU	Lossiemouth Elgin	Wellington I
21 OTU	Moreton-in-Marsh Edgehill	Wellington I
22 OTU	Wellesbourne Mountford Gaydon	Wellington I, III
23 OTU	Pershore Stratford	Wellington I
24 OTU	Honeybourne Long Marston	Whitley V

No 92 Group, HQ: Winslow, Bucks

11 OTU	Westcott Oakley	Wellington I
12 OTU	Chipping Warden Turweston	Wellington I
13 OTU	Bicester Finmere	Blenheim I, IV
14 OTU	Cottesmore Saltby	Hampden; Hereford
16 OTU	Upper Heyford Barford St John Hinton-in-the-Hedges	Wellington I, III
17 OTU	Upwood	Blenheim I, IV
26 OTU	Wing Little Horwood	Wellington I, III
28 OTU	Wymeswold Castle Donington	Wellington I, III
29 OTU	North Luffenham	Wellington I, III
81 OTU	Tilstock	Whitley V

No 93 Group, HQ: Egginton Hall, Derby

18 OTU	Bramcote Bitteswell Nuneaton	Wellington I, III
27 OTU	Lichfield Church Broughton	Wellington I, III
30 OTU	Hixon Seighford	Wellington III, X

February 1944

No 1 Group, HQ: Bawtry Hall, Yorks

1662 HCU	Blyton	Halifax I, II, V
1667 HCU	Sandtoft	Halifax II, V
1 LFS	Hemswell	Lancaster I, III

No 3 Group, HQ: Exning, Suffolk

1651 HCU	Wratting Common	Stirling I, III
1653 HCU	Chedburgh	Stirling I, III
1657 HCU	Stradishall	Stirling I, III
3 LFS	Feltwell	Lancaster I, III

No 4 Group, HQ: Heslington Hall, Yorks

1652 HCU	Marston Moor	Halifax I, II, V; Stirling III
1658 HCU	Riccall	Halifax I, II, V
1663 HCU	Rufforth	Halifax II

No 5 Group, HQ: Moreton Hall, Swinderby, Lincs

1654 HCU	Wigsley	Stirling III; Lancaster I, III
1656 HCU	Lindholme	Halifax V; Lancaster I, III
1660 HCU	Swinderby	Stirling I, III
1661 HCU	Winthorpe	Stirling III
5 LFS	Syerston	Lancaster I, III

No 6 (RCAF) Group, HQ: Allerton Park, Yorks

| 1664 HCU | Dishforth | Halifax II, V |
| 1666 HCU | Wombleton | Halifax II; Lancaster I,II |

No 8 (PFF) Group, HQ: Castle Hill House, Hunts

| PFF Navigation Training Unit | Upwood | Lancaster; Mosquito |

No 91 Group, HQ: Abingdon, Berks

10 OTU	Abingdon Stanton Harcourt	Whitley V, VII
15 OTU	Harwell Hampstead Norris	Wellington III, X
19 OTU	Kinloss Forres	Wellington III, X
20 OTU	Lossiemouth Elgin	Wellington III, X
21 OTU	Moreton-in-Marsh Enstone	Wellington III, X
22 OTU	Wellesbourne Mountford Gaydon	Wellington III, X
23 OTU	Pershore Stratford	Wellington III, X
24 OTU	Honeybourne Long Marston	Wellington III, X

No 92 Group, HQ: Winslow, Bucks

11 OTU	Westcott Oakley	Wellington III, X
12 OTU	Chipping Warden Edgehill	Wellington III, X
14 OTU	Market Harborough Husbands Bosworth	Wellington III, X
16 OTU	Upper Heyford Barford St John	Wellington III, X
17 OTU	Silverstone Turweston	Wellington III, X
26 OTU	Wing Little Horwood	Wellington III, X
28 OTU	Wymeswold Castle Donington	Wellington III, X
29 OTU	Bruntingthorpe Bitteswell	Wellington III, X
84 OTU	Desborough	Wellington III, X

No 93 Group, HQ: Egginton Hall, Derby

18 OTU	Finningley / Worksop / Doncaster	Wellington III, X
27 OTU	Lichfield / Church Broughton	Wellington III, X
30 OTU	Hixon / Seighford	Wellington III, X
82 OTU	Ossington / Gamston	Wellington III, X
83 OTU	Peplow / Wellington	Wellington III, X

February 1945

No 7 Group, HQ: St Vincent's, Grantham, Lincs

1651 HCU	Woolfox Lodge	Lancaster I, III
1652 HCU	Marston Moor	Halifax II, V, III
1653 HCU	North Luffenham	Lancaster I, III
1654 HCU	Wigsley	Stirling III; Lancaster I, III
1656 HCU	Lindholme	Halifax V; Lancaster I, III
1658 HCU	Riccall	Halifax II, V, III
1659 HCU	Topcliffe	Halifax V, III; Lancaster I, III
1660 HCU	Swinderby	Stirling III; Lancaster I, III
1661 HCU	Winthorpe	Stirling III; Lancaster I, III
1662 HCU	Blyton	Lancaster I, III
1663 HCU	Rufforth	Halifax III
1664 HCU	Dishforth	Halifax II, V; Lancaster I, III, X
1666 HCU	Wombleton	Lancaster I, III, X
1667 HCU	Sandtoft	Halifax V; Lancaster I, III
1668 HCU	Bottesford	Lancaster I, III
1669 HCU	Langar	Halifax II, V; Lancaster I, III
Bomber Instructors' School,	Finningley	Wellington X; Halifax; Lancaster I, III

No 91 Group, HQ: Abingdon, Berks

10 OTU	Abingdon	Wellington X
19 OTU	Kinloss	Wellington X
20 OTU	Lossiemouth / Elgin	Wellington X
21 OTU	Moreton-in-Marsh / Enstone	Wellington X
22 OTU	Wellesbourne Mountford / Gaydon	Wellington III, X
24 OTU	Honeybourne / Long Marston	Wellington X
27 OTU	Lichfield / Church Broughton	Wellington X
30 OTU	Gamston / Hixon	Wellington III, X

No 92 OTU, HQ: Winslow, Bucks

11 OTU	Westcott / Oakley	Wellington X
12 OTU	Chipping Warden / Edgehill	Wellington X
14 OTU	Market Harborough	Wellington X
16 OTU	Upper Heyford / Barford St John	Wellington X; Mosquito III, IV, VI, XVI, XX, XXV
17 OTU	Silverstone / Turweston	Wellington X
26 OTU	Wing / Little Horwood	Wellington III, X
29 OTU	Bruntingthorpe	Wellington X
84 OTU	Desborough	Wellington X
85 OTU	Husbands Bosworth	Wellington X

No 8 (PFF) Group, HQ: Castle Hill House, Hunts

PFF Navigation Training Unit	Warboys	Lancaster I, III; Mosquito IV, XVI, XX, XXV

No 100 Group, HQ: Bylaugh Hall, East Dereham, Norfolk

1699 HCU	Oulton	Fortress II, III; Liberator IV

Below:
Missing . . .

Bibliography

Unpublished Primary Source Material:

PUBLIC RECORD OFFICE, KEW
AIR 14 — Bomber Command Records
AIR 14/554 No 6 Group Summary of Events
AIR 14/1847 The Effect of Experience on Bomber Losses: December 1943-August 1946
AIR 14/2504 No 6 Group Analysis of Operations: January 1944-May 1945
AIR 14/2791 Missing Aircraft Register: January 1943-January 1945
AIR 14/3069 Group Summary of Operations: September 1944 — Day
AIR 14/3076 Group Summary of Operations: December 1944 — Night
AIR 14/3234 No 4 Group Raid Assessments and Flight Plans: November 1944-February 1945
AIR 14/3453 Bomber Command Quarterly Review No 10: July-September 1944
AIR 14/3454 Bomber Command Quarterly Review No 11: October-December 1944

AIR 24 — Bomber Command Operations Record Books (ORBs)
AIR 24/300 Bomber Command HQ ORB Vol 3: Intelligence Reports and Narrative of Operations — November 1944

AIR 27 — Squadrons ORBs
AIR 27/1853 No 429 Squadron: January 1943-December 1944
AIR 27/1858 No 431 Squadron: January 1944-May 1945
AIR 27/2050 No 578 Squadron
AIR 27/2155 No 635 Squadron

AIR 28 — Station ORBs
AIR 28/451 RCAF Station Leeming: January 1943-December 1944

PUBLIC ARCHIVES OF CANADA, OTTAWA: NATIONAL PERSONNEL RECORDS CENTRE
RCAF Attestation Papers and Records of Service
RCAF Casualty Notification — 27 November 1944
Circumstantial Report re: Halifax LW136 — 24 September 1944
Letter from AOC-in-C RCAF Overseas to Director General Graves Regisration and Enquiries — 10 August 1945
RAF Form 551: Report on Accidental Injuries or Death — 15 March 1945

MINISTRY OF DEFENCE, NEW ZEALAND
Royal New Zealand Air Force Record of Service

Published Primary Source Material:

Sgn Ldr L. Harding (Ed), *Transport Command Flying Control Aircrew Manual* (January 1945)

Published Secondary Source Material:

S. Willis & B. Hollis, *Military Airfields in the British Isles 1939-1945 (Omnibus Edition)* (Enthusiast Publications 1987)
Michael J. F. Bowyer, *Action Stations 1: East Anglia* (PSL 1990)
Bruce Barrymore Halpenny, *Action Stations 2: Lincolnshire and the East Midlands* (PSL 1981)
David J. Smith, *Action Stations 3: Wales and the North-West* (PSL 1990)
Bruce Barrymore Halpenny, *Action Stations 4: Yorkshire,* (PSL 1984)
Michael J. F. Bowyer, *Action Stations 6: Cotswolds and the Central Midlands* (PSL 1983)
David J. Smith, *Action Stations 7: Scotland, the North-East and Northern Ireland* (PSL 1989)
Bruce Barrymore Halpenny, *Action Stations 8: Greater London* (PSL 1984)
David J. Smith, *Britain's Military Airfields 1939-45* (PSL 1989)
Sir Charles Webster & Noble Frankland, *The Strategic Air Offensive Against Germany 1939-1945,* Vols I-IV (HMSO 1961)
Wg Cdr C. G. Jefford, *RAF Squadrons* (Airlife 1988)
Philip Moyes, *Bomber Squadrons of the RAF and their Aircraft* (Macdonald 1964)
Philip Congdon, *Per Ardua Ad Astra: A Handbook of the Royal Air Force* (Airlife 1987)
Anthony Verrier, *The Bomber Offensive* (Pan 1974)
Stephen Brooks, *Bomber: Strategic Air Power in Twentieth Century Conflict* (Imperial War Museum 1983)
AVM D. C. T.Bennett, *Pathfinder* (Goodall Publications 1988)
Serving A Nation at War 1939-1945 — A Review of the Building and Civil Engineering Work of John Laing & Son Ltd (John Laing & Son Ltd 1946)
G. L. 'Larry' Donnelly, *The Whitley Boys: 4 Group Bomber Operations 1939-1940* (Air Research Publications 1991)
Peter B. Gunn, *RAF Great Massingham: A Norfolk Airfield at War* (Peter B. Gunn 1990)
Geoff D. Copeman, *Silksheen: The History of East Kirkby Airfield* (Midland Counties Publications 1989)
Chaz Bowyer, *Mosquito Squadrons of the Royal Air Force* (Ian Allan Ltd 1984)
Francis K. Mason, *The Avro Lancaster* (Aston Publications 1990)
John Foreman, *Battle of Britain, The Forgotten Months: November and December 1940* (Air Research Publications 1988)
John F. Hamlin, *The Royal Air Force at Newmarket 1939-1947* (J. F. Hamlin 1985)
Anon, *The History of Royal Air Force Finningley* (1969)
Air Historical Branch Monographs: *Works* (AP3236) (HMSO 1956)

Journal Articles:

Malcolm Smith, 'A Matter of Faith: British Strategic Air Doctrine Before 1939', *Journal of Contemporary History* Vol 15, No 3, 1980
Uri Bialer, 'Humanisation of Air Warfare in British Foreign Policy on the Eve of World War Two', *Journal of Contemporary History* Vol 13, No 1, 1978

Magazines and Periodicals:

Various editions/issues of *Air Britain Digest, Air Ministry News Letter, Air Pictorial, Aviation News*